The Complete Book
of Business Math

The Complete Book of Business Math

**Every Manager's Guide
to Analyzing Facts and Figures
for Smart Business Decisions**

Joel G. Siegel, Ph.D., CPA

Jae K. Shim, Ph.D.

David Minars, J.D., M.B.A., CPA

McGraw-Hill, Inc.

New York   San Francisco   Washington, D.C.   Auckland   Bogotá
Caracas   Lisbon   London   Madrid   Mexico City   Milan
Montreal   New Delhi   San Juan   Singapore
Sydney   Tokyo   Toronto

Library of Congress Cataloging-in-Publication Data

Siegel, Joel G.
 The complete book of business math : every manager's guide to
analyzing facts and figures for smart business decisions / Joel G.
Siegel, Jae K. Shim, David Minars.
     p.   cm.
   Includes index.
   ISBN 0-07-057624-6
   1. Business mathematics.   I. Shim, Jae K.   II. Minars, David.
III. Title.
HF5691.S4327   1995
650'.01'513—dc20   94-38110
                                                              CIP

1 2 3 4 5 6 7 8 9 0   AGM/AGM   9 0 0 9 8 7 6 5

ISBN 0-07-057624-6

*The sponsoring editor for this book was David J. Conti, the editing supervisor
was Stephen M. Smith, and the production supervisor was Suzanne W. B.
Rapcavage. It was set in Century Schoolbook by Estelita F. Green of
McGraw-Hill's Professional Book Group composition unit.*

Printed and bound by Quebecor/Martinsburg.

BK
$59.95

counts to use as premi-
ing programs. For more
, McGraw-Hill, Inc., 11
ocal bookstore.

r containing a minimum

To

Theodore Nardin
With Utmost Regard and Respect

Roberta M. Siegel
Loving Wife and Colleague

Chung Shim
Loving and Dedicated Wife

Iris Minars
My Best Partner and Friend

Contents

Part 5   Controlling Inventory

Part 6   Buying and Selling Products and Services

Part 11   Measuring Business Performance

Part 16   Buying or Selling a Small Business

Preface

The Complete Book of Business Math provides the small business entrepreneur with the information, analyses, and insights necessary to analyze and calculate the consequences of a wide range of business financial strategies and problems. The ability to select the right operational technique is vital if the small business is to survive, profit, and grow in today's uncertain economic environment. The owner of a small business must be able to make the right financial decision based on sound mathematical reasoning in order to run the business efficiently. He or she must understand the problem, and then apply math skills to solve it.

This book is a comprehensive, one-stop desk reference for managers and owners of small businesses who must use quantitative calculations to make daily operating and investing decisions. Its purpose is to provide the fundamentals of business math techniques that can be quickly applied to *real-word* problems. This unique resource will save countless hours of research time by making sound financial planning truly easy. It provides analyses as well as clear and understandable explanations of complex small business problems. Basic mathematical techniques are presented in a *step-by-step* fashion that takes the reader through each stage of the problem-solving process. The examples in this book provide an invaluable and effective operating tool. This book also contains *user-friendly* personal computer techniques. The examples enable the businessperson to measure results and to report the data in an easy-to-understand format.

Each section begins with an overview of the mathematics necessary to solve the problem under discussion. This book covers every facet of business math that is vital to the small business owner. The presentation of the data will enable the small business owner to select and use the appropriate statistical method to make cost-effective and profitable business decisions. The language associated with the mathematical techniques can also be adopted by the manager when circumstances require communication with investors, lenders, vendors, customers, employees, and other parties associated with the enterprise.

The objectives and methods illustrated in this book cover a wide range of areas, including management, marketing, accounting, taxes, finance, operations, insurance, and economics. This book provides solutions to traditional as well as new operating and financial problems created by today's uncertain economic environment. It also advises the business manager and/or business consultant about ways to respond to sudden and unexpected problems. Complex business problems are broken down into smaller ones for easier solution.

This book is divided into parts, each of which covers an area that is important in starting and running a small business. Part topics include managing cash and inventory, evaluating loans and credit, researching the market and competition, and preparing financial statements. Each part is broken down into sections. For example, budgeting and profit planning is made up of sections that discuss such important areas as predicting sales and costs, cash flow analysis, the allocation of financial resources, and finding the payback period. This book also contains illustrative and practical mathematical formulas, equations, models, ratios, and other statistical techniques that can be used to make sound and profitable business decisions. The examples in each section focus on financial problems and highlight the importance of using mathematical and financial management principles. Where required, mathematical techniques for solving the problem are presented.

Other topics covered in *The Complete Book of Business Math* include the methods used to find the correct level of inventory, determining the amount and rate of production, computing profits, finding the rate of return, monitoring and controlling costs, allocating financial resources, analyzing the financial position of the business, identifying trends, comparing performance to that of competitors, evaluating supervisors and employee productivity, using human and physical resources efficiently, determining how much and when to reorder, computing the necessary amount of merchandise safety stock, whether to offer a discount to customers, computing the cost of financing, determining cash requirements, computing the breakeven point, calculating the debt level, finding the variances between budgeted and actual revenues and/or costs, forcasting sales accurately, calculating adequate insurance coverage, finding the tax liability, computing the potential cash flows for projects, analyzing floor space, evaluating the effects of inflation, appraising customer relationships and transactions such as average order size and the number of backorders, computing the value of the business, and identifying potential bankruptcy so steps may be taken to avoid it. The small business operator will also learn how to use a computer to assemble data and perform rapid calculations which will promote the effective use of the mathematical procedures. There are also in-depth discussions of both simple and complex mathematical applications that may be applicable to a particular problem. Each quantitative approach is described clearly and concisely. In some cases, the reader will be directed to the use of financial calculators, spreadsheet programs such as Lotus 1-2-3, Lotus 1-2-3 add-ins, stand-alone specialized computer software, accounting and tax software, and cash management software.

The authors do not assume that the reader has any mathematical expertise. Thus both the novice and the experienced businessperson will profit from the methodology contained in this action-oriented book. The *applications* will make the small business manager competent in the use of the most up-to-date managerial tools. The presentation is easy to understand and is *user-friendly*. This book shows what the mathematical technique measures, why it is important, when it should be used, how it should be used, and what the numbers mean.

The field of financial management has recently witnessed a dangerous period of rapid change, stagnation, and contraction. Uncertainty about the future growth of the economy has forced the small business operator to be more prudent and sophisticated in the allocation of financial resources. It is therefore imperative that small business owners employ new mathematical and financial management techniques to aid their decision making. The authors are aware of these vital and complex techniques and cover them in clear and concise detail.

The small business manager must also be aware of both the usefulness and the limitations of the particular mathematical technique employed to solve a problem. This book points out, when required, that a particular technique may be appropriate in one situation but not in others. This book also contains hundreds of filled-in examples, illustrations, practical applications, measures, procedures, rules of thumb, statistical data, exhibits, tables, graphs, and diagrams. They are presented to aid in the comprehension and successful solution of a particular problem. The reader will also learn when and how to use the appropriate computational method, why it is used, when computer techniques such as spreadsheets should be used, and how to read and analyze the computer printout. Typical questions of concern to small business managers are answered, such as: How much sales are needed to justify the cost of a proposed advertising program? How many factory workers are required to meet production needs? Is the business growing, and how does it compare to competition?

In today's marketplace, economic downturns force small business managers to face new challenges. This book will minimize the effects of these potentially disastrous periods. It is designed to maximize both the profits and the value of the firm for its owners. This is a central objective of this book, and each financial procedure discussed is linked to the impact it has on the value of the firm. The reader will find this book useful, practical, comprehensive, and profitable. Keep it handy as an easy-to-use reference. There is cross-referencing of topics and mathematical techniques. The index can be used to find a specific area of interest. The glossary defines important mathematical terms.

In summation, this book is an invaluable addition to any library and will provide quick and accurate answers to the small business entrepreneur. It will make an individual "savvy," comfortable, and proficient in both the business math and the financial applications required for the successful operation of any small business.

Joel G. Siegel
Jae K. Shim
David Minars

Acknowledgments

We thank Caroline Carney, David J. Conti, Stephen Smith, and Maggie Stuckey for their advice on the organization, structure, and writing of this book.

We also acknowledge with much thanks Theodore Nardin. The lead author has been fortunate to have authored eleven other books with Ted for at least ten years. He is a man who is very much admired and respected.

Thanks goes to René Ramelow-Porter of California State University, Long Beach, for her outstanding computer assistance and excellent quantitative advice.

Thanks goes to Brian Oeding, a research assistant at California State University, Long Beach, for his assistance.

Finally, we thank Abraham J. Simon, Ph.D., CPA, for coauthoring Sec. 142 on the valuation of a business.

The Complete Book
of Business Math

Evaluating the Cost of Bank Loans, Business Loans, Trade Credit, and Other Financing

1 Understanding Simple Interest

INTRODUCTION. The fee charged for the use of money, or principal, is called interest. It is the amount charged by a lender to a borrower. The interest rate is usually stated on an annual basis. The sum of the principal and the interest due is called the *accumulated value, amount due,* or *maturity value.* Compound interest is discussed in Sec. 60, How Do You Calculate Future Values? How Money Grows.

HOW IS IT COMPUTED? The amount of interest due is based on three factors: the principal, the rate of interest, and the time period during which the principal is used. One year is generally used as the time period. Simple interest is calculated on original principal only. The formula for simple interest is:

$$\text{Interest} = \text{principal} \times \text{rate} \times \text{time}$$

$$I = Prt$$

The maturity value S is given as:

$$\text{Maturity value} = \text{principal} + \text{interest}$$

Although the time span of a loan may be given in days, months, or years, the rate of interest is an annual rate. Thus, when the duration of a loan is given in months or days, the time must be converted to years. When the time is given in months, the formula is:

$$t = \frac{\text{number of months}}{12}$$

Example 1 A small business owner obtains a 2-year loan of $10,000 from the Amalgamated Bank. The bank charges an annual simple interest rate of 10 percent. The rate of interest charged for 1 year is $1000, calculated as follows:

$$\$10,000 \times 10\% \times 1 \text{ year} = \$1000$$

The total simple interest for the 2-year period is $2000, calculated as follows:

$$\$1000 \times 2 \text{ years} = \$2000$$

The maturity value (S) of the loan is $12,000, calculated as follows:

$$I = Prt$$

$$S = P + I = \$10,000 + \$2,000 = \$12,000$$

Example 2 A small business owner obtains a 3-month loan of $10,000 from the Fidelity bank. The bank charges an annual simple interest rate of 10 percent. The interest charged for the 3-month period is $250, and the maturity value of the loan is $10,250, calculated as follows:

$$P = \$10,000 \qquad r = 10\% \text{ or } 0.10 \qquad t = \text{}^{3}\!/_{12} \text{ month}$$

$$I = Prt$$

$$\$10,000 \times 0.10 \times \text{}^{3}\!/_{12} \text{ month} = \$250$$

The maturity value of the loan is

$$S = P + I$$

$$\$10,000 + \$250 = \$10,250$$

HOW IS IT USED AND APPLIED? The owner must know how to determine the cost of money in a debt or lease agreement. By knowing the cost of borrowing, the owner can better plan a business strategy to obtain an adequate return on his or her money and to provide sufficient funds to pay principal and interest.

The small business owner who seeks a loan should shop around to obtain the best interest terms possible. Excessive interest rates, although they are tax deductible, are a drain on an owner's profits. Large outstanding loans, coupled with high interest rates, can substantially reduce an owner's profits and impair a business's credit rating. A balance sheet showing high interest-bearing loans can also result in lenders charging even higher rates of interest because of the possibility of default and even bankruptcy if the loans are not paid at their maturity date.

See Sec. 2, Real (Effective) Interest Rate.

2 Real (Effective) Interest Rate

INTRODUCTION. The stated rate of interest does not tell the whole story: you need to be sure you understand all the fees and charges that might affect the real interest rate. The real rate of interest on a loan is expressed as an annual percentage applicable for the life of the loan.

HOW IS IT COMPUTED?

$$\text{Real interest rate} = \frac{\text{nominal interest on face of loan}}{\text{net proceeds of loan}}$$

For a discounted loan, which is a common form of loan, interest is deducted immediately in arriving at the net proceeds—which increases the effective interest rate. A bank may require a compensating balance, i.e., a deposit that offsets the unpaid loan. In this case, no interest is earned on the compensating balance, which is stated as a percentage of the loan. A compensating balance also increases the effective interest rate.

Example A small business takes out a $10,000, 1-year, 10 percent discounted loan. The compensating balance is 5 percent. The effective interest rate is:

$$\frac{\$1,000}{\$10,000 - \$1,000 - \$500} = \frac{1,000}{8,500} = 11.8\%$$

HOW IS IT USED AND APPLIED? Small business owners compute the effective interest rate to determine the true cost of borrowing. See Sec. 3, The Cost of Credit: Annual Percentage Rate.

3 The Cost of Credit: Annual Percentage Rate

INTRODUCTION. The annual percentage rate (APR) is a true measure of the effective cost of credit. It is the ratio of the finance charge to the average amount of credit in use during the life of the loan, and is expressed as a percentage rate per year.

HOW IS IT COMPUTED? We present below a discussion of the way the effective APR is calculated for various types of loans.

Single-Payment Loans. The single-payment loan is paid in full on a given date. There are two ways of calculating APR on single-payment loans: the simple interest method and the discount method.

1. Simple interest method. Recall from Sec. 1 that, under the simple interest method, interest is calculated only on the amount borrowed (proceeds):

$$APR = \frac{\text{average annual finance charge}}{\text{amount borrowed or proceeds}}$$

Example 1 A small business owner took out a single-payment loan of $1000 for 2 years at a simple interest rate of 15 percent. The interest charge is: $300 ($1000 × 0.15 × 2 years). Hence the APR is:

$$\text{APR} = 15\% \left(\frac{150}{1000} \right)$$

Under the simple interest method, the stated simple interest rate and the APR are always the same for single-payment loans.

2. Discount method. Under the discount method, interest is determined and then deducted from the amount of the loan. The difference is the actual amount the borrower receives. In other words, the borrower prepays the finance charges.

Example 2 Using the same figures as in Example 1, the actual amount received is $700 ($1000 − $300), not $1000. The APR is:

$$\text{APR} = 21.43\% \left(\frac{150}{700} \right)$$

The rate the lender must quote on the loan is 21.43 percent, not 15 percent.

The discount method always gives a higher APR than the simple interest method for single-payment loans at the same interest rates because the proceeds received are less.

Installment Loans. Most consumer loans use the add-on method. One popular method of calculating the APR for add-on loans is the *constant-ratio method*. The constant-ratio formula is:

$$\text{APR} = \frac{2MC}{P(N + 1)}$$

where M = number of payment periods in 1 year
N = number of scheduled payments
C = finance charges in dollars (dollar cost of credit)
P = original proceeds

Example 3 Assume that a small business owner borrows $1000 to be repaid in 12 equal monthly installments of $93.00 each for a finance charge of $116.00. The APR under the constant-ratio method is computed as follows:

$$\text{APR} = \frac{2MC}{P(N + 1)}$$

$$= \frac{2 \times 12 \times 116}{1,000(12 + 1)} = \frac{2,784}{13,000} = 21.42\%$$

Note that some lenders charge fees for a credit investigation, a loan application, or for life insurance. When these fees are required, the lender must include them in addition to the finance charge in dollars as part of the APR calculations.

HOW IS IT USED AND APPLIED? The lender is required by the Truth in Lending Act (Consumer Credit Protection Act) to disclose to a borrower the effective annual percentage rate (APR) as well as the finance charge in dollars.

Banks often quote their interest rates in terms of dollars of interest per hundred dollars. Other lenders quote in terms of dollars per payment. This leads to confusion on the part of borrowers. Fortunately, APR can eliminate this confusion. By comparing the APRs of different loans, a borrower can determine the best deal.

Example 4 Bank A offers a 7 percent car loan if a small business owner puts down 25 percent. That is, if she buys a $4000 auto, she will finance $3000 over a 3-year period with carrying charges that amount to $630 ($0.07 \times \$3000 \times 3$ years). She will make equal monthly payments of $100.83 for 36 months.

Bank B will lend $3500 on the same car. In this case the small business owner must pay $90 per month for 48 months.

Which of the two quotes offers the best deal?

The APR calculations (using the constant-ratio formula) follow.

$$\text{Bank A:} \quad \text{APR} = \frac{2 \times 12 \times 630}{3,000(36 + 1)} = \frac{15,120}{111,000} = 13.62\%$$

$$\text{Bank B:} \quad \text{APR} = \frac{2 \times 12 \times 820}{3,500(48 + 1)} = \frac{19,680}{171,500} = 11.48\%$$

In the case of Bank B, it is necessary to multiply 90×48 months to arrive at a total cost of $4320. Therefore, the total credit cost is $820 ($4320 - $3500).

Based on the APR, the small business owner should choose Bank B over Bank A.

4 Calculating Due Dates

INTRODUCTION. The due date, also called maturity date, is the exact date when a loan must be repaid.

HOW IS IT COMPUTED? Some loans specify the maturity date while other loans state the period of the loan in days or months. When the maturity date is given in days, the date is determined by counting the days from the day the loan was secured. The day on which the loan is procured is not counted. For example, a 120-day loan obtained on October 17, 19X1, is due on February 15, 19X2. When the period is given in months, the loan's maturity date falls on the same day of the month as the date the loan is issued. For example a 6-month loan dated March 15 matures on September 15. If the due date of the loan falls on a nonbusiness day, the maturity date is the next business day, with an additional day(s) added to the period for which interest is charged.

Example Motor Parts, Inc., obtained a 90-day loan dated March 16, 19X1. The maturity date of the loan is June 14, 19X1, as determined below.

To determine the maturity date, calculate forward for the exact number of days in the loan period. Do not count the day on which you actually received the loan. Remember that some months have 30 days and some have 31.

Time period of loan				90 days
	March	31		
Issuance date		16	15 days	
	April		30 days	
	May		31 days	
Total				76 days
Maturity date	June			14 days

HOW IS IT USED AND APPLIED? Due dates are not approximations; they are precise and final. On that date, you must be prepared to make full payment. Failure to do so means that you have defaulted on a loan, and that can have disastrous consequences for your business.

It is critical, therefore, that you know the exact date well in advance so you can make certain you will have the funds available.

5 Promissory Notes and Bank Discounts

INTRODUCTION. A business may both make a promissory note and receive one. Notes receivable and notes payable are formal arrangements promising payment. Often a debtor signs a *promissory note,* which serves as evidence of a debt. The promissory note is a written promise to pay principal with interest at a maturity date. A small business owner might discount a note if cash is needed quickly and he or she does not wish to hold the note until its maturity date.

HOW IS IT COMPUTED? As with loans, some notes specify the maturity date, while others state the period of the note, in days or months. When the maturity value is given in days, the maturity date is determined by counting the days from issue. Interest is usually computed on the basis of a 360-day year (12 months × 30 days per month). Recall from Sec. 1 that the following formula is used:

$$\text{Interest} = \text{principal} \times \text{interest rate} \times \text{time}$$

For example, the maturity date of a 90-day note issued May 6, 19X1, is August 4, 19X1, computed as follows:

Time period of note				90
	May	31		
Issuance date		6	25	
	June		30	
	July		31	
Total				86
Maturity date	August			4

When the period is given in months, the note's maturity date falls on the same day of the month as the date the note is issued. For example a 6-month note dated January 15 matures on July 15. If the due date of the note falls on a nonbusiness day, the maturity date is the next business day, with the additional day(s) added to the period for which interest is charged.

If you are holding a promissory note from a supplier or other party, you may find yourself in the position of needing more money before the due date, in which case you may discount the note receivable at a bank or finance company.

The proceeds received by the holder at the time the note is discounted are equal to the maturity value less the bank discount (interest charge). The bank discount is based on the period of time the bank will hold the note and the note's interest rate. The interest rate charged by the bank need not be the same as the interest rate on the maker's note. In fact, it is usually higher, because the bank generally charges a higher interest rate. The rate may also be different because of changes in the going interest rate since the note was originally written. The maturity value of the note is found as follows:

$$\text{Maturity value} = \text{face value of note} + \text{interest income}$$

The bank discount is:

$$\text{Bank discount} = \text{maturity value} \times \text{bank discount} \\ \times \text{period of time held by bank}$$

Example 1 On June 30, 19XX, Susan Ray, a small business owner, issued a 180-day, 18 percent note to the Denmark Company to pay a short-term business loan. The note's interest 6 months later will be $900, calculated as follows:

$$\text{Principal} \times \text{rate of interest} \times \text{time} = \text{interest}$$

$$\$10,000 \times 18\% \times 6 \text{ months} = \$900$$

The maturity value of the note is $10,900, calculated as follows:

$$\text{Maturity value} = \text{face value of note} + \text{interest income}$$

$$\$10,900 = \$10,000 + \$900$$

Example 2 The Solvay Tool Company received the following notes:

Date	Term	Interest rate (%)	Face amount
(a) Aug. 2	4 months	6	$1000
(b) Aug. 11	60 days	8	7500
(c) Sept. 9	45 days	9	2000
(d) May 20	90 days	12	5000

The due date and amount of interest on each note is:

Due date	Interest due	Maturity value
(a) Nov. 30	$ 20 ($1000 \times \frac{4}{12} \times 6\%$)	$1020.00
(b) Oct. 10	100 ($7500 \times \frac{60}{360} \times 8\%$)	7600.00
(c) Oct. 24	22.50 ($2000 \times \frac{45}{360} \times 9\%$)	2022.50
(d) Aug. 18	150.00 ($5000 \times \frac{90}{360} \times 12\%$)	5150.00

Example 3 On June 20, 19XX, the Bunyan Grass Seed Company received a 90-day, 12 percent note receivable for $5000. On August 5 the company, in need of cash, discounts the note at its bank. The bank

charges a discount rate of 15 percent. The proceeds from the discounted note are 5077.04 calculated as follows:

Bank discount = maturity value × discount rate

$$\times \text{ period note is held by bank}$$

Face value of note dated June 20	$5000.00
Add: Interest on note ($5000 × 12% × $^{90}/_{360}$)	150.00
Maturity value of note due Sept. 18	$5150.00
Bank discount on maturity value ($5150 × 15% × $^{34}/_{360}$)	72.96

The net proceeds received by the payee at the time of discounting are:

Net proceeds = maturity value − bank discount

Maturity value of note due Sept. 18	$5150.00
Less: Discount period (Aug. 5–Sept. 18 = 34 days)	
Discount on maturity value (34 days at 15%)	72.96
Net proceeds of note after discounting	$5077.04

HOW IS IT USED AND APPLIED? When a note receivable is sold or discounted to a bank or other financial institution, the seller (small business owner) of the note remains *contingently liable* until the maker pays at maturity. If the original maker of the note does not pay the note at its maturity, the bank will seek payment from the seller of the note. The party who originally discounted the note will now be forced to pay and must seek reimbursement from the original maker of the note.

6 Trade Credit

INTRODUCTION. When you buy supplies or materials on credit, you are agreeing to pay the supplier within a certain period after receiving the goods. This is called *trade credit,* because it is a sale within the trade (as opposed to a sale to the public at large), and it is in effect a form of loan: You get the materials now and pay for them later. Many suppliers also offer a discount if you pay early.

HOW IS IT COMPUTED? Trade credit is usually extended for a specific period of time; 30 days is common. This means that payment is due 30 days after you receive the merchandise. If a supplier offers a discount, there is also a specific period during which the discount may be taken. One very common arrangement is 2/10, net 30, sometimes written 2/10, n/30, which means that if you pay the invoice within 10 days, you can take a 2 percent discount; otherwise the full amount is due within 30 days. The cost of *not* taking the discount is referred to as the *opportunity cost of credit*; it can be substantial.

The cost of credit if a cash discount is not taken is:

$$\text{Credit cost} = \frac{\text{percent discount}}{100 - \text{percent discount}}$$

$$\times \frac{360}{\text{credit period} - \text{discount period}}$$

Example 1 Suppose that a supplier has extended $900 of trade credit to a small business owner on terms of 2/10, net 30. The owner can either pay $900 \times 0.98 = $882 at the end of the 10-day period, or wait for the full 30 days and pay the full $900. By waiting the full 30 days, the owner effectively borrows $882 for an additional 20 days, paying $900 − $882 or $18 in interest. Now, $18 may not seem like much of a savings, but if you put it in annual terms, it is significant.

This information can be used to compute the credit cost of borrowing this money:

$$\text{Credit cost} = \frac{\text{percent discount}}{100 - \text{percent discount}}$$

$$\times \frac{360}{\text{credit period} - \text{discount period}}$$

$$= \frac{2}{100 - 2} \times \frac{360}{30 - 10}$$

$$= \frac{2}{98} \times \frac{360}{20}$$

$$= 36.73\%$$

It is important for a buyer to take advantage of all available discounts, even though it may be necessary to borrow the money to make the payment.

Example 2 Andover Supply receives a $2000 invoice, discount terms 2/10, n/30, for goods purchased from Czar Wholesalers. Andover borrows the money for the remaining 20 days of the discount period at an annual interest rate of 12% and saves $26.93, computed as follows:

Discount of 2% on $2000	$40.00
Interest for 20 days, at rate of 12% on $1960 ($2000 − $40)	13.07
Savings effected by borrowing	$26.93

HOW IS IT USED AND APPLIED? Computing the cost of credit is an essential part of doing business. You should always be weighing the savings gained by paying early against the benefit of holding onto your money longer. Which is more advantageous to you: Paying a smaller mount sooner, or paying more later but having the use of the funds in the meantime? The only way to answer that question is to work through the numbers both ways, and compare the results.

If you do not take the discount, you are losing the savings; the amount lost is the true cost of credit. However, that cost may be of secondary importance to you if other forms of financing are not available. On the other hand, if bank credit is not a problem, you may be better off to forgo the discount and invest the money short term in something that generates revenue.

Doing this now/later analysis is a continual process. Your decisions may change from one month to the next, as your cash flow changes. You should also be aware that the amounts of discount offered to you will often change to reflect the overall economic climate. Thus the cost of not taking trade credit usually increases during relatively good economic periods, with more generous discounts being offered; in periods of economic downturn, however, the cost of not taking trade credit usually declines as discount terms are reduced. Also, you may be able to negotiate with your major suppliers for a more favorable discount, especially if you have a strong record with them or they are particularly eager for cash.

7 Receivables and Inventory Financing

INTRODUCTION. You may be able to improve your business's cash flow by using receivables or inventory as collateral for loans. Both these assets represent important financing sources because they are significant in amount and relate to recurring business activities.

1 RECEIVABLES FINANCING. Receivables financing is the use of short-term financing backed by receivables, under either a *factoring* or an *assignment* arrangement. The financing of accounts receivable is facilitated if customers are financially strong, sales returns are minimal, and title to the goods is received by the buyer at shipment.

Factoring of Accounts Receivable. *Factoring* is the outright sale of accounts receivable to a third party *without recourse*; the purchaser assumes all credit and collection risks. The factor will usually advance you up to 80 percent, meaning that the factor buys the receivables for 80 percent of face value. The factor collects the full amount from the customer and keeps the difference. The proceeds you receive equal face value minus commission, fee, and discount. The amount the factor will advance depends on the quality of the accounts receivable. The cost of factoring includes the factor's commission for credit investigation of the customer, interest charges, and the discount from the face value of the receivables. The factor's total fee depends on the volume of business you give the factor and the creditworthiness of your customers. Billing and collection are done by the factor.

How is it computed? The cost of a factoring agreement is computed as follows:

$$\text{Factor fee} + \text{cost of borrowing} = \text{total cost}$$

Example 1 You have $10,000 per month in accounts receivable that a factor will buy, advancing you up to 75 percent of the receivables for an annual charge of 15 percent and a 1.0 percent fee on receivables purchased. The cost of this factoring arrangement is:

Factor fee [0.01 × ($10,000 × 12)]	$1200
Cost of borrowing [0.15 × ($10,000 × 0.75)]	1125
Total cost	$2375

Assignment of Accounts Receivable. *Assignment* is the transfer of accounts receivable to a finance company *with recourse:* If the customer does not pay, you (as borrower) have to pay. The accounts receivable act as collateral, and new receivables substitute for receivables collected. Ownership of accounts receivable is not transferred. Customer payments continue to be made directly to you.

How is it computed? The finance company usually advances between 50 and 85 percent of the face value of the receivables in cash. You incur a service charge and interest on the advance, and you absorb any bad debt losses. The cost is computed as follows:

$$\text{Service charge} + \text{interest} + \text{bad debts} = \text{total cost}$$

2 INVENTORY FINANCING. *Inventory financing* is the use of inventory as collateral for a loan. This typically occurs when you have fully exhausted your borrowing capacity on receivables.

Inventory financing requires the existence of marketable, nonperishable, standardized goods with fast turnover. Inventory should preferably be stable in price; expenses associated with its sale should be minimal.

How Is It Computed? The cost of inventory financing is computed as:

$$\text{Interest} + \text{warehouse cost} = \text{total cost}$$

Example 2 You want to finance $250,000 of inventory. Funds are required for 2 months. An inventory loan may be taken out at 14 percent with an 80 percent advance against the inventory's value. The warehousing cost is $2000 for the 2-month period. The cost of financing the inventory is:

Interest ($0.14 \times 0.80 \times \$250,000 \times \frac{2}{12}$)	$4667
Warehousing cost	2000
Total cost	$6667

HOW IS IT USED AND APPLIED? The advantages of receivables financing are that it (1) avoids the need for long-term financing and (2) provides needed cash flow. Its major disadvantage is its high administrative cost if the business has many small accounts.

The advantages of factoring are that (1) you receive immediate cash, (2) overhead is reduced because credit investigation is no longer needed, (3) you can obtain advances as needed on a seasonal basis, and (4) there are no loan restrictions or required account balances. Disadvantages are that factoring involves (1) high cost, (2) possible negative customer reaction, and (3) possible antagonism from customers who are past due and who are subject to pressure from the factor.

Advantages of assignment are that (1) cash is immediately available, (2) cash advances are received on a seasonal basis, and (3) it avoids negative customer reaction. Its disadvantages are (1) its high cost, (2) the continued credit function, and (3) significant credit risks.

The advance on inventory financing is usually higher for readily marketable goods. A bank will typically lend about 50 percent of the market value of merchandise at an interest rate about 3 to 5 points over the prime interest rate.

Disadvantages of inventory financing include its high interest rate and the restrictions often placed on the inventory.

8 Estimating the Cost of Debt and Equity Financing

INTRODUCTION. The small business owner should observe that if she invests money today to receive benefits in the future, she must be absolutely certain that the business earns at least as much as it costs to acquire the funds for the business. This amount is called the *minimum acceptable return.* If funds cost the business 10 percent, the owner must be sure that she is earning at least this rate of return. To satisfy this test, the business must determine the cost of its funds or, more properly stated, the cost of capital.

The small business owner must ascertain which combination of debt and equity will result in the lowest cost of capital.

HOW IS IT COMPUTED? The best way to calculate a business's cost of capital is to examine each element of its capital structure. The capital structure of a small business may be based on long-term debt, preferred stock, and common stock. (Stock may only be issued by a corporation.) Capital structure is the mix of long-term debt and equity used by the business to finance.

The cost of debt is the interest rate paid to noteholders. The simplest case would be a $1000 note paying $100 annually and thus costing the business 10 percent. The holder of the note would then say that the note's *yield* is 10 percent. The after-tax cost of the debt to the business is the yield to maturity times 1 minus the tax rate. The formula is:

$$\text{Cost of debt} = Y(1 - \text{tax})$$

where Y is the yield.

The cost of preferred stock is similar to the cost of debt in that a constant annual payment is made only if the stock pays dividends. Note, however, that preferred stock has no maturity date, so the small business owner merely has to divide the annual dividend by the current price to calculate the annual percentage cost of the preferred stock. Costs are converted to percentages so that they may be compared. The formula is:

$$\text{Cost of preferred stock} = \frac{\text{annual dividend}}{\text{price of preferred stock}}$$

The cost of common stock is similar to the cost of preferred stock in that an annual dividend payment may exist. Like preferred stock, common stock has no maturity date, so the small business owner merely has to divide the annual dividend by the current price to calculate the annual cost of the common stock. The formula is:

$$\text{Cost of common stock} = \frac{\text{annual dividend}}{\text{price of common stock}}$$

A small business corporation that issues notes, preferred stock, and common stock would combine all elements to arrive at a weighted-average cost of capital. It would be calculated as follows:

	(1) Cost (after tax)	(2) Percentage of capital structure	(3) Weighted cost
Debt			
Preferred stock			
Common stock			_____
Weighted average cost of capital			======

Example 1 The Max Clothing Company signed a note for $10,000 at 10 percent. The business is in the 15 percent corporate tax bracket. The after-tax cost of the note is 8.5 percent, calculated as follows:

$$\begin{aligned}
\text{Cost of debt} &= Y(1 - \text{tax}) \\
&= 10\%(1 - 0.15) \\
&= 10\%(0.85) \\
&= 8.5\%
\end{aligned}$$

Example 2 The Palo Wire Company sold 100 shares of preferred stock for $100 a share to an investor. The preferred stock will pay a guaranteed annual dividend of $9 per share. The cost of the preferred stock is 9 percent annually, calculated as follows:

$$\text{Cost of preferred stock} = \frac{\text{annual dividend}}{\text{price of preferred stock}}$$

$$= \frac{\$9}{\$100} = 9\%$$

Example 3 The Rex Photo Development Company sold 100 shares of its common shares for $100 a share to an investor. All common shareholders expect a guaranteed annual dividend of $7.50 per share. The cost of the common stock is 7.5 percent annually, calculated as follows:

$$\text{Cost of common stock} = \frac{\text{annual dividend}}{\text{price of common stock}}$$

$$= \frac{\$7.50}{\$100} = 7.5\%$$

Example 4 The Halo Paint Company raised capital by issuing a $20,000 bond at 11 percent; selling $20,000 of $100-par-value, 8 percent preferred stock, and selling $10,000 of 6 percent common stock. The company is in the 25 percent tax bracket and estimates that it will earn 10 percent on its capital. The company's weighted-average cost of capital is 7.7 percent, and it is earning 2.3 percent more than its cost of financing. Halo's weighted-average cost of capital is determined as follows:

Cost of $20,000 bond: Cost of debt $= Y(1 - \text{tax})$

$$= 11\%(1 - 0.25)$$

$$= 11\%(0.75)$$

$$= 8.25\%$$

Cost of $20,000 in preferred stock:

$$\text{Cost of preferred stock} = \frac{\text{annual dividend}}{\text{price of preferred stock}}$$

$$= \frac{\$8}{\$100} = 8\%$$

Cost of $10,000 in common stock:

$$\text{Cost of common stock} = \frac{\text{annual dividend}}{\text{price of common stock}}$$

$$= \frac{\$6}{\$100} = 6\%$$

	(1) Cost (after tax)	(2) Percentage of capital structure	(3) Weighted cost
Debt	8.25%	($20,000) 40%	$3.30
Preferred stock	8.00	($20,000) 40%	3.20
Common stock	6.00	($10,000) 20%	1.20
Weighted-average cost of capital			$7.70

HOW IS IT USED AND APPLIED? The weighted-average cost of capital is compared to the businesses's return on capital to see whether the small business owner is at least earning the cost of financing her operations.

A small business owner may need a certain amount of money to develop a new product and in so doing has to weigh the costs of various funding sources.

The minimum expected rate of return of any small business must exceed its cost of capital if the business is to survive. While debt is usually the easiest form of financing because it merely entails borrowing money, excessive debt may increase the financial risk of the business and drive up the costs from all sources of financing.

Budgeting and Profit Planning

9 Establishing a Budgeting System for Profit Planning

INTRODUCTION. Managers of small businesses should adopt a budgeting procedure almost immediately after they start in business. Deviations from what has been budgeted enable business managers to anticipate potential serious financial problems early enough to take corrective action. A comprehensive (master) budget is a formal statement of management's expectations regarding sales, expenses, volume, and other financial transactions of an organization for the coming period. Simply put, a budget is a set of pro forma (projected or planned) financial statements.

HOW IS IT COMPUTED? Budgets are classified broadly into two categories:

1. Operating budgets, which reflect the results of operating decisions
2. Financial budgets, which reflect the financial decisions of the business

The operating budget consists of:

- Sales budget
- Production budget
- Direct materials budget
- Direct labor budget
- Factory overhead budget
- Selling and administrative expense budget
- Pro forma income statement

The financial budget consists of:

- Cash budget
- Pro forma balance sheet

The major steps in preparing the budget are:

1. Prepare a sales forecast.
2. Determine expected production volume.
3. Estimate manufacturing costs and operating expenses.
4. Determine cash flow and other financial effects.
5. Formulate projected financial statements.

Figure 9.1 shows a simplified diagram of the various parts of the comprehensive (master) budget, the master plan of the business.

Begin the budget by estimating sales, then production, then product costs, and finally operating expenses. Sales significantly influence most of what is to follow, so much time and effort should be put into the forecast for each product. Sales revenue is sales volume times the sales price of the product. In a service business, service revenue equals service hours multiplied by the hourly charge. Volume and price do influence each other, so you need to try to balance the two to make the most amount of money.

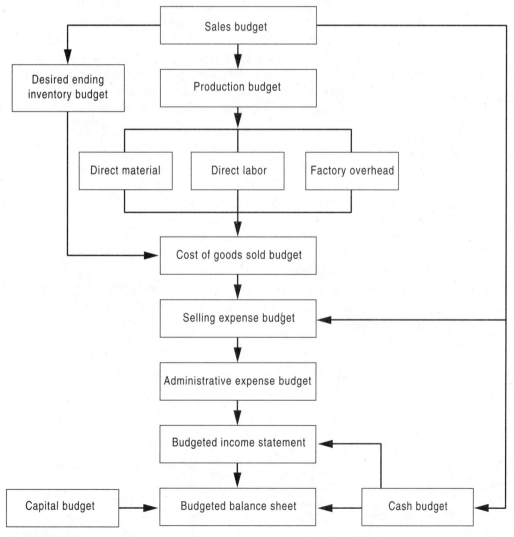

Figure 9.1 Comprehensive (master) budget.

A knowledge of how efficient and capable your production is and how much inventory you need leads to the production budget. With knowledge of how much you are going to produce, you can start to determine product cost. Product costs are a function of direct materials, direct labor, and production (factory) overhead. *Direct* means anything that is used in the production of the product (not advertising, administration, research and development, or other indirect expenses). Selling and administrative expenses are budgeted after production costs.

ILLUSTRATION. To illustrate how all these budgets are put together, we will focus on a manufacturing business called Packard Manufacturers, which produces and markets a single product. We will assume that the business develops the master budget in contribution format for 19B on a quarterly basis. We will highlight the variable cost–fixed cost breakdown throughout the illustration. Variable costs, such as direct labor and production costs, change with volume. Fixed costs, such as rent and insurance, are constant regardless of the volume produced.

The Sales Budget. The sales budget is the starting point in preparing the master budget, since estimated sales volume influences nearly all the other items that appear in the master budget. The sales budget should show total sales in quantity and value. The expected total sales can be breakeven or target income sales or projected sales. Sales may be analyzed further by product, by territory, by customer, and, of course, by seasonal pattern of expected sales.

Generally, the sales budget includes a computation of expected cash collections from credit sales, which will be used later for cash budgeting.

Example 1

PACKARD MANUFACTURERS
Sales Budget
For the Year Ending December 31, 19B

| | Quarter | | | | |
	1	2	3	4	Total
Expected sales in units	800	700	900	800	3,200
Unit sales price	× $80	× $80	× $80	× $80	× $80
Total sales	$64,000	$56,000	$72,000	$64,000	$256,000

	Quarter				
	1	2	3	4	Total

Schedule of Expected Cash Collections

	1	2	3	4	Total
Accounts receivable, 12/31/19A, $9,500*	$ 9,500				
1st-quarter sales ($64,000)	44,800†	$17,920‡			$ 62,720
2d-quarter sales ($56,000)		39,200	$15,680		54,880
3d-quarter sales ($72,000)			50,400	$20,160	70,560
4th-quarter sales ($64,000)				44,800	44,800
Total cash collections	$54,300	$57,120	$66,080	$64,960	$242,460

*All of the $9500 accounts receivable balance is assumed to be collectible in the first quarter.
†70% of a quarter's sales are collected in the quarter of sale.
‡28% of a quarter's sales are collected in the quarter following, and the remaining 2% are uncollectible.

The Production Budget.   The production budget is a statement of the output by product and is generally expressed in units. It should take into account the sales budget, plant capacity, whether stocks are to be increased or decreased, and outside purchases. The number of units expected to be manufactured to meet budgeted sales and inventory requirements is set forth in the production budget. The expected volume of production is determined by subtracting the estimated inventory at the beginning of the period from the sum of the units expected to be sold and the desired inventory at the end of the period. The production budget is illustrated in the following example.

Example 2

PACKARD MANUFACTURERS
Production Budget
For the Year Ending December 31, 19B

	Quarter				
	1	2	3	4	Total
Planned sales (Example 1)	800	700	900	800	3200
Desired ending inventory*	70	90	80	100†	100
Total needs	870	790	980	900	3300
Less: Beginning inventory‡	80	70	90	80	80
Units to be produced	790	720	890	820	3220

*10% of the next quarter's sales.
†Estimated.
‡The same as the previous quarter's ending inventory.

The Direct Materials Budget. When the level of production has been computed, a direct materials budget should be constructed to show how much material will be required for production and how much material must be purchased to meet this production requirement. The purchase will depend on both expected usage of materials and inventory levels. The formula for computation of the purchase is:

Purchase in units =
usuage + desired ending material inventory units
− beginning inventory units

The direct materials budget is usually accompanied by a computation of expected cash payments for materials.

Example 3

PACKARD MANUFACTURERS
Direct Materials Budget
For the Year Ending December 31, 19B

	Quarter				
	1	2	3	4	Total
Units to be produced (Example 2)	790	720	890	820	3,220
Material needs per unit (lb)	× 3	× 3	× 3	× 3	× 3
Material needs for production	2,370	2,160	2,670	2,460	9,660
Desired ending inventory of materials*	216	267	246	250†	250
Total needs	2,586	2,427	2,916	2,710	9,910
Less: Beginning inventory of materials‡	237	216	267	246	237
Materials to be purchased	2,349	2,211	2,649	2,464	9,673
Unit price	× $2	× $2	× $2	× $2	× $2
Purchase cost	$4,698	$4,422	$5,298	$4,928	$19,346

Schedule of Expected Cash Disbursements

	1	2	3	4	Total
Accounts payable, 12/31/19A	$2,200				$ 2,200
1st-quarter purchases ($4,698)	2,349	$2,349§			4,698
2d-quarter purchases ($4,422)		2,211	$2,211		4,422
3d-quarter purchases ($5,298)			2,649	$2,649	5,298
4th-quarter purchases ($4,928)				2,464	2,464
Total disbursements	$4,549	$4,560	$4,860	$5,113	$19,082

*10% of the next quarter's units needed for production.
†Estimated.
‡The same as the prior quarter's ending inventory.
§50% of a quarter's purchases are paid for in the quarter of purchase; the remainder are paid for in the following quarter.

The Direct Labor Budget. The production requirements as set forth in the production budget also provide the starting point for the preparation of the direct labor budget. To compute direct labor requirements, expected production volume for each period is multiplied by the number of direct labor hours required to produce a single unit. The number of direct labor hours to meet production requirements is then multiplied by the direct labor cost per hour to obtain budgeted total direct labor costs.

Example 4

PACKARD MANUFACTURERS
Direct Labor Budget
For the Year Ending December 31, 19B

	Quarter				
	1	2	3	4	Total
Units to be produced (Example 2)	790	720	890	820	3,220
Direct labor hours per unit	× 5	× 5	× 5	× 5	× 5
Total hours	3,950	3,600	4,450	4,100	16,100
Direct labor cost per hour	× $5	× $5	× $5	× $5	× $5
Total direct labor cost	$19,750	$18,000	$22,250	$20,500	$80,500

The Factory Overhead Budget. The factory overhead budget provides a schedule of all manufacturing costs other than direct materials and direct labor. Examples are factory rent, factory insurance, and factory depreciation. Using the contribution approach to budgeting requires the development of a predetermined overhead rate for the variable portion of the factory overhead. (The contribution margin format is sales − variable costs = contribution margin − fixed costs = net income.)

Remember that depreciation does not entail a cash outlay and therefore must be deducted from the total factory overhead in computing cash disbursements for factory overhead.

Example 5 To illustrate the factory overhead budget, we will assume that:

- Total factory overhead budgeted = $6000 fixed (per quarter), plus $2 per hour of direct labor.
- Depreciation expenses are $3250 each quarter.
- All overhead costs involving cash outlays are paid for in the quarter incurred.

PACKARD MANUFACTURERS
Factory Overhead Budget
For the Year Ending December 31, 19B

	Quarter				
	1	2	3	4	Total
Budgeted direct labor hours (Example 4)	3,950	3,600	4,450	4,100	16,100
Variable overhead rate	× $2	× $2	× $2	× $2	× $2
Variable overhead budgeted	$ 7,900	$ 7,200	$ 8,900	$ 8,200	$32,200
Fixed overhead budgeted	6,000	6,000	6,000	6,000	24,000
Total budgeted overhead	$13,900	$13,200	$14,900	$14,200	$56,200
Less: Depreciation	3,250	3,250	3,250	3,250	13,000
Cash disbursement for overhead	$10,650	$ 9,950	$11,650	$10,950	$43,200

The Ending Inventory Budget. The desired ending inventory budget provides the information required for the construction of budgeted financial statements. Specifically, it helps in computing the cost of goods sold for the budgeted income statement. Second, it gives the dollar value of the ending materials and finished goods inventory, which appear on the budgeted balance sheet.

Example 6

PACKARD MANUFACTURERS
Ending Inventory Budget
For the Year Ending December 31, 19B

	Ending inventory units	Unit cost	Total
Direct materials	250 lb (Example 3)	$ 2	$ 500
Finished goods	100 units (Example 2)	$41*	$4100

*The unit variable cost of $41 is computed as follows:

	Unit cost	Units	Total
Direct materials	$2	3 lb	$ 6
Direct labor	5	5 hr	25
Variable overhead	2	5 hr	10
Total variable manufacturing cost			$41

The Selling and Administrative Expense Budget. The selling and administrative expense budget lists the operating expenses involved in selling the products and in managing the business. In order to complete the budgeted income statement in contribution format, variable selling and administrative expense per unit must be computed.

Example 7

PACKARD MANUFACTURERS
Selling and Administrative Expense Budget
For the Year Ending December 31, 19B

	Quarter				
	1	2	3	4	Total
Expected sales in units	800	700	900	800	3,200
Variable selling and administrative expense per unit*	× $4	× $4	× $4	× $4	× $4
Budgeted variable expense	$ 3,200	$ 2,800	$ 3,600	$ 3,200	$12,800
Fixed selling and administrative expenses:					
Advertising	$ 1,100	$ 1,100	$ 1,100	$ 1,100	$ 4,400
Insurance	2,800				2,800
Office salaries	8,500	8,500	8,500	8,500	34,000
Rent	350	350	350	350	1,400
Taxes			1,200		1,200
Total budgeted selling and administrative expenses†	$15,950	$12,750	$14,750	$13,150	$56,600

*Includes sales agents' commissions, shipping, and supplies.
†Paid for in the quarter incurred.

The Cash Budget. The cash budget is prepared for the purpose of cash planning and control. It presents the expected cash inflows and cash outflows for a designated time period. The cash budget helps management keep cash balances in reasonable relationship to its needs. It aids in avoiding unnecessary idle cash and possible cash shortages. The cash budget consists typically of four major sections:

1. The receipts section, which is the beginning cash balance, cash collections from customers, and other receipts

2. The disbursements section, which comprises all cash payments made, by purpose

3. The cash surplus or deficit section, which simply shows the difference between the cash receipts section and the cash disbursements section

4. The financing section, which provides a detailed account of the borrowings and repayments expected during the budgeting period

Example 8   To illustrate, we will make the following assumptions:

- The business desires to maintain a $5000 minimum cash balance at the end of each quarter.
- All borrowing and repayment must be in multiples of $500 at an interest rate of 10 percent per annum. Interest is computed and paid as the principal is repaid. Borrowing takes place at the beginning of each quarter and repayment at the end of each quarter.

PACKARD MANUFACTURERS
Cash Budget
For the Year Ending December 31, 19B

	Example	Quarter 1	2	3	4	Total
Cash balance, beginning	Given	$10,000	$ 9,401	$ 5,461	$ 9,106	$10,000
Add: Receipts						
Collected from customers	1	54,300	57,120	66,080	64,960	242,460
Total cash available		$64,300	$66,521	$71,541	$74,066	$252,460
Less: Disbursements						
Direct materials	3	$4,549	$ 4,560	$ 4,860	$ 5,113	$19,082
Direct labor	4	19,750	18,000	22,250	20,500	80,500
Factory overhead	5	10,650	9,950	11,650	10,950	43,200
Selling and administrative	7	15,950	12,750	14,750	13,150	56,600
Machinery purchase	Given	—	24,300	—	—	24,300
Income tax	Given	4,000	—	—	—	4,000
Total disbursements		$54,899	$ 69,560	$53,510	$49,713	$227,682
Cash surplus (deficit)		$ 9,401	$ (3,039)	$18,031	$24,353	$ 24,778
Financing:						
Borrowing		—	8,500	—	—	$8,500
Repayment		—	—	$(8,500)	—	(8,500)
Interest		—	—	(425)	—	(425)
Total financing		—	$ 8,500	$(8,925)	—	$(425)
Cash balance, ending		$ 9,401	$ 5,461	$ 9,106	$24,353	$24,353

The Budgeted Income Statement.   The budgeted income statement summarizes the various component projections of revenue and expenses for the budgeting period. However, for control purposes the budget can be divided into quarters or even months, depending on the need.

Example 9

PACKARD MANUFACTURERS
Budgeted Income Statement
For the Year Ending December 31, 19B

	Example no.		
Sales (3,200 units @ $80)	1		$256,000
Less: Variable expenses			
Variable cost of goods sold			
(3,200 units @ $41)	6	$131,200	
Variable selling and administrative	7	12,800	144,000
Contribution margin			$112,000
Less: Fixed expenses			
Factory overhead	5	$ 24,000	
Selling and administrative	7	43,800	67,800
Net operating income			$ 44,200
Less: Interest expense	8		425
Income before taxes			$ 43,775
Less: Income taxes	20%		8,755
Net income			$ 35,020

The Budgeted Balance Sheet. The budgeted balance sheet is developed by beginning with the balance sheet for the year just ended and adjusting it, using all the activities that are expected to take place during the budgeting period. Some of the reasons why the budgeted balance sheet must be prepared are:

- It could disclose some unfavorable financial conditions that management might want to avoid.
- It serves as a final check on the mathematical accuracy of all the other schedules.
- It helps management perform a variety of ratio calculations.
- It highlights future resources and obligations.

Example 10 To illustrate, we will use the following balance sheet for the year 19A.

PACKARD MANUFACTURERS
Balance Sheet
December 31, 19A

Assets		Liabilities and Stockholders' Equity	
Current Assets:		Current Liabilities:	
Cash	$ 10,000	Accounts Payable	$ 2,200
Accounts Receivable	9,500	Income Tax Payable	4,000
Materials Inventory	474	Total Current Liabilities	$ 6,200
Finished Goods Inventory	3,280		
Total Current Assets	$ 23,254		

PACKARD MANUFACTURERS
Balance Sheet (*Continued*)
December 31, 19A

Assets		**Liabilities and Stockholders' Equity**	
Fixed Assets:		Stockholders' Equity:	
Land	$ 50,000	Common Stock (no par)	$ 70,000
Buildings and Equipment	100,000	Retained Earnings	37,054
Accumulated Depreciation	(60,000)		
	$ 90,000		
Total Assets	$113,254	Total Liabilities and Stockholders' Equity	$113,254

PACKARD MANUFACTURERS
Budgeted Balance Sheet
December 31, 19B

Assets		**Liabilities and Stockholders' Equity**	
Current Assets:		Current Liabilities:	
Cash	$ 24,353 (a)	Accounts Payable	$ 2,464 (h)
Accounts Receivable	23,040 (b)	Income Tax Payable	8,755 (i)
Materials Inventory	500 (c)	Total Current Liabilities	$ 11,219
Finished Goods Inventory	4,100 (d)		
Total Current Assets	$ 51,993		
Fixed Assets:		Stockholders' Equity:	
Land	$ 50,000 (e)	Common Stock (no par)	70,000 (j)
Buildings and Equipment	124,300 (f)	Retained Earnings	72,074 (k)
Accumulated Depreciation	(73,000) (g)		
	$101,300		
Total Assets	$153,293	Total Liabilities and Stockholders' Equity	$153,293

Computations:
(a) From Example 8 (cash budget).
(b) $9,500 + $256,000 sales − $242,460 receipts = $23,040.
(c), (d) From Example 6 (ending inventory budget).
(e) No change.
(f) $100,000 + $24,300 (from Example 8) = $124,300.
(g) $60,000 + $13,000 (from Example 5) = $73,000.
(h) $2,200 + $19,346 − $19,082 = $2,464 (all accounts payable relate to material purchases), or 50% of 4th-quarter purchase = 50%($4,928) = $2,464.
(i) From Example 9 (budgeted income statement).
(j) No change.
(k) $37,054 + $35,020 net income = $72,074.

HOW IS IT USED AND APPLIED? A budget is a tool for both planning and control. At the beginning of the period, the budget is a plan or standard; at the end of the period, it serves as a control device to help the business manager measure performance against the plan so that future performance may be improved.

The major objectives of a budgeting system are to:

1. Set acceptable targets for revenues and expenses.
2. Increase the likelihood that targets will be reached.
3. Provide time and opportunity to formulate and evaluate options should obstacles arise.
4. Evaluate a variety of "what-if" scenarios (especially with the aid of computer software) in an effort to find the best possible course of action.

It is important to realize that with the aid of computer technology, budgeting can be used as an effective device for evaluation of "what-if" scenarios. This way managers should be able to move toward finding the best course of action among various alternatives through simulation. If the manager does not like what he sees in analyzing the budgeted financial statements in terms of various financial ratios such as liquidity, activity (turnover), leverage, profit margin, and market value ratios, he can always alter the contemplated decision and planning set. A ratio is a relationship of one amount to another. It relates financial statement components to each other.

10 What Is the Cost Structure?

INTRODUCTION. The ratio of variable costs to fixed costs measures the relationship between costs that change with volume and costs that do not change within the short term.

HOW IS IT COMPUTED?

$$\frac{\text{Total variable costs}}{\text{Total fixed costs}}$$

Examples of variable costs are direct materials and direct labor used in producing a product. Examples of fixed costs are rent, insurance, and property taxes.

Example A small business reports total variable costs of $800,000 and total fixed costs of $8,000,000. The ratio is 0.10. This is unfavorable, because it is difficult to reduce fixed costs in the short run when business falls off.

HOW IS IT USED AND APPLIED? When there is idle capacity, additional volume may be produced but total fixed cost remains constant. However, fixed cost per unit decreases because total fixed cost is spread over more units. Total variable cost increases as more units are produced, but the variable cost per unit remains the same. In a nonmanufacturing environment, service hours are substituted for units produced.

The cost structure of the business indicates what costs may be cut if needed, as in a recessionary environment (e.g., the early 1990s). The owner can more readily control and adjust variable costs than fixed costs.

See Sec. 54, Cost-Volume-Profit Analysis; Sec. 55, Contribution Margin Analysis; and Sec. 107, Operating Leverage.

11 Using Budgeting to Control Cash

INTRODUCTION. The *cash budget* presents the amount and timing of the expected cash inflows and outflows for a specified time period. It is a tool for cash planning and control and should be detailed enough that you know how much is required to run your small business. If you can estimate cash flows reliably, you will be able to keep cash balances near a target level using fewer transactions.

The cash budget should be prepared for the shortest time period for which reliable financial information can be obtained. In the case of many small businesses, this may be one week. However, it is also possible to predict major cash receipts and cash payments for a specific day.

HOW IS IT PREPARED? The cash budget usually consists of four major sections:

1. The *receipts section,* which is the beginning cash balance, cash collections from customers, and other receipts

2. The *disbursements section,* which comprises all cash payments that are expected for the budgeting period

3. The *cash surplus or deficit section,* which shows the difference between the cash receipts section and the cash disbursements section

4. The *financing section,* which provides a detailed account of the borrowings and repayments anticipated during the budgeting period

TABLE 11.1   Important Components of a Cash Budget

Cash inflows
  Operating: Cash sales, collections from customers on account
  Nonoperating: Investment income (dividend income, interest income),
  rental income, sales of assets, amount received from debt incurrence,
  royaly income

Cash outflows
  Operating: Salaries expense, rent expense, purchases of materials and supplies, payments to vendors, utilities expense
  Nonoperating: Purchases of fixed assets, repayments of loans, tax expense,
  purchases of stocks and bonds in other companies

If further financing is needed, the cash budget projections allow adequate lead time for the necessary arrangements to be made.

Cash budgets are often prepared monthly, but there are no strict rules for determining the length of the budget period. In general, it should be long enough to show the effects of your business policies, yet short enough so that estimates can be made with reasonable accuracy. Table 11.1 shows the major elements of a cash budget.

The basis for predicting cash receipts is *sales,* whether from cash sales or collections from customer balances. An incorrect sales estimate will result in erroneous cash estimates. The sales prediction also influences the projected cash outlays for manufacturing costs, since production is tied to sales. The projection of operating expenses may be tied to the supplier's payment terms.

Example

FRED'S SPORTS CENTER
Cash Budget
January 19X8

Cash balance, Jan. 1	$ 50,000
Add: Cash receipts from customers	150,000
Cash available	$200,000
Less: Cash payments	
For inventory	$ 40,000
Rent	10,000
Insurance	5,000
Supplies	3,000
Utilities	2,000
Purchase of equipment	8,000
Salaries	12,000
Taxes	10,000
Total cash payments	$ 90,000
Cash balance, Jan. 31	$110,000

HOW IS IT USED AND APPLIED? The cash budget allows you to review future cash receipts and cash payments to identify possible *patterns of cash flows.* In this way, you can examine your collection and disbursement efforts to ascertain if you are maximizing your net cash flows. Further, the cash budget reveals when and how much to borrow and when you will be able to pay the money back. For instance, if your cash budget indicates that a large cash outlay will be needed to purchase assets such as store fixtures, you may have to borrow money and determine a debt repayment schedule. In order to obtain a credit line, lenders usually require you to submit a cash budget, along with your financial statements.

Comparing estimated and actual cash figures allows you to study the reasons for any major discrepancies and to take any corrective action. *Variance analysis* gives you an idea of your cash position and provides insight in improving cash estimates in the next budgeting period. It also aids in the periodic revision of projections. This updating usually occurs at the beginning of each budget segment (e.g., the first day of a quarter, or the first day of a month). Budgets should be modified immediately for significant changes. Table 11.2 shows a format that may be used for variance analysis.

Variance analysis is important for a small business, whether it be a retailer, wholesaler, manufacturer, or service concern. Evaluation of cash variances may be performed yearly, quarterly, monthly, or daily. If theft is suspected, variance analysis should be done frequently. After all, cash is the easiest asset to steal.

TABLE 11.2   Variance Analysis Report for Cash Budgeting

	Budget	Actual	Percentage	Change	Reason
Cash balance, Jan. 1					
Add: Cash receipts					
Cash sales					
Collections on account					
Cash available					
Less: Cash payments					
Wages					
Utilities					
Rent					
Insurance					
Purchase assets					
Miscellaneous					
Taxes					
Total cash paid					
Cash balance, Jan. 31					

12 Forecasting Cash Collections

INTRODUCTION. A forecast of cash collections and potential bad debts is an essential part of cash budgeting. The critical step in making such a forecast is estimating the cash collection and bad debt *percentages* and applying them to sales or accounts receivable balances.

HOW IS IT COMPUTED? The historical trend in cash collections relative to sales should be examined for the past 3 years. An example illustrates the technique.

Example 1 Assume that an analysis by Mr. Jones, the owner of a clothing store, of collection experience for August sales revealed the following collection data:

Description	Percent of total credit sales
Collected in August	2.3
September	80.2
October	9.9
November	5.1
December	0.5
Cash discounts	1.0
Bad debt losses	1.0
Total	100.0

If next year's August sales are expected to fall into the same pattern, then the calculated percentage for August credit sales can be used to determine the probable monthly distribution of collections. The same analysis applied to each month of the year will give a reasonably reliable basis for collection forecasting. The worksheet (August column) for cash collections might look as follows:

Month of sale	Percent of total	Net sales	August collections
April	0.5	$168,000	$ 840
May	4.2	192,000	8,064
June	8.9	311,100	27,688
July	82.1	325,600	267,318
August	2.3	340,000	7,820
Total collections			$311,730
Cash discounts (July)	1.0	325,600	(3,256)
Losses	1.0	340,000	(3,400)
Total			$305,074

The following example illustrates how cash collection rates are used to generate a forecast of the cash collection portion of the cash budget.

Example 2 The following data are given for Sharpe's Clothing Store:

	September actual	October actual	November estimated	December estimated
Cash sales	$ 7,000	$ 6,000	$ 8,000	$ 6,000
Credit sales	50,000	48,000	62,000	80,000

Past experience based on the aging of accounts receivable indicates that collections normally occur in the following pattern:

- No collections are made in the month of sale.
- 80 percent of the sales of any month are collected in the following month.
- 19 percent of sales are collected in the second following month.
- 1 percent of sales are uncollectible.

The total cash receipts for November and December are computed as follows:

	November	December
Cash receipts		
Cash sales	$ 8,000	$ 6,000
Cash collections		
September sales		
$50,000 × 19%	9,500	
October sales		
$48,000 × 80%	38,400	
$48,000 × 19%		9,120
November sales		
$62,000 × 80%		49,600
Total cash receipts	$55,900	$64,720

HOW IS IT USED AND APPLIED?   The forecasting of cash collections is important in predicting whether sufficient cash will be available to meet expenditure needs. Further, the more quickly cash is received from customers, the less is the risk of noncollection. In addition, a return can be earned on the cash received early.

13 "What-if" Analysis

INTRODUCTION.   Managers make decisions in the fact of uncertainty or risk. The environments in which they operate are subject to change without notice. It is therefore advisable to set up "what-if" scenarios and analyze them with the aid of computer software.

HOW IS IT COMPUTED?   Many "what-if" scenarios can be evaluated using the concepts of contribution margin as a tool for profit planning. *Contribution margin* is the difference between sales and the variable cost of a product or service; it is the amount of money available to cover fixed costs and generate profits.

Example 1   To illustrate a "what-if" analysis, consider the following data for the Allison Toy Store:

	Total	Per unit	Percentage
Sales (1,500 units)	$37,500	$25	100%
Less: Variable costs	15,000	10	40
Contribution margin	$22,500	$15	60%
Less: Fixed costs	15,000		
Net income	$ 7,500		

Let us suppose that, in an effort to stimulate sales, the owner is considering cutting the unit price by $5 and increasing the advertising budget by $1000. If these two steps are taken, she feels that unit sales will go up by 60 percent. Should the two steps be taken? To answer the question, you may construct a proposed income statement as follows:

	(A) Present (1,500 units)	(B) Proposed (2,400 units)	(B – A) Difference
Sales	$37,500 (@ $25)	$48,000 (@ $20)	$10,500
Less: Variable cost	15,000 (@ $10)	24,000 (@ $10)	9,000
Contribution margin	$22,500	$24,000	$ 1,500
Less: Fixed costs	15,000	16,000	1,000
Net income	$ 7,500	$ 8,000	$ 500

The answer is yes, since these two steps will increase net income by $500.

Example 2   Delta Gamma Manufacturers wishes to prepare a 3-year projection of net income using the following information:

1. 19X4 base-year amounts are as follows:

Sales revenues	$4,500,000
Cost of sales	2,900,000
Selling and administrative expenses	800,000
Net income before taxes	800,000

2. Use the following "what-if" assumptions:

- Sales revenues increase by 6 percent in 19X5, 7 percent in 19X6, and 8 percent in 19X7.
- Cost of sales increases by 5 percent each year.
- Selling and administrative expenses increase only 1 percent in 19X5 and will remain at the 19X5 level thereafter.
- The income tax rate is 46 percent.

Figure 13.1 shows a spreadsheet for the pro forma income statement for the next 3 years. Using a spreadsheet program such as Lotus 1-2-3 allows managers to evaluate various "what-if" scenarios.

CAN A COMPUTER HELP?   Performing "what-if" analyses without the aid of a computer is almost impossible. "What-if" software includes:

1. Spreadsheet programs such as Lotus 1-2-3, Microsoft's Excel, and Quattro Pro.

2. Cash management and accounting software such as Quicken and Up Your Cash Flow.

3. Decision-support and budgeting software such as COMSHARE's Interactive Financial Planning System (IFPS), @Risk, and Encore Plus.

HOW IS IT USED AND APPLIED?   The cash budget would be incomplete if it were based on only one set of estimated cash inflows and cash outflows. These figures may well be *expected* cash flows or even *most likely* estimates, but we need to consid-

	19X4	19X5	19X6	19X7
Sales	$4,500,000	$4,770,000	$5,103,900	$5,512,212
Cost of sales	$2,900,000	$3,045,000	$3,197,250	$3,357,113
Gross profit	$1,600,000	$1,725,000	$1,906,650	$2,155,100
Selling & adm. exp.	$ 800,000	$ 808,000	$ 816,080	$ 824,241
Earnings before tax	$ 800,000	$ 917,000	$1,090,570	$1,330,859
Tax	$ 368,000	$ 421,820	$ 501,662	$ 612,195
Earnings after tax	$ 432,000	$ 495,180	$ 588,908	$ 718,664

Figure 13.1   Delta Gamma Manufacturers: three-year income projections (19X4–19X7).

TABLE 13.1   Certain and Uncertain Cash Flows

Known cash flows	Uncertain cash flows
Interest receipts	Cash sales
Rents	Collections
Payroll	Payable payments
Tax payments	
Interest payments	
Loan repayments	
Purchase of long-term assets	

er the possibility of errors or variability in cash flow estimates. Table 13.1 lists the principal known and uncertain cash flows.

The variability in cash flows can be handled by "what-if" analysis or by optimistic/pessimistic forecasts. For example, what if your cash sales were, say, 10 percent higher, or lower, than originally expected? A cash budget prepared for a worst-case scenario might be quite useful. If may also allow you to plan better for difficult times.

14 Budget Accuracy Ratios

INTRODUCTION.   The accuracy of a budget may be evaluated by comparing budget figures to actual figures. The closer the actual amounts are to the estimates, the better is the budget process and the greater is the reliance that may be placed on future projections.

HOW IS IT COMPUTED?

$$\text{Budget sales accuracy} = \frac{\text{actual sales}}{\text{budget sales}}$$

$$\text{Budget cost compliance} = \frac{\text{actual costs}}{\text{budgeted costs}}$$

$$\text{Budget profit reliability} = \frac{\text{actual profit}}{\text{budgeted profit}}$$

Example   An owner budgeted profit for $800,000, but the business actually earned $1,000,000. The reasons for this favorable result might be one or more of the following:

- Higher revenue and/or fewer expenses than predicted. The higher revenue might be due to excellent salesperson efforts. The lower expenses may have arisen from a cost-reduction program.

- The intentional underestimation of the budgeted profit, so that when actual sales exceed budgeted sales the manager looks good.
- Poor planning due to the failure to properly take historical and current factors into account when making up the budget.

HOW IS IT USED AND APPLIED?   There is no assurance that a plan designed to increase earnings will in fact do so. However, if actual profit exceeds budgeted profit, the owner has achieved the profit goal. This may arise because of greater revenue than expected, or better control over costs than anticipated.

By comparing actual to budgeted amounts, the owner can determine whether the business plans are sound. If not, improvements in the planning process are needed. Perhaps the planning is overoptimistic or unrealistic. On the other hand, the problem may lie with an inclination to overspend and/or waste. The expense deviation should be related to that of sales. Perhaps all that has happened is simply that expenses went up because sales revenue increased. In that case, the result is expected and no negative sign exists.

Business Forecasting Methods

15 Projecting Financing Needs

INTRODUCTION. Forecasts of future sales and their related expenses provide the business with the information needed to project its future needs for financing. The percentage-of-sales method is widely used. It involves estimating the various expenses, assets, and liabilities for a future period as a percentage of the sales forecast and then using these percentages, together with the projected sales, to construct pro forma balance sheets.

HOW IS IT COMPUTED? The basic steps involved in projecting financing needs are as follows.

1. Project sales. The sales forecast is the initial and most important step. Most other forecasts (budgets) follow the sales forecast.
2. Project additional variables such as expenses.
3. Estimate the level of investment in current and fixed assets that are required to support the projected sales.
4. Calculate financing needs.

The following example illustrates how to develop a pro forma balance sheet and determine the amount of external financing needed.

Example Assume that sales for 19X1 = $20 million, projected sales for 19X2 = $24 million, net income = 5 percent of sales, and the dividend payout ratio = 40 percent. Figure 15.1 is a step-by-step illustration of the method for calculating external financing needs. (All dollar amounts are in millions.)

The steps for the computations are outlined as follows:

Step 1. Express those balance sheet items that vary directly with sales as a percentage of sales. Any item such as long-term debt that does not vary directly with sales is designated "n.a." or "not applicable."

Step 2. Multiply these percentages by the 19X2 projected sales = $24 to obtain the projected amounts as shown in the last column.

Step 3. Insert figures for long-term debt, common stock and capital surplus from the 19X1 balance sheet.

Step 4. Compute 19X2 retained earnings as shown in note (*b*).

Step 5. Sum the asset accounts, obtaining a total projected assets of $7.2, and add the projected liabilities and equity to obtain $7.12, the total financing provided. Since liabilities and equity must total $7.2 but only $7.12 is projected, there is a shortfall of $0.08 "external financing needed."

	Present (19X1)	Percent of sales (19X1 sales = $20)	Projected (19X2 sales = $24)	
Assets				
Current assets	2	10	2.4	
Fixed assets	4	20	4.8	
Total assets	6		7.2	
Liabilities and stockholders' equity				
Current liabilities	2	10	2.4	
Long-term debt	2.5	n.a.	2.5	
Total liabilities	4.5		4.9	
Common stock	0.1	n.a.	0.1	
Capital surplus	0.2	n.a.	0.2	
Retained earnings	1.2		1.92 (a)	
Total equity	1.5		2.22	
Total liabilities and stockholders' equity	6		7.12	Total financing provided
			0.08 (b)	External financing needed
			7.2	Total

Notes:
(a) 19X2 retained earnings = 19X1 retained earnings + projected net income − cash dividends paid = $1.2 + 5%($24) − 40%[5%($24)] = $1.2 + $1.2 − $0.48 = $2.4 − $0.48 = $1.92.
(b) External financing needed = projected total assets − (projected total liabilities + projected equity) = $7.2 − ($4.9 + $2.22) = $7.2 − $7.12 = $0.08.

Figure 15.1 Pro forma balance sheet (in millions of dollars).

Any external financing needed may be raised by issuing notes payable, bonds, stocks, or any combination of these financing sources.

HOW IS IT USED AND APPLIED? Business owners should determine the portion of next year's fund requirements that has to be raised externally. By doing so they can get a head start on arranging a least-cost financing plan. The major advantage of the percentage-of-sales method of financial forecasting is that it is simple and inexpensive to use. To obtain a more precise projection of future financing needs, however, the preparation of a cash budget is required. One important assumption behind the use of the percentage-of-sales method is that the business is operating at full capacity. This means that the business has no production capacity to absorb a projected increase in sales and thus requires additional investment in assets.

16 Naive Forecasting Models

INTRODUCTION. Naive forecasting models are based exclusively on historical observation of sales or other variables such as earnings and cash flows. They do *not* attempt to explain the underlying causal relationships which produce the variables being forecast. Naive models may be classified into two groups. One group consists of simple projection models. These models require inputs of data from recent observations, but no statistical analysis is performed. The second group is made up of models that, while naive, are complex enough to require a computer. Traditional methods such as classical decomposition, moving-average, and exponential smoothing models are some examples. (See Secs. 17 and 18.)

The *advantages* of naive forecasting models are that they are quick and inexpensive to develop, store, and operate. The *disadvantages* are that they do not consider possible causal relationships that underlie the forecasted variable.

HOW IS IT COMPUTED?

1. A simple type of naive model uses actual sales for the current period as the forecast for the next period. Let us use the symbol F as the forecast value and the symbol A_t as the actual value for time t. Then

$$F = A_t$$

2. If we consider trends, then

$$F = A_t + (A_t - A_{t-1})$$

This model adds the latest observed absolute period-to-period change to the most recent actual data of the variable.

3. If we want to incorporate the rate of change rather than the absolute amount, then

$$F = A_t \left(\frac{A_t}{A_{t-1}} \right)$$

Example Consider the following quarterly sales data for Rex Tool Stores in 19X1:

Month	Monthly sales of product
1	$5504
2	5810
3	6100

We will develop forecasts for the fourth quarter of 19X1 based on the three models we have discussed.

1. $F = A_t = \$6100$
2. $F = A_t + (A_t - A_{t-1})$
   $= \$6100 + (\$6100 - \$5810)$
   $= \$6100 + \$290 = \$6390$
3. $F = A_t \left(\dfrac{A_t}{A_{t-1}} \right)$

   $= \$6100 \left(\dfrac{\$6100}{\$5810} \right)$

   $= \$6100(1.05)$
   $= \$6405$

HOW IS IT USED AND APPLIED?   The naive models can be applied, with very little use of a computer, to develop forecasts for sales, earnings, and cash flows. These models, however, must be used in conjunction with more complex naive models such as classical decomposition and exponential smoothing, and more sophisticated models such as regression analysis. See Sec. 17, Moving Averages; Sec. 18, Exponential Smoothing; Sec. 19, Regression Analysis; Sec. 20, Regression Statistics; Sec. 21, Simple Regression; Sec. 22, Trend Equation; Sec. 23, Decompo-sition of Time Series; and Sec. 24, Measuring Accuracy of Forecasts.

17 Moving Averages

INTRODUCTION.   A moving average is an average that is updated as new information is received. A manager employs the most recent observations to calculate an average, which is used as the forecast for the next period.

HOW IS IT COMPUTED?   For a moving average, simply take the most recent observations and calculate an average. Moving averages are updated continually as new data are available.

Example   Assume that the manager of Drake Hardware Store has the following sales data:

Month	Sales (000)
April	20
May	21
June	24
July	22
August	26
September	25

Using a 5-month moving average, predicted sales for October are computed as follows:

$$\frac{21 + 24 + 22 + 26 + 25}{5} = \frac{118}{5} = 23.60 \quad \text{or} \quad \$23{,}600$$

HOW IS IT USED AND APPLIED? Moving averages are used, for example, to project future sales. Once sales are projected, needed financing for production and inventory may be planned. Business owners can choose the number of periods to use on the basis of the relative importance attached to old versus current data.

For example, one can compare two possibilities, a 5-month and a 3-month period. In terms of the relative importance of new versus old data, the old data receive a weight of $\frac{4}{5}$ and current data $\frac{1}{5}$. In the second possibility, the old data receive a weight of $\frac{2}{3}$, while current observation receive a $\frac{1}{3}$ weight. This is a special case of the exponential smoothing method, in which a smoothing constant is in effect the weight given to the most recent data. See Sec. 18, Exponential Smoothing.

Sales forecasts can be fairly accurate if the right number of observations to be averaged is picked. In order to pick the right number, the business manager may have to experiment with different moving-average periods. Measures of forecasting accuracy, such as the *mean absolute deviation* (MAD), can be used to pick the optimal number of periods. See Sec. 24, Measuring Accuracy of Forecasts.

18 Exponential Smoothing

INTRODUCTION. Exponential smoothing is a popular technique for short-run business forecasting. It uses a weighted average of past data as the basis for a forecast. The procedure gives heaviest weight to recent information and smaller weights to observations in the distant past. The reason for this is that the future is more dependent on the recent past than on the distant past.

HOW IS IT COMPUTED? The formula for exponential smoothing is

$$Y'_{t+1} = \alpha Y_t + (1 - \alpha)Y'_t$$

or

$$Y'_{new} = \alpha Y_{old} + (1 - \alpha)Y'_{old}$$

where Y'_{new} = exponentially smoothed average to be used as
the forecast
Y_{old} = most recent actual data
Y'_{old} = most recent smoothed forecast
α = smoothing constant

The higher the α, the greater is the weight given to the more recent information.

Example The following data on sales are given for an appliance business:

Time period, t	Actual sales (1000), Y_t
1	$60.0
2	64.0
3	58.0
4	66.0
5	70.0
6	60.0
7	70.0
8	74.0
9	62.0
10	74.0
11	68.0
12	66.0
13	60.0
14	66.0
15	62.0

To initialize the exponential smoothing process, we must have the initial forecast. The first smoothed forecast to be used can be

1. First actual observations
2. An average of the actual data for a few periods

For illustrative purposes, let us use a 6-period average as the initial forecast Y'_7 with a smoothing constant of $\alpha = 0.40$. Then

$$Y'_7 = \frac{Y_1 + Y_2 + Y_3 + Y_4 + Y_5 + Y_6}{6}$$

$$= \frac{60 + 64 + 58 + 66 + 70 + 60}{6}$$

$$= 63$$

Note that $Y_7 = 70$. Then Y'_8 is computed as follows:

$$Y'_8 = \alpha Y_7 + (1 - \alpha)Y'_7$$
$$= (0.40)(70) + (0.60)(63)$$
$$= 28.0 + 37.80$$
$$= 65.80$$

Similarly,

$$Y'_9 = \alpha Y_8 + (1 - \alpha)Y'_8$$
$$= (0.40)(74) + (0.60)(65.80)$$
$$= 29.60 + 39.48$$
$$= 69.08$$

and

$$Y'_{10} = \alpha Y_9 + (1 - \alpha)Y'_9$$
$$= (0.40)(62) + (0.60)(69.08)$$
$$= 24.80 + 41.45$$
$$= 66.25$$

By using the same procedure, the values of Y'_{11}, Y'_{12}, Y'_{13}, Y'_{14}, and Y'_{15} can be calculated. Table 18.1 shows a comparison between the actual sales and predicted sales under the exponential smoothing method.

Because of the negative and positive differences between actual sales and predicted sales, the forecaster can use a higher or lower

TABLE 18.1 Comparison of Actual Sales and Predicted Sales

Time period, t	Actual sales, Y_t	Predicted sales, Y'_t	Difference $(Y_t - Y'_t)$	Difference^2 $(Y_t - Y'_t)^2$
1	$60.0			
2	64.0			
3	58.0			
4	66.0			
5	70.0			
6	60.0			
7	70.0	$63.00	$7.00	$ 49.00
8	74.0	65.80	8.20	67.24
9	62.0	69.08	−7.08	50.13
10	74.0	66.25	7.75	60.06
11	68.0	69.35	−1.35	1.83
12	66.0	68.81	−2.81	7.90
13	60.0	67.69	−7.69	59.14
14	66.0	64.61	1.39	1.93
15	62.0	65.17	−3.17	10.05
				$307.28

smoothing constant α, in order to adjust the prediction as quickly as possible to large fluctuations in the data series. For example, if the forecast is slow in reacting to increased sales (that is, if the difference is negative), the forecaster might want to try a higher value. For practical purposes, the optimal α may be picked by minimizing what is known as the *mean squared error* (MSE):

$$MSE = \frac{\Sigma \, (Y_t - Y'_t)^2}{n - i}$$

where i is the number of observations used to determine the initial forecast (in our example, $i = 6$). (See Sec. 24, Measuring Accuracy of Forecasts.) In our example,

$$MSE = \frac{307.28}{15 - 6} = \frac{307.28}{9} = 34.14$$

The idea is to select the α that minimizes the MSE, which is the average sum of the variations between the historical sales data and the forecast values for the corresponding periods.

CAN A COMPUTER HELP? As a manager, you will be confronted with complex problems requiring large sample data. You will also need to try different values of a for exponential smoothing. A computer program is readily available. Figure 18.1 is a sample output from a computer program for exponential smoothing. Notice that the best a for this particular example is 0.9, because it gives the lowest MSE.

HOW IS IT USED AND APPLIED? The exponential smoothing method is effective when there is randomness and no seasonal fluctuations in the data. Finding the best a is key to success in using this method.

The method is simple and effective in that it does not require a whole lot of data other than the variable itself. One disadvantage, however, is that the method does not consider industrial or economic factors such as market conditions, prices, or the effects of competitors' actions.

19 Regression Analysis

INTRODUCTION. Regression analysis is a statistical procedure for estimating mathematically the average relationship between the dependent variable and the independent variable(s). The least-squares method is widely used in regression analysis to estimate the parameter values in a regression equation. *Simple regression* involves only one independent variable,

```
PLEASE ENTER THE NUMBER OF OBSERVATIONS

?10
ENTER YOUR DATA NOW.
THE DATA SHOULD BE SEPARATED BY COMMAS.

?117,120,132,141,140,156,169,171,174,182
ENTER THE NUMBER OF PERIODS OVER WHICH
YOU COMPUTE THE AVERAGE TO BE USED AS THE FIRST
FORECAST VALUE.

?1
**********EXPONENTIAL SMOOTHING PROGRAM -SINGLE SMOOTHING**********
JAE K. SHIM


PERIOD     ACTUAL VALUE     ESTIMATED VALUE     ERROR
   1           117.00              .00
   2           120.00           117.00


THE VALUE OF THE EXPONENTIAL SMOOTHER IS .1
   3           132.00           117.30          14.70
   4           141.00           118.77          22.23
   5           140.00           120.99          19.01
   6           156.00           122.89          33.11
   7           169.00           126.20          42.80
   8           171.00           130.48          40.52
   9           174.00           134.54          39.46
  10           182.00           138.48          43.52
THE TOTAL ABSOLUTE ERROR IN ESTIMATE IS 255.34
THE MEAN SQUARED ERROR IS 1136.48


THE VALUE OF THE EXPONENTIAL SMOOTHER IS .2
   3           132.00           117.60          14.40
   4           141.00           120.48          20.52
   5           140.00           124.58          15.42
   6           156.00           127.67          28.33
   7           169.00           133.33          35.67
   8           171.00           140.47          30.53
   9           174.00           146.57          27.43
  10           182.00           152.06          29.94
THE TOTAL ABSOLUTE ERROR IN ESTIMATE IS 202.24
THE MEAN SQUARED ERROR IS 690.23


THE VALUE OF THE EXPONENTIAL SMOOTHER IS .3
   3           132.00           117.90          14.10
   4           141.00           122.13          18.87
   5           140.00           127.79          12.21
   6           156.00           131.45          24.55
   7           169.00           138.82          30.18
   8           171.00           147.87          23.13
   9           174.00           154.81          19.19
  10           182.00           160.57          21.43
THE TOTAL ABSOLUTE ERROR IN ESTIMATE IS 163.66
THE MEAN SQUARED ERROR IS 447.49


THE VALUE OF THE EXPONENTIAL SMOOTHER IS .4
   3           132.00           118.20          13.80
   4           141.00           123.72          17.28
   5           140.00           130.63           9.37
   6           156.00           134.38          21.62
   7           169.00           143.03          25.97
   8           171.00           153.42          17.58
   9           174.00           160.45          13.55
  10           182.00           165.87          16.13
THE TOTAL ABSOLUTE ERROR IN ESTIMATE IS 135.31
THE MEAN SQUARED ERROR IS 308.97
```

Figure 18.1 Sample output from an exponential smoothing computer program.

```
PERIOD       ACTUAL VALUE      ESTIMATED VALUE        ERROR
THE VALUE OF THE EXPONENTIAL SMOOTHER IS .5
   3           132.00              118.50            13.50
   4           141.00              125.25            15.75
   5           140.00              133.12             6.88
   6           156.00              136.56            19.44
   7           169.00              146.28            22.72
   8           171.00              157.64            13.36
   9           174.00              164.32             9.68
  10           182.00              169.16            12.84
THE TOTAL ABSOLUTE ERROR IN ESTIMATE IS 114.16
THE MEAN SQUARED ERROR IS 226.07

THE VALUE OF THE EXPONENTIAL SMOOTHER IS .6
   3           132.00              118.80            13.20
   4           141.00              126.72            14.28
   5           140.00              135.29             4.71
   6           156.00              138.12            17.88
   7           169.00              148.85            20.15
   8           171.00              160.94            10.06
   9           174.00              166.98             7.02
  10           182.00              171.19            10.81
THE TOTAL ABSOLUTE ERROR IN ESTIMATE IS 98.13
THE MEAN SQUARED ERROR IS 174.23

THE VALUE OF THE EXPONENTIAL SMOOTHER IS .7
   3           132.00              119.10            12.90
   4           141.00              128.13            12.87
   5           140.00              137.14             2.86
   6           156.00              139.14            16.86
   7           169.00              150.94            18.06
   8           171.00              163.58             7.42
   9           174.00              168.77             5.23
  10           182.00              172.43             9.57
THE TOTAL ABSOLUTE ERROR IN ESTIMATE IS 85.76
THE MEAN SQUARED ERROR IS 140.55

THE VALUE OF THE EXPONENTIAL SMOOTHER IS .8
   3           132.00              119.40            12.60
   4           141.00              129.48            11.52
   5           140.00              138.70             1.30
   6           156.00              139.74            16.26
   7           169.00              152.75            16.25
   8           171.00              165.75             5.25
   9           174.00              169.95             4.05
  10           182.00              173.19             8.81
THE TOTAL ABSOLUTE ERROR IN ESTIMATE IS 76.05
THE MEAN SQUARED ERROR IS 117.91
```

Figure 18.1 (*Continued*)

such as price or advertising in a demand function. *Multiple regression* involves two or more variables, such as *both* price and advertising in predicting sales.

HOW IS IT COMPUTED?   We will assume a simple linear regression to illustrate the least-squares method, which means that we will assume the relationship $Y = a + bX$.

The regression method includes all the observed data and attempts to find a line of best fit. To find this line, a technique called the least-squares method is used.

```
PERIOD      ACTUAL VALUE     ESTIMATED VALUE       ERROR
THE VALUE OF THE EXPONENTIAL SMOOTHER IS .9
   3           132.00            119.70          12.30
   4           141.00            130.77          10.23
   5           140.00            139.98            .02
   6           156.00            140.00          16.00
   7           169.00            154.40          14.60
   8           171.00            167.54           3.46
   9           174.00            170.65           3.35
  10           182.00            173.67           8.33
THE TOTAL ABSOLUTE ERROR IN ESTIMATE IS 68.30
THE MEAN SQUARED ERROR IS 102.23
SUMMARY RESULTS

THE EXPONENTIAL SMOOTHER .1 WITH A MEAN SQUARED ERROR OF 1136.48
THE EXPONENTIAL SMOOTHER .2 WITH A MEAN SQUARED ERROR OF  690.23
THE EXPONENTIAL SMOOTHER .3 WITH A MEAN SQUARED ERROR OF  447.49
THE EXPONENTIAL SMOOTHER .4 WITH A MEAN SQUARED ERROR OF  308.97
THE EXPONENTIAL SMOOTHER .5 WITH A MEAN SQUARED ERROR OF  226.07
THE EXPONENTIAL SMOOTHER .6 WITH A MEAN SQUARED ERROR OF  174.23
THE EXPONENTIAL SMOOTHER .7 WITH A MEAN SQUARED ERROR OF  140.55
THE EXPONENTIAL SMOOTHER .8 WITH A MEAN SQUARED ERROR OF  117.91
THE EXPONENTIAL SMOOTHER .9 WITH A MEAN SQUARED ERROR OF  102.23
```

Figure 18.1 (*Continued*)

To explain the least-squares method, we define the error as the difference between the observed value and the estimated one and denote it by u. See Fig. 19.1.

In symbols,

$$u = Y - Y'$$

where Y = observed value of the dependent variable
Y' = estimated value based on $Y' = a + bX$

The least-squares criterion requires that the line of best fit be such that the sum of the squares of the errors (or the verti-

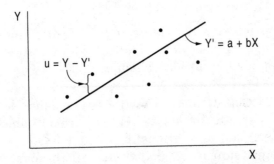

Figure 19.1 Actual (Y) and estimated (Y').

cal distance in Fig. 19.1 from the observed data points to the line) is a minimum, i.e.,

$$\text{Minimum: } \Sigma u^2 = \Sigma (Y - Y')^2$$

Using differential calculus we obtain the following equations, called normal equations:

$$\Sigma Y = na + b\Sigma X$$

$$\Sigma XY = a\Sigma X + b\Sigma X^2$$

where n = number of observations. Solving the equations for b and a yields

$$b = \frac{n\Sigma XY - (\Sigma X)(\Sigma Y)}{n\Sigma X^2 - (\Sigma X)^2}$$

$$a = \overline{Y} - b\overline{X}$$

where $\overline{Y} = \Sigma Y/n$ and $\overline{X} = \Sigma X/n$.

Example 1 To illustrate the computation of b and a, we will refer to the following data: All the sums required are computed and shown below.

Advertising, X (000)	Sales, Y (000)	XY	X^2
$ 9	$ 15	135	81
19	20	380	361
11	14	154	121
14	16	224	196
23	25	575	529
12	20	240	144
12	20	240	144
22	23	506	484
7	14	98	49
13	22	286	169
15	18	270	225
17	18	306	289
$174	$225	3414	2792

From the table,

$$\Sigma X = 174 \quad \Sigma Y = 225 \quad \Sigma XY = 3414 \quad \Sigma X^2 = 2792$$

$$\overline{X} = \frac{\Sigma X}{n} = \frac{174}{12} = 14.5 \quad \overline{Y} = \frac{\Sigma Y}{n} = \frac{225}{12} = 18.75$$

Substituting these values into the formula for b first:

$$b = \frac{n\Sigma XY - (\Sigma X)(\Sigma Y)}{n\Sigma X^2 - (\Sigma X)^2} = \frac{(12)(3414) - (174)(225)}{(12)(2792) - (174)^2} = \frac{1818}{3228} = 0.5632$$

Next:

$$a = \overline{Y} - b\overline{X} = 18.75 - (0.5632)(14.5) = 18.75 - 8.1664 = 10.5836$$

Thus,

$$Y' = 10.5836 + 0.5632X$$

CAN A COMPUTER HELP? Spreadsheet programs such as Lotus 1-2-3 include regression routines which can be used without difficulty. As a matter of fact, you do not need to compute the parameter values a and b manually. Figure 19.2 shows, step by step, how to use the Lotus regression command. Other statistics that appear in Fig. 19.2 are discussed in Sec. 20, Regression Statistics.

Step 1. Enter the data on X and Y as shown below:

(X) Adv. (000)	(Y) Sales (000)
9	15
19	20
11	14
14	16
23	25
12	20
12	20
22	23
7	14
13	22
15	18
17	18

Step 2. Press "/Data Regression."
Step 3. Define X and Y range.
Step 4. Define output range.
Step 5. Hit Go.

Lotus 1-2-3 Regression Result

Constant	10.58364 ←a
Std Err of Y Est	2.343622
R Squared	0.608373
No. of Observations	12
Degree of Freedom	10
X Coefficient(s)	0.563197 ←b
Std Err of Coef.	0.142893
t-value	3.941389

The result shows that

$$Y' = 10.58364 + 0.563197X$$

Figure 19.2 Using Lotus 1-2-3 regression command.

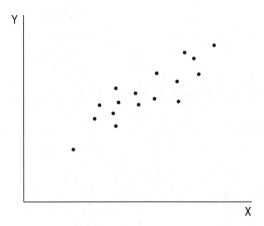

Figure 19.3 Scattergraph.

HOW IS IT USED AND APPLIED? Before attempting a least-squares regression approach, it is important to plot the observed data on a diagram, called a *scattergraph* (see Fig. 19.3). The reason is that you might want to make sure that a linear (straight-line) relationship existed between Y and X in the past sample. If for any reason there was a nonlinear relationship in the sample, the linear relationship we assumed ($Y = a + bX$) would not give a good fit.

Regression analysis is a powerful statistical technique used to develop a model for predicting sales, expenses, and earnings.

> **Example 2** For the data of Example 1, assume that advertising of $10,000 is to be expended for next year. The projected sales for the next year are computed as follows:
>
> $$Y' = 10.5836 + 0.5632X$$
>
> $$= 10.5836 + 0.5632(10)$$
>
> $$= \$16.216 \quad \text{or} \quad \$16,216$$

In order to pick the best possible model with a good fit and a high degree of forecasting accuracy, businesspeople should be familiar with regression statistics such as R-squared (R^2) and the t-statistic. See Sec. 20, Regression Statistics; and Sec. 21, Simple Regression.

20 Regression Statistics

INTRODUCTION. Regression analysis is a statistical procedure for estimating the average relationship between the dependent variable (e.g., sales) and the independent variable(s) (e.g., price or advertising, or both). It uses a variety of statistics to tell about the accuracy and reliability of the regression results.

HOW ARE THEY COMPUTED? Regression statistics include:

1. Correlation coefficient (R) and coefficient of determination (R^2)
2. Standard error of the estimate (S_e)
3. Standard error of the regression coefficient (S_b) and t-statistic

1. Correlation Coefficient (R) and Coefficient of Determination (R²).

The correlation coefficient R measures the degree of correlation between Y and X. The range of values it takes is between -1 and $+1$. More widely used, however, is the coefficient of determination, designated R^2 (read as R-squared). Simply put, R^2 tells how good the estimated regression equation is. In other words, it is a measure of "goodness of fit" in the regression. Therefore, the higher the R^2, the more confidence we have in our estimated equation.

More specifically, the coefficient of determination represents the proportion of the total variation in Y that is explained by the regression equation. It has the range of values between 0 and 1.

Example 1 The statement "Sales is a function of advertising dollars with $R^2 = 70$ percent," can be interpreted as "70 percent of the total variation of sales is explained by the regression equation or the change in advertising and the remaining 30 percent is accounted for by something other than advertising."

The coefficient of determination is computed as

$$R^2 = 1 - \frac{\Sigma(Y - Y')^2}{\Sigma(Y - \bar{Y})^2}$$

In a simple regression situation, however, there is a shortcut method available:

$$R^2 = \frac{[n\Sigma XY - (\Sigma X)(\Sigma Y)]^2}{[n\Sigma X^2 - (\Sigma X)^2][n\Sigma Y^2 - (\Sigma Y)^2]}$$

Example 2 To illustrate the computations of various regression statistics, we will use the same data as the example of Sec. 19, Regression Analysis. All the sums required are computed and shown below.

Advertising, X (000)	Sales, Y (000)	XY	X^2	Y^2
$ 9	$ 15	135	81	225
19	20	380	361	400
11	14	154	121	196
14	16	224	196	256
23	25	575	529	625
12	20	240	144	400
12	20	240	144	400
22	23	506	484	529
7	14	98	49	196
13	22	286	169	484
15	18	270	225	324
17	18	306	289	324
$174	$225	3414	2792	4359

From the table:

$$\Sigma X = 174 \qquad \Sigma Y = 225 \qquad \Sigma XY = 3414 \qquad \Sigma X^2 = 2792 \qquad \Sigma Y^2 = 4359$$

$$\overline{X} = \frac{\Sigma X}{n} = \frac{174}{12} = 14.5 \qquad \overline{Y} = \frac{\Sigma Y}{n} = \frac{225}{12} = 18.75$$

Using the shortcut method for R^2,

$$R^2 = \frac{(1,818)^2}{(3,228)[(12)(4,359) - (225)^2]} = \frac{3,305,124}{(3,228)(52,308 - 50,625)}$$

$$= \frac{3,305,124}{(3,228)(1,683)} = \frac{3,305,124}{5,432,724} = 0.6084 = 60.84\%$$

This means that about 60.84 percent of the total variation in total sales is explained by advertising and the remaining 39.16 percent is still unexplained. A relatively low R^2 indicates that there is a lot of room for improvement in the forecasting equation ($Y' = \$10.5836 + \$0.5632X$). Advertising or a combination of price and advertising might improve R^2.

Note: A low R^2 is an indication that the model is inadequate for explaining the Y variable. The usual causes for this problem are:

1. Use of a wrong functional form
2. Poor choice of an X variable as the predictor
3. Omission of some important variable or variables from the model

2. Standard Error of the Estimate (S_e). The standard error of the estimate, designated S_e, is defined as the standard deviation of the regression. It is computed as

$$S_e = \sqrt{\frac{\Sigma(Y - Y')^2}{n - 2}} = \sqrt{\frac{\Sigma Y^2 - a\Sigma Y - b\Sigma XY}{n - 2}}$$

This statistic can be used to gain some idea of the accuracy of the predictions.

Example 3   Returning to our example data, S_e is calculated as:

$$S_e = \sqrt{\frac{4359 - (10.5836)(225) - (0.5632)(3414)}{12 - 2}} = \sqrt{\frac{54.9252}{10}}$$

$$= 2.3436$$

If you want to be 95 percent confident in your prediction, the confidence interval would be the estimated cost,

$$Y' \pm t \cdot S_e$$

where t is the critical value for the level of significance employed. For example, for a significance level of 0.025 (or 95 percent confidence interval), the critical value of t for 10 degrees of freedom is 2.228 (see Table 8 in the Appendix). As a rule of thumb, we use $t = 2$.

Example 4   From Sec. 19, Regression Analysis, $Y' = \$16.2156$. Therefore, the 95 percent confidence interval for the prediction, given an advertising expenditure of $10,000, is

$$\$16.2156 \pm 2.228(2.3436) = \$16.2156 \pm 5.2215$$

which means

$$\$10.9941 - \$21.4371$$

Note: The confidence interval is the linear distance bounded by limits on either side of the prediction.

3. Standard Error of the Regression Coefficient (S_b) and the t-Statistic.   The standard error of the regression coefficient, designated S_b, and the t-statistic are closely related. S_b is calculated as:

$$S_b = \frac{S_e}{\sqrt{\Sigma(X - \bar{X})^2}}$$

or, in shortcut form,

$$S_b = \sqrt{\frac{S_e}{\Sigma X^2 - X \Sigma X}}$$

S_b gives an estimate of the range where the true coefficient will "actually" fall.

The t-statistic (or t-value) is a measure of the statistical significance of an independent variable X in explaining the dependent variable Y. It is determined by dividing the estimated regression coefficient b by its standard error S_b. This value is then compared with the table t-value. Thus, the t-statistic measures how many standard errors the coefficient is away from zero.

Example 5 The S_b for our example is:

$$S_b = \sqrt{\frac{2.3436}{2792 - (14.5)(174)}}$$

$$= \sqrt{\frac{2.3436}{2792 - 2523}}$$

$$= \sqrt{\frac{2.3436}{269}} = 0.143$$

Thus,

$$t\text{-statistic} = \frac{b}{S_b} = \frac{0.5632}{0.143} = 3.94$$

Since $t = 3.94 > 2$, we conclude that the b coefficient is statistically significant.

Rule of thumb: Any t-value greater than $+ 2$ or less than $- 2$ is acceptable. The higher the t-value, the greater is the confidence we have in the coefficient as a predictor. Low t-values are indications of low reliability of the predictive power of that coefficient.

CAN A COMPUTER HELP? We can use a spreadsheet program such as Lotus 1-2-3 in order to develop a model and estimate most of the statistics we discussed thus far. Figure 20.1 shows the relevant statistics.

HOW IS IT USED AND APPLIED? The least-squares method is used to estimate simple and multiple regressions. In reality,

```
Constant                    10.58364    (a)
Std Err of Y Est            2.343622    (S )
                                           e
R Squared                   0.608373    (R²)
No. of Observations         12
Degree of Freedom           10
X Coefficient(s)            0.563197    (b)
Std Err of Coef.            0.142893    (S )
                                           b
t-statistic                 3.941389    (calculated independently)
```

The result shows that

$$Y' = 10.58364 + 0.563197X$$

with
(1) $R^2 = 0.608373 = 60.84\%$
(2) Standard error of the estimate $S_e = 2.343622$
(3) Standard error of the coefficient $S_b = 0.142893$
(4) t-Statistic $= 3.941389$

All of the above are the same as the values obtained manually.

Figure 20.1   Lotus 1-2-3 regression result.

however, managers face more multiple-regression situations than simple regressions. They have to use computer software including spreadsheet software such as Lotus 1-2-3 to estimate b's and various statistics discussed thus far. Note the following:

1. The t-statistic is more relevant to multiple regressions which have more than one b.

2. R^2 tells how good the forest (overall fit) is, while the t-statistic tells how good an individual tree (an independent variable) is.

Note that the table t-value (Table 8 in the Appendix) is used:

1. To set the prediction range—upper and lower limits—for the predicted value of the dependent variable.

2. To set the confidence range for regression coefficients.

3. As a cutoff value for the t-test.

21 Simple Regression

INTRODUCTION.   A simple regression involves one independent (explanatory) variable in regression analysis.

HOW IS IT COMPUTED?   Simple regression takes the form:

$$Y = a + bX$$

where Y = dependent variable
X = independent variable

$$a = \text{constant}$$
$$b = \text{slope}$$

The least-squares estimation method is typically used to estimate the parameter values a and b.

Example Assume that data on VCR sales and advertising expenditures have been collected over the past 7 periods by a small business owner. Using the *least-squares method,* which was discussed in Sec. 19, we will be able to estimate the linear regression equation. A Lotus 1-2-3 regression printout is shown in Fig. 21.1.

As shown in Fig. 21.1, the sales/advertising regression for VCRs is estimated to be:

$$\text{VCR sales} = Y = 19.88 + 4.72X$$

$$R^2 = 0.7630 = 76.30\%$$

HOW IS IT USED AND APPLIED? Simple regression equations can be developed in order to forecast such important variables as sales and total expenses.

1. Sales is regressed against price or advertising.

2. Total expenses is regressed against one activity variable (such as either production volume or direct labor hours).

VCR Sales

Sales (Y)	Advertising (X)
(both in millions)	
37.00	4.50
48.00	6.50
45.00	3.50
36.00	3.00
25.00	2.50
55.00	8.50
63.00	7.50

Regression Output:

Constant	19.88 ← a
Std Err of Y Est	6.79
R Squared	0.76
No. of Observations	7.00
Degrees of Freedom	5.00
X Coefficient(s)	4.72 ← b
Std Err of Coef.	1.18

The estimated sales forecasting equation is:

$$Y' = 19.88 + 4.72X \text{ with } R^2 = 76.30\%$$

Figure 21.1 Lotus 1-2-3 simple regression output.

In order to pick the best possible model with a good fit and a high degree of forecasting accuracy, the business manager should check regression statistics such as R^2 and the t-value and measures of accuracy such as the mean absolute error (MAD). See Sec. 19, Regression Analysis; Sec. 20, Regression Statistics; and Sec. 24, Measuring Accuracy of Forecasts.

22 Trend Equation

INTRODUCTION. Trends are the general upward or downward movements of the average over time. These movements may require many years of data to determine or describe them. The basic forces underlying trends include technological advances, productivity changes, inflation, and population change.

HOW IS IT COMPUTED? The trend equation is a common method for forecasting sales or earnings. It involves a regression whereby a trend line is fitted to a time series of data.

The *linear* trend line equation can be shown as

$$Y = a + bt$$

where t = time.

The formulas for the coefficients a and b are essentially the same for *simple regression*. They are estimated using the least-squares method, which was discussed in Sec. 19, Regression Analysis.

However, for regression purposes, a time period can be given a number so that $\Sigma t = 0$. When there is an odd number of periods, the period in the middle is assigned a value of 0. If there is an even number, then -1 and $+1$ are assigned to the two periods in the middle, so that again $\Sigma t = 0$.

With $\Sigma t = 0$, the formulas for b and a reduce to:

$$b = \frac{n\Sigma tY}{n\Sigma t^2}$$

$$a = \frac{\Sigma Y}{n}$$

Example 1

Case 1 (odd number):

	19X1	19X2	19X3	19X4	19X5
$t =$	-2	-1	0	$+1$	$+2$

Case 2 (even number):

	19X1	19X2	19X3	19X4	19X5	19X6
$t =$	-3	-2	-1	$+1$	$+2$	$+3$

In each case $t = 0$.

Example 2 Consider ABC Store, whose historical sales are:

Year	Sales (in millions)
19X1	$10
19X2	12
19X3	13
19X4	16
19X5	17

Since the business has 5 years of data, which is an odd number, the year in the middle is assigned a value of 0.

Year	t	Sales (in millions), Y	tY	t^2
19X1	-2	$10	-20	4
19X2	-1	12	-12	1
19X3	0	13	0	0
19X4	$+1$	16	16	1
19X5	$+2$	17	34	4
	0	$68	18	10

$$b = \frac{(5)(18)}{(5)(10)} = \frac{90}{50} = 1.8$$

$$a = \frac{68}{5} = 13.6$$

Therefore, the estimated trend equation is

$$Y' = \$13.6 + \$1.8t$$

To project 19X6 sales, we assign $+3$ to the t-value for the year 19X6.

$$Y' = \$13.6 + \$1.8(3)$$

$$= \$19$$

HOW IS IT USED AND APPLIED? Managers use the trend equation for forecasting purposes, such as to project future sales, earnings, and expenses. They should use the trend equation, however, only if the time series data reflect the gradual shifting or growth pattern over time. See also Sec. 23, Decomposition of Time Series.

23 Decomposition of Time Series

INTRODUCTION. When sales exhibits seasonal or cyclical fluctuation, we use a forecasting method called *classical decomposition* to deal with seasonal, trend, and cyclical components together.

HOW IS IT COMPUTED? We assume that a time series is combined into a model that consists of the four components: trend (T), cyclical (C), seasonal (S), and random (R). The model we assume is of a multiplicative type, i.e.,

$$Y_t = T \times C \times S \times R$$

We illustrate the classical decomposition method step by step, working with quarterly sales data. The approach basically involves the following four steps:

1. Determine seasonal indices, using a four-quarter moving average.
2. Deseasonalize the data.
3. Develop the linear least-squares equation in order to identify the trend component of the forecast.
4. Forecast the sales for each of the four quarters of the coming year.

Example We illustrate the classical decomposition approach by working with the quarterly sales data presented in Table 23.1 and Fig. 23.1. These data show sales of VCR sets (in thousands of units) for a particular manufacturer over the past 4 years.

We begin our analysis by showing how to identify the seasonal component of the time series. Looking at Fig. 23.1, we can easily see a seasonal pattern of VCR sales. Specifically, we observe that sales are lowest in the second quarter of each year, followed by higher sales in quarters 3 and 4. The computational procedure used to eliminate the seasonal component is explained below, step by step.

Step 1. We use a *moving average* to measure the combined trend cyclical (TC) components of the time series. This way we eliminate the seasonal and random components, S and R.

More specifically, step 1 involves the following sequences of steps:

a. Calculate the four-quarter moving average for the time series. Note, however, that the moving-average values that are computed do not correspond directly to the original quarters of the time series.

b. We resolve this difficulty by using the midpoints between successive moving-average values. For example, since 6.35 corresponds to the first half of quarter 3 and 6.6 corresponds to the last half of quarter 3, we use $(6.35 + 6.6)/2 = 6.475$ as the moving-average value of

TABLE 23.1   Quarterly Sales Data for VCRs over the Past 4 Years

Year	Quarter	Sales
1	1	5.8
	2	5.1
	3	7.0
	4	7.5
2	1	6.8
	2	6.2
	3	7.8
	4	8.4
3	1	7.0
	2	6.6
	3	8.5
	4	8.8
4	1	7.3
	2	6.9
	3	9.0
	4	9.4

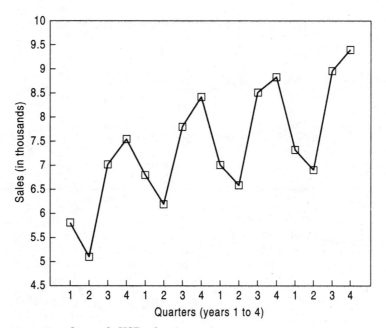

Figure 23.1   Quarterly VCR sales time series.

quarter 3. Similarly, we associate $(6.6 + 6.875)/2 = 6.7375$ with quarter 4. A complete summary of the moving-average calculation is shown in Table 23.2.

c. Next, we calculate the ratio of the actual value to the moving-average value for each quarter in the time series having a four-quarter moving-average entry. This ratio in effect represents the season-

TABLE 23.2 Moving-Average Calculations for the VCR Sales Time Series

Year	Quarter	Sales	Four-quarter moving average	Centered moving average
1	1	5.8		
	2	5.1		
			6.35	
	3	7.0		6.475
			6.6	
	4	7.5		6.7375
			6.875	
2	1	6.8		6.975
			7.075	
	2	6.2		7.1875
			7.3	
	3	7.8		7.325
			7.35	
	4	8.4		7.4
			7.45	
3	1	7.0		7.5375
			7.625	
	2	6.6		7.675
			7.725	
	3	8.5		7.7625
			7.8	
	4	8.8		7.8375
			7.875	
4	1	7.3		7.9375
			8	
	2	6.9		8.075
			8.15	
	3	9.0	0	
	4	9.4		

al–random component, $SR = Y/TC$. The ratios calculated this way appear in Table 23.3.

d. Arrange the ratios by quarter and then calculate the average ratio by quarter in order to eliminate the random influence.

For example, for quarter 1,

$$\frac{0.975 + 0.929 + 0.920}{3} = 0.941$$

e. The final step adjusts the average ratio slightly (for example, for quarter 1, 0.941 becomes 0.940), which will be the seasonal index, as shown in Table 23.4.

Step 2. After obtaining the seasonal index, we must first remove the effect of season from the original time series. This process is referred to as *deseasonalizing* the time series. For this, we must divide the original series by the seasonal index for that quarter. This is shown in Table 23.5 and graphed in Fig. 23.2.

TABLE 23.3 Seasonal Random Factors for the Series

Year	Quarter	Sales	Four-quarter moving average	Centered moving average, TC	Seasonal-random moving average, $SR = Y/TC$
1	1	5.8			
	2	5.1			
			6.35		
	3	7.0		6.475	1.081
			6.6		
	4	7.5		6.738	1.113
			6.875		
2	1	6.8		6.975	0.975
			7.075		
	2	6.2		7.188	0.863
			7.3		
	3	7.8		7.325	1.065
			7.35		
	4	8.4		7.400	1.135
			7.45		
3	1	7.0		7.538	0.929
			7.625		
	2	6.6		7.675	0.860
			7.725		
	3	8.5		7.763	1.095
			7.8		
	4	8.8		7.838	1.123
			7.875		
4	1	7.3		7.938	0.920
			8		
	2	6.9		8.075	0.854
			8.15		
	3	9.0			
	4	9.4			

TABLE 23.4 Seasonal Component Calculations

Quarter	Seasonal–random, SR	Seasonal factor S	Adjusted S
1	0.975		
	0.929		
	0.920	0.941	0.940
2	0.863		
	0.860		
	0.854	0.859	0.858
3	1.081		
	1.065		
	1.095	1.080	1.079
4	1.113		
	1.135		
	1.123	1.124	1.123
		4.004	4.000

TABLE 23.5 Deseasonalized Data

Year	Quarter	Sales	Seasonal, S	Deseasonalized data	t	tY	t^2
1	1	5.8	0.940	6.17	1	6.17	1
	2	5.1	0.858	5.94	2	11.89	4
	3	7.0	1.079	6.49	3	19.46	9
	4	7.5	1.123	6.68	4	26.72	16
2	1	6.8	0.940	7.23	5	36.17	25
	2	6.2	0.858	7.23	6	43.35	36
	3	7.8	1.079	7.23	7	50.59	49
	4	8.4	1.123	7.48	8	59.86	64
3	1	7.0	0.940	7.45	9	67.01	81
	2	6.6	0.858	7.69	10	76.91	100
	3	8.5	1.079	7.88	11	86.64	121
	4	8.8	1.123	7.84	12	94.07	144
4	1	7.3	0.940	7.76	13	100.94	169
	2	6.9	0.858	8.04	14	112.57	196
	3	9.0	1.079	8.34	15	125.09	225
	4	9.4	1.123	8.37	16	133.98	256
				117.82	136	1051.43	1496

t-bar = 8.5 y-bar = 7.3638
$b = 0.1469$
$a = 6.1147$

which means that $y = 6.1147 + 0.1469t$ for the forecast periods:

$$t = 17$$
$$18$$
$$19$$
$$20$$

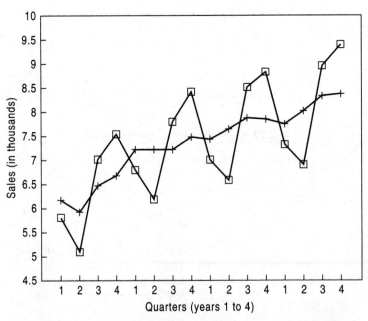

Figure 23.2 Quarterly VCR sales time series: original versus deseasonalized.

TABLE 23.6   Quarter-to-Quarter Sales Forecasts for Year 5

Year	Quarter	Trend forecast	Seasonal factor	Quarterly forecast
5	1	8.6128 (a)	0.940	8.0971
	2	8.7598	0.858	7.5170
	3	8.9067	1.079	9.6121
	4	9.0537	1.123	10.1632

Note: (a) $y = 6.1147 + 0.1469t = 6.1147 + 0.1469(17) = 8.6128$.

Step 3. Looking at Fig. 23.2, we see that the time series seems to have an upward linear trend. To identify this trend, we develop the least-squares trend equation. This procedure is also shown in Table 23.5.

Step 4. Develop the forecast using the trend equation and adjust the forecast to account for the effect of season. The quarterly forecast, as shown in Table 23.6, can be obtained by multiplying the forecast based on trend by the seasonal factor.

HOW IS IT USED AND APPLIED?   The classical decomposition model is a time series model used for forecasting. This means that the method can only be used to fit time series data, whether they are monthly, quarterly, or annual. The types of time series data a company may deal with include sales, earnings, cash flows, market share, and costs. As long as the time series displays the patterns of seasonality and cyclicality, the model constructed will be very effective in projecting the future variable.

24 Measuring Accuracy of Forecasts

INTRODUCTION.   The performance of a forecast should be checked against its own record or against that of other forecasts. There are various statistical measures that can be used to measure performance of the model.

HOW IS IT COMPUTED?   Performance is measured in terms of forecasting error, where error is defined as the difference between a predicted value and the actual result: Error $(e) =$ actual (A) − forecast (F).

There are three common measures for summarizing historical errors.

1. *Mean absolute deviation* (MAD) is the mean or average of the sum of the errors for a given data set taken without regard to sign. The formula for calculating MAD is:

$$\text{MAD} = \frac{\Sigma |e|}{n}$$

2. *Mean squared error* (MSE) is a measure of accuracy computed by squaring the individual errors for each item and then finding the average value of the sum of those squares. MSE gives greater weight to large errors than to small errors, since the errors are squared before being summed. The formula for calculating MSE is:

$$\text{MSE} = \frac{\Sigma e^2}{n - 1}$$

3. *Mean absolute percentage error* (MAPE): Sometimes it is more useful to compute the forecasting errors in percentages rather than in amounts. The MAPE is calculated by finding the absolute error in each period, dividing this by the actual value of that period, and then averaging these absolute percentage errors, as shown below.

$$\text{MAPE} = \frac{\Sigma |e|}{A/n}$$

The following example illustrates the computation of MAD, MSE, and MAPE.

Example 1   Sales data for a microwave oven manufacturer are as folows:

Period	Actual, A	Forecast, F	$e(A - F)$	$|e|$	e^2	Absolute percent error, $|e|/A$
1	217	215	2	2	4	0.0092
2	213	216	− 3	3	9	0.0014
3	216	215	1	1	1	10.0046
4	210	214	− 4	4	16	0.0190
5	213	211	2	2	4	0.0094
6	219	214	5	5	25	0.0023
7	216	217	− 1	1	1	0.0046
8	212	216	− 4	4	16	0.0019
			− 2	22	76	0.0524

Using the figures above,

$$\text{MAD} = \frac{\Sigma |e|}{n} = \frac{22}{8} = 2.75$$

$$\text{MSE} = \frac{\Sigma e^2}{n - 1} = \frac{76}{7} = 10.86$$

$$\text{MAPE} = \frac{\Sigma |e|}{A/n} = \frac{0.0525}{8} = 0.0066$$

One way these measures are used is to evaluate the forecasting ability of alternative forecasting methods. For example, using MAD, MSE, or MAPE, a forecaster could compare the results of exponential smoothing with α (see Sec. 18) and elect the one that performs best in terms of the lowest MAD, MSE, or MAPE for a given set of data. Also, it can help select the best initial forecast value for exponential smoothing.

HOW IS IT USED AND APPLIED?   It is important to monitor forecast errors to ensure that the forecast is performing well. If the model is performing poorly based on some criterion, the forecaster might reconsider the use of the existing model or switch to another forecasting model or technique. Forecasting control can be accomplished by comparing forecasting errors to predetermined values or limits. Errors that fall within the limits are judged acceptable, while errors outside the limits signal that corrective action is desirable (see Fig. 24.1).

MONITORING FORECASTS.   Forecasts can be monitored using either tracking signals or control charts.

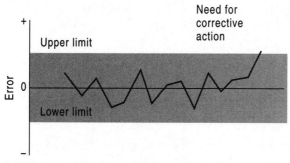

Figure 24.1   Monitoring forecast errors.

Tracking Signals. A tracking signal is based on the ratio of cumulative forecast error to the corresponding value of MAD:

$$\text{Tracking signal} = \frac{\Sigma A - F}{\text{MAD}}$$

The resulting tracking signals are compared to predetermined limits. These are based on experience and judgment and often range from plus or minus 3 to plus or minus 8. The values within the limits suggest that the forecast is performing adequately. By the same token, when the signal goes beyond this range, corrective action is appropriate.

Example 2 Returning to Example 1, the deviation and cumulative deviation have already been computed:

$$\text{MAD} = \frac{\Sigma A - F}{n} = \frac{22}{8} = 2.75$$

$$\text{Tracking signal} = \frac{\Sigma A - F}{\text{MAD}} = -\frac{2}{2.75} = -0.73$$

The tracking signal is -0.73, which is substantially below the limit (-3 to -8). This does not suggest that any action is necessary at this time.

Note: After an initial value of MAD has been computed, the estimate of the MAD can be continually updated using exponential smoothing:

$$\text{MAD}_t = \alpha(A - F) + (1 - \alpha)\text{MAD}_{t-1}$$

Control Charts. The control chart approach involves setting upper and lower limits for individual forecasting errors rather than cumulative errors. The limits are multiples of the estimated standard deviation of forecast, S_f, which is the square root of the mean squared error. Frequently, control limits are set at 2 or 3 standard deviations:

$$\pm 2 \text{ (or 3)}S_f$$

Note: Plot the errors and see if all errors are within the limits, so that you can visualize the process and determine if the method being used is in control.

Example 3 For the following sales data, using the naive forecast, we will determine if the forecast is in control. For illustrative purposes, we will use 2σ control limits.

Year	Sales	Forecasts	Error	Error^2
1	320			
2	326	320	6	36
3	310	326	− 16	256
4	317	310	7	49
5	315	317	− 2	4
6	318	315	3	9
7	310	318	− 8	64
8	316	310	6	36
9	314	316	− 2	4
10	317	314	3	9
			− 3	467

First, compute the standard deviation of forecast errors:

$$S_f = \sqrt{\frac{e^2}{n-1}} = \sqrt{\frac{467}{9-1}} = 7.64$$

Two sigma limits are then ± 2(7.64) = − 15.28 to + 15.28.

Note that the forecast error for year 3 is below the lower bound, so the forecast is not in control (see Fig. 24.2). Another method, such as moving average, exponential smoothing, or regression, might produce a better forecast.

Note: A system for monitoring forecasts needs to be developed. The computer may be programmed to print a report showing the past history when the tracking signal "trips" a limit. For

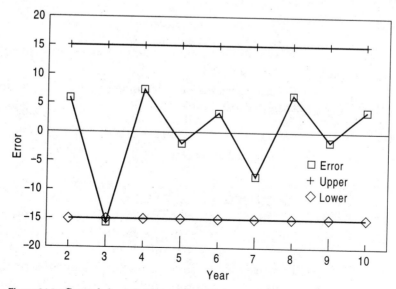

Figure 24.2 Control chart for forecasting errors.

example, when a type of exponential smoothing is used, the system may try a different value of α (so that the forecast will be more responsive) and continue forecasting.

25 Cost of Prediction Errors

INTRODUCTION. There is always a cost involved in a failure to predict a certain variable accurately. The cost of prediction errors associated with sales, expenses, and purchases can be significant.

HOW IS IT COMPUTED? The cost of the prediction error is basically the contribution or profit lost because of an inaccurate prediction. It can be measured in terms of lost sales, disgruntled customers, or idle machines.

> **Example** Assume that a retail store has been selling a toy doll having a cost of $0.60 for $1.00 each. The fixed cost is $300. The store has no privilege to return any unsold dolls. It has predicted sales of 2000 dolls. However, unforeseen competition has reduced sales to 1500 dolls. The cost of its prediction error—that is, its failure to predict demand accurately, is calculated as follows:

1. Initial predicted sales = 2000 dolls
   Optimal decision: purchase 2000 dolls
   Expected net income = $500 [(2000 dolls $\times$ $0.40 contribution) $-$ $300 fixed costs]

2. Alternative parameter value = 1500 dolls
   Optimal decision: purchase 1500 dolls
   Expected net income = $300 [(1500 dolls $\times$ $0.40 contribution) $-$ $300 fixed costs]

3. Results of original decision under alternative parameter value
   Expected net income:
   Revenue (1500 dolls $\times$ $1.00) $-$ cost of dolls (2000 dolls $\times$ $0.60) $-$ $300 fixed costs = $1500 $-$ $1200 $-$ $300 = $0

4. Cost of prediction error = (2) $-$ (3) = $300

HOW IS IT USED AND APPLIED? It is important to determine the cost of the prediction error in order to minimize the potential detrimental effect on future profitability. The cost of the prediction error can be substantial, depending on the circumstances. For example, failure to make an accurate projection of sales could result in poor production planning, too much or too little purchase of labor, and so on, thereby causing potentially huge financial losses.

Businesspeople need to keep track of past prediction records to ensure that (1) future costs can be minimized and (2) better forecasting methods can be developed.

26 χ^2 (Chi-Square) Test

INTRODUCTION. The χ^2 (chi-square) test is a statistical test of the significance of a difference between classifications or sub-classifications. The test is applied to sample data in testing whether or not two qualitative population variables are independent.

HOW IS THE TEST PERFORMED? The χ^2 test involves three steps.

Step 1. Calculate the χ^2 statistic, which is defined as:

$$\chi^2 = \frac{\Sigma (f_0 - f_e)^2}{f_e}$$

where f_o = individual observed frequencies of each class
f_e = individual expected frequencies of each class

Step 2. Find the table value at a given level of significance (see Table 6 in the Appendix).

Step 3. If the calculated value is greater than the table value, we reject the null hypothesis, which means that the two variables or classifications are associated.

Example Consider the following survey regarding restaurants:

	With outdoor cafe	Without outdoor cafe	Total
With à la carte menu	466	169	635
With prix fixe menu	180	29	209
Total	646	198	844

The null hypothesis is: The menu and the indoor/outdoor cafes are independent.

In order to calculate χ^2, we need to construct an expected value table on the basis of the assumption that menu and indoor/outdoor cafes are independent of each other. If no association exists, it is to be expected that the proportion of à la carte and prix fixe restaurants with outdoor cafes or tables will be the same as that without outdoor cafes. First, we compute the expected frequencies based on the premise of independence:

$$635/844 = 0.7524 \qquad 209/844 = 0.2476$$

Now, we can compute the expected values from the proportions of totals as follows:

$$0.7524 \times 646 = 486$$

$$0.2476 \times 646 = 160$$

$$0.7524 \times 198 = 149$$

$$0.2476 \times 198 = 49$$

These expected values give the following table:

	With outdoor cafe	Without outdoor cafe	Total
With à la carte menu	486	149	635
With prix fixe menu	160	49	209
Total	646	198	844

Step 1. Calculate χ^2. We are interested in how far the observed table differs from the expected table.

$$\chi^2 = \frac{(466 - 486)^2}{486} + \frac{(180 - 160)^2}{160} + \frac{(169 - 149)^2}{149} + \frac{(29 - 49)^2}{49}$$

$$= 14.171$$

Step 2. χ^2 value at the 0.05 level of significance with one degree of freedom (from Table 6 in the Appendix) is 3.841. The degree of freedom is calculated as (no. rows − 1) × (no. of columns − 1) = (2 − 1) × (2 − 1) = 1.

Step 3. As shown in Fig. 26.1, since the calculated value is greater than the table value (14.171 > 3.841), we reject the null hypothesis,

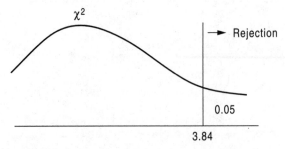

Figure 26.1 Chi-square test and rejection area.

which means that the menu is associated with the outdoor/indoor restaurant setup.

HOW IS IT USED AND APPLIED? The chi-square test has many applications in business. It is a statistical test of independence (or association), to determine if membership in categories of one variable is different as a function of membership in the categories of a second variable. It is important to note, however, that there are limitations to this test: (1) The sample must be big enough for the expected frequencies for each cell (rule of thumb: at least 5); and (2) the test does not tell anything about the *direction* of an association.

Managers need to know whether the differences they observe among several sample proportions are significant or due only to chance.

For example, marketing managers are concerned that their brand's share may be unevenly distributed throughout the country. They conduct a survey in which the country is divided into a specific number of geographic regions and see if consumers' decisions as to whether or not to purchase the company's brand has anything to do with the geographic location.

As another example, a financial manager might be interested in the differences in capital structure within different firm sizes in a certain industry. To see if firm sizes have the same capital structure (or firm sizes have nothing to do with the capital structure), what he or she needs to do is to survey a group of firms with assets of different amounts and divide them into groups. Each firm can be classified according to predetermined debt/equity ratio groups.

Managing Cash and Receivables

27 Cash Flow Statement

INTRODUCTION. Current profitability is only one important factor in success. Also essential is cash flow. In fact, a business can be profitable and still have a cash crisis. An example is a small business with a high level of credit sales but with a very long collection period. The business shows a profit but does not have the cash from those sales.

It is essential to know your cash flow in order to plan adequately. Should you cut back on cash payments? Where are you obtaining cash flow? Where are you spending your money? What products are cash drains or cash surpluses? Is there adequate money to pay bills and purchase required equipment? Are you liquid?

A *statement of cash flows* is useful because it provides valuable data that are not available in the balance sheet and income statement. The statement presents the sources and uses of cash and is a basis for cash flow analysis.

HOW IS IT COMPUTED? The statement of cash flows classifies cash receipts and cash payments from (1) operating, (2) investing, and (3) financing activities. Let's look at each of these major sections.

1. *Operating activities* relate to the manufacturing and selling of or the rendering of services. Cash inflows that come from operating activities include *(a)* cash sales or collections on receivables and *(b)* cash receipts from interest income and dividend income. Cash outflows include *(a)* cash paid for merchandise and *(b)* cash paid for expenses.

2. *Investing activities* relate to the purchase and sale of fixed assets (such as equipment and machinery) and the purchase of stocks and bonds of other businesses. Cash inflows comprise *(a)* amounts received from selling fixed assets and *(b)* receipts from sales of stocks and bonds of other companies. Cash outflows include *(a)* payments to purchase fixed assets and *(b)* disbursements to buy stocks and bonds of other entities.

3. *Financing activities* relate to borrowing and repayment and to issuing stock and reacquiring previously issued shares. Cash inflows comprise *(a)* funds obtained from loans and *(b)* funds received from the sale of stock. Cash outflows include *(a)* paying off debt, and *(b)* repurchase of stock.

Example Consider Mr. Paul, who owns a small business that sells appliances. The statement of cash flows for this small business follows:

Cash flow from operating activities:		
Net income		$30,500
Add (deduct) items not impacting cash:		
Depreciation	$ 3,500	
Decrease in accounts receivable	2,500	
Increase in prepaid insurance and rent	(1,000)	
Increase in accounts payable	2,000	7,000
Net cash flow from operating activities		$37,500
Cash flow from investing activities:		
Purchase of land	$(17,500)	
Purchase of building	(15,000)	
Purchase of store furnishings	(9,000)	
		(41,500)
Cash flow from financing activities:		
Long-term loans	$ 15,000	15,000
Net increase in cash		$11,000

An evaluation of the statement shows that earnings and cash flow have improved. This indicates good earnings performance as well as the fact that earnings are backed up by cash. The decrease in accounts receivable may reveal better collection efforts. The increase in accounts payable is a sign that suppliers have confidence in the business and are willing to provide interest-free financing. The acquisition of land, a building, and furnishings indicates a growing business undertaking capital expansion. The long-term loan indicates that part of the financing of assets is through debt. Overall, there was an increase in cash of $11,000 along with a net income of $30,500. This is a favorable sign taking into account the significant capital expenditures made.

HOW IS IT USED AND APPLIED?

Cash flow analysis is a valuable tool. The cash flow statement provides information about the way your small business generates and uses cash. An analysis of the statement is helpful in appraising past performance, showing why cash flow increased or decreased, as well as looking at future direction, forecasting liquidity trends, and evaluating the ability to pay debt at maturity.

An analysis of the operating section determines the adequacy of cash flow generated from sales to satisfy operating expenses. Are you obtaining positive future net cash flows from your daily activities?

In examining the investing section, an increase in fixed assets indicates expansion and future growth. A contraction in business occurring from the sale of fixed assets without adequate replacement is a negative sign.

An appraisal of the financing section reveals the type of financing used. A determination should be made of the risk and the cost of obtaining those funds.

The statement of cash flows is different from the income statement. The statement of cash flows presents the cash receipts and cash payments of the business by source. It reveals where the cash is coming from and where it is going. The statement emphasizes *cash flows*; its bottom line is the cash balance at the end of the period.

The income statement looks not at cash flows but at the *profitability* of the business. It reveals net income—revenue less expenses. Revenue, which is income earned from operations and may or may not involve cash receipts, is earned from sales of merchandise and the rendering of services. A credit sale is recorded as revenue, although it does not involve receiving money; expenses which are incurred to obtain revenue and may or may not involve cash payment, may result from either conducting operations (e.g., operating expenses) or financing the business (e.g., interest expense). Bills received for accrued expenses during the year (e.g., utilities) reduce profit but do not involve cash payments until such later time when these bills are actually paid. For example, a telephone bill covering the month of December 1996 is an expense for the year 1996. This expense reduces net income. However, the bill may not be paid until January 1997.

28 Using Float

INTRODUCTION. *Float* is defined as the difference between the cash balance your records show and the cash balance the bank's records show. Float results from writing checks that have not yet cleared (disbursement float). Float makes it possible for your bank book balance to be negative while the bank shows your balance as being positive.

There are several types of delays in processing checks:

1. *Mail float*—the time required for a check to move from someone to you

2. *Processing float*—the time needed for you to enter the payment in your records

3. *Deposit collection float*—the time for a check to clear

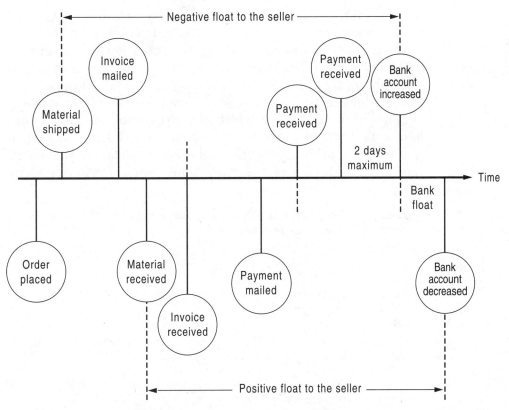

Figure 28.1 Schematic float calendar. [*Source:* Keith V. Smith, *Guide to Working Capital Management* (New York: McGraw-Hill, 1979), p. 83.]

Figure 28.1 is a schematic float calendar for a small business.

HOW IS IT COMPUTED? The acceleration of cash inflow enables you to profit through reduced collection float. If deposits average $20,000 per day and the collection time can be reduced by 3 days, the business will have $60,000 in additional usable funds. Assuming a rate of return of 10 percent, the value of those funds is $6000 per year in savings.

If float is used effectively, you may get an "interest-free" loan from the bank. For example, assume you have a $5000 balance in your checking account (non-interest-bearing) and $150,000 in your money market account. You write a check for $20,000, which you expect to clear in 5 days. On the fifth day, you transfer $15,000 from the savings account to the checking account to cover the check. You have successfully used 5 days' float to earn interest on the $15,000 for 5 days. The check will clear because your checking account balance is $20,000 ($15,000 + $5,000).

The amount of float depends on both (1) the *time lag* and (2) the *dollars involved*. Float may be determined in dollar-days, multiplying the lag in days by the dollar amount delayed. The *cost* of float is the interest lost because the money was not available for investment or the interest paid because money had to be borrowed during the lag period. The cost of float is computed by multiplying the average daily float by the cost of capital (opportunity cost) for the time period under consideration.

Example George Harris owns a mail-order business and is concerned about cash float. He examines the following information:

Item	Dollar amount		Number of days		Dollar days
X	$35,000	×	2	=	$ 70,000
Y	15,000	×	1	=	15,000
Z	40,000	×	5	=	200,000
	$90,000				$285,000

$$\text{Average daily float} = \frac{\$285,000}{30} = \$9,500$$

$$\text{Average daily receipts} = \frac{\$90,000}{30} = \$3,000$$

$$\text{Average daily days} = \frac{\$285,000}{\$90,000} = 3.1667 \text{ days}$$

$$\text{Average daily float} = \$3,000 \times 3.1667 = \$9,500$$

$$\text{Average cost of float} = \$9,500 \times 0.09 = \$855$$

HOW IS IT USED AND APPLIED? It is in your best interest to receive payments from your customers as quickly as possible and to make payments to your creditors as slowly as possible so that you can invest the funds and maximize your investment return. When you receive checks from customers, deposit them immediately. This allows you to have use of the funds as soon as the checks clear and minimizes the possibility that the check will be returned for insufficient funds. If you suspect the payor is in financial difficulty, it is best to make your claim against any available funds as quickly as possible. Similarly, it is smart to delay payments to creditors for as long as possible so that you can retain use of the money until the last minute.

Determine the causes for delays in depositing cash receipts and take corrective action. Ascertain *how* and *where* the cash receipts come; how cash is transferred to your bank account, the bank's policy regarding funds availability, and the length of time between when a check is received and when it is deposited. You want money available to you as soon as possible so you can earn interest.

See Sec. 29, Using a Lockbox to Get Money Sooner.

29 Using a Lockbox to Get Money Sooner

INTRODUCTION. If your business receives many checks from customers, time and money are spent in processing these deposits. A lockbox arrangement may be appropriate.

A *lockbox* is a collection point (such as a post office box) placed near customers. Customer payments are mailed to strategic post office boxes in their local areas in order to shorten mailing and depositing time. Banks collect from these boxes several times a day and make deposits to your account.

HOW IS IT COMPUTED? The following computation will help to determine whether a lockbox arrangement is feasible:

Return on early collection of cash
Less: Cost of lockbox
Advantage or disadvantage

Example 1 If it takes about 7 days to receive and deposit payments from customers, a lockbox arrangement for Beautiful Furniture may reduce the float time to 5 days. Assume that average daily collections are $50,000 and the return rate is 13 percent.

If a lockbox system is initiated, the decline in outstanding cash balances would be:

$$2 \text{ days} \times \$50,000 = \$100,000$$

The return that could be earned on these funds is:

$$\$100,000 \times 0.13 = \$13,000$$

The maximum monthly charge that should be paid for the lockbox system is:

$$\frac{\$13,000}{12} = \$1,083$$

Example 2   A small business owner is thinking of using a lockbox system costing $14,000 per year. Daily collections average $40,000. The lockbox arrangement will reduce the float period by 3 days. The rate of return is 12 percent.

The cost–benefit analysis is:

Return on early collection of cash	$14,400
Less: Cost	14,000
Advantage of lockbox	$ 400

HOW IS IT USED AND APPLIED?   To help determine whether you should use a lockbox, calculate the average dollar amount of checks received, the cost of clerical operations that would be eliminated, and the reduction in "mail float" days. Because per-item processing costs are typically significant, it is most beneficial to use a lockbox with low-volume, high-dollar collections. The system is becoming available to small businesses with high-volume, low-dollar receipts as technological advances lower the per-item cost of lockboxes.

30 Bank Reconciliation

INTRODUCTION.   Preparation of a bank reconciliation is based on information included in the bank statement: deposits made, checks cleared, and charges or credits (deductions or additions) to the account. For example, a bank charge is a deduction from an account, whereas the amount collected on a customer's note is an addition. Canceled checks, debit memoranda for charges, and credit memoranda for credits are typically enclosed with the bank statement.

The ending balance on the bank statement rarely agrees with the ending balance in the cash account according to the books; thus, a bank reconciliation is needed to reflect the reconciling items. Once the reconciliation is completed, the adjusted bank balance must agree with the adjusted book balance. When this occurs, both records are correct.

HOW IS IT COMPUTED?   The cash balance per the books must be the same as the balance in the bank account at the end of the period. Reconciling differences relate to (1) items shown on the business's books but not on the bank statement and (2) items shown on the bank statement but not on the business's books. Examples and explanations of each follow.

Reconciling Items for the Bank Statement. The bank balance is adjusted for several types of items that are reflected on the business's books but not on the bank statement.

Outstanding checks. Checks that have been issued by the business but have not yet cleared the bank. The total of the outstanding checks is deducted from the bank balance. (An exception is an uncleared certified check—a check for which the bank immediately sets aside funds for payment. A certified check is not deemed outstanding, since both parties—the business and the bank—know about it.)

Deposits in transit. Cash that has been received at the end of the period but is either not yet deposited or was deposited after the bank prepared its statement. Deposits in transit are added to the bank balance.

Errors in recording checks. Mistakes include transposition errors made in the recording of checks. An item should be added to the bank balance, for instance, if it was previously overstated on the books.

Bank errors in charging or crediting the business's account. If a business's account is charged in error for another firm's cleared check, the business's bank balance is understated, so the business should add the amount of this check to its own bank balance. However, if a deposit made by the small business was incorrectly credited to the account of another business, the other business should make the adjustment and reduce its bank balance.

Reconciling Items for the Books. The book balance (cash account) is adjusted for items that are shown on the bank statement but are not reflected on the books. Such items include the following:

Bank charges. Bank service fees reduce the book balance, but these amounts are not known until the bank statement is received. Examples include monthly service charges, cost per check, check printing costs, and stop-payment fees.

NSF (not sufficient funds) checks. Checks that have "bounced" due to insufficient funds in the customer's checking account. In such a case, the small business's bank issues a debit memorandum for the dishonored amount and the book balance is reduced.

Collections. Notes and other items collected by the bank for a nominal fee. The proceeds received less the charge (in the form of a credit memorandum) are credited to the business's account. The net amount is added to the book balance.

Interest earned. Interest income credited by the bank on the checking account increases the book balance.

Errors on the books. Various kinds of mistakes may occur on the books. Two examples of mistakes and corrections follow (assume that the amount of the check is correct).

1. A $100 check is written, which is more than the $90 amount entered as a cash disbursement. In this case, cash disbursements are understated by $10; thus, the balance per books should be reduced by this amount.

2. A $50 check is written, which is less than the $60 amount shown as a cash disbursement. Here, cash disbursements are overstated, and the book balance should be increased by $10 to correct the error.

After the bank reconciliation has been prepared, journal entries are made for the reconciling items that affect the book balance. A journal entry is needed because the amounts on the books must be updated to reflect any items on the bank statement of which the business was unaware during the period. Reconciling items entered as adjustments to the bank balance are not journalized, however, because they are already on the books. Such reconciling items will probably be shown on the next bank statement.

Example A small business provides the following data in connection with the preparation of its bank reconciliation on June 30, 19XX:

Balance per bank	$4889
Balance per books	4400
Outstanding checks:	
Check 410	500
Check 423	200
Deposit in transit	300
Collection on note:	
Principal	200
Interest	16
Collection fee on note	12
NSF check	100
Monthly service charge	15

The following shows the proper form for the bank reconciliation:

A SMALL BUSINESS
Bank Reconciliation
June 30, 19XX

Balance per bank		$4889
Add: Deposits in transit		300
		$5189
Less: Outstanding checks		
410	$500	
423	200	700
Adjusted bank balance		$4489
Balance per books		$4400
Add: Proceeds on note		216
		$4616
Less:		
NSF check	$100	
Collection fee	12	
Service charge	15	127
Adjusted book balance		$4489

HOW IS IT USED AND APPLIED? A bank's reconciliation is prepared and used by a small business to assure that the balance per the depositor's records agrees with the balance per the bank's records after accounting for all reconciling items. If a discrepancy exists after the bank reconciliation has been prepared, an investigation should be made to uncover any errors or irregularities, such as fraud perpetrated by the bookkeeper.

31 Putting Excess Cash to Work

INTRODUCTION. The small business owner should invest excess cash for a return but still retain liquidity. Marketable securities are readily tradeable securities with short-term debt maturities (i.e., 1 year or less). The management of marketable securities is a major part of cash management. Some small businesses have a marketable security portfolio in excess of their cash balance. The objectives of investing in marketable securities are to ensure that cash is readily available, to ensure the safety of principal, and to minimize the risk of loss.

HOW IS IT COMPUTED? Holding-period return (HPR) is the total return earned from holding an investment (such as stock) for a period of time. It is determined from current income (dividend income or interest income) and capital gain or loss. Holding-period return is computed as:

$$\text{HPR} = \frac{\text{current income} + \text{capital gain (or loss)}}{\text{purchase price}}$$

Example. Consider the following investments in Stock X and Stock Y over a 1-year period of ownership:

	Stock X	Stock Y
Purchase price (beginning of year)	$100	$100
Cash dividend received (during the year)	8	12
Sales price (end of year)	110	95

Combining the capital gain (or loss) with the current income, the total return on each investment is found as follows.

	Stock X	Stock Y
Cash dividend	$ 8	$12
Capital gain (loss)	10	(5)
Total return	$18	$ 7

$$\text{HPR (Stock X)} = \frac{\$8 + \$10}{\$100} = \frac{\$18}{\$100} = 18\%$$

$$\text{HPR (Stock Y)} = \frac{\$12 - \$5}{\$100} = \frac{\$7}{\$100} = 7\%$$

HOW IS IT USED AND APPLIED? In selecting marketable securities, consider the type, marketability, maturity date, rate of return, transaction cost, default risk, maximum amount to be invested, maximum/minimum dollar amount to be traded, and trend in interest rates. The small business owner must balance the return desired against the risk he or she is willing to assume. As a general rule, the return on marketable securities is low, but they are liquid and safe. Risk takes the form of a lack of marketability, possible loss of principal (the amount invested), and the susceptibility to changing interest rates (e.g., as interest rates rise, the price of fixed-income securities declines). The small business owner should demand a higher return when default risk is greater and the maturity period is longer.

32 What Is the Equivalent Tax Yield?

INTRODUCTION. The equivalent taxable yield is the rate of return on a nontaxable investment as it would be on a taxable basis. Today, all small business owners are tax conscious. The highest maximum tax rate for a corporation is 35 percent, and it is 39.6 percent for individuals. Since the profits of a sole proprietorship or partnership automatically flow through to the owners, any profits earned by these entities will be taxed at a rate no higher than 39.6 percent.

Bonds issued by states, school districts, port authorities, counties, and fire districts are tax exempt. On the other hand, bonds issued by corporations yield taxable income. As a result, a municipal bond investment remains an attractive tax savings opportunity for all small business owners.

HOW IS IT COMPUTED?

$$\text{Equivalent taxable yield} = \frac{\text{tax-free return}}{1 - \text{marginal tax rate}}$$

The small business owner is usually faced with the decision of whether to purchase taxable or exempt bonds. The decision is easy if the risk of the investments is assumed to be equal. A small business owner should invest in exempt bonds instead of taxable bonds if the interest on the exempt bonds is greater than the interest on the taxable bonds times 1 minus the taxpayer's marginal tax rate expressed as a decimal. This means that the small business owner should invest in tax-exempt municipal bonds if

Return on the tax-exempt bonds > Return on the taxable bonds
$$\times (1 - \text{marginal tax bracket})$$

Example 1 Jack Tryon operates as a sole proprietorship and is in the 28 percent tax bracket. He is offered a tax-exempt bond paying 9 percent interest, and a taxable corporate bond paying 12 percent. Jack should invest in the tax-exempt bond paying 9 percent because its yield will be greater than the 8.64 percent generated by the corporate taxable bond computed as follows:

$$12\% \times (1 - 0.28) = 8.64\%$$

Example 2 Amanda Clinton is a 50 percent partner in a partnership that plans to purchase bonds. Both she and her partner are in the 31 percent tax bracket. The partnership is offered a tax-exempt bond paying 7 percent interest, and a taxable corporate bond paying 11 percent. The partnership should invest in the taxable bond paying 11 percent because its yield will be greater at 7.59 percent than the 7 percent yield generated by the tax-exempt municipal bond computed as follows:

$$11\% \times (1 - 0.31) = 7.59\%$$

Example 3 The Payout Corporation is in the 25 percent tax bracket. The corporation is offered a tax-exempt bond paying 7 percent interest, and a taxable corporate bond paying 10 percent. The corporation should invest in the taxable bond paying 10 percent because its yield will be greater at 7.50 percent than the 7 percent yield generated by the tax-exempt municipal bond computed as follows:

$$10\% \times (1 - 0.25) = 7.50\%$$

HOW IS IT USED AND APPLIED? Individuals use the equivalent taxable yield to determine what their tax-free rate of return would be on a taxable basis. This enables them to compare alternative tax-free and taxable investments.

The main factor in deciding whether to make an investment is the determination of equivalent taxable yield. If the income generated by the investment is fully taxable, then any earnings must be further reduced by the applicable tax rate to determine after-tax earnings. Other factors such as liquidity and marketability also influence the risk pertaining to the investment.

Many small business owners consider the exclusion of interest on municipal bonds to be one of the few remaining tax shelters for them. This means that if the small business owner operated as a corporation, it would avoid taxes of as much as 35 percent on bond interest. If the enterprise operated as either a sole proprietorship or a partnership, the tax savings would be as much as 39.6 percent.

33 Determining the Optimal Cash Balance

INTRODUCTION. There are two techniques for deciding how much cash to maintain at any given time, considering that both holding cash and investing it have both advantages and disadvantages. The purpose of cash models is to satisfy cash requirements at the least cost.

HOW IS IT COMPUTED?

The Baumol's Model. The Baumol's model attempts to determine the optimum amount of transaction cash under conditions of certainty. The objective is to minimize the sum of the fixed costs of transactions and the opportunity cost of holding cash balances. These costs are expressed as:

$$F \times \frac{T}{C} + i\,\frac{C}{2}$$

where F = the fixed cost of a transaction, T = the total cost needed for the time period involved, i = the interest rate on marketable securities, and C = cash balance.

The optimal level of cash is determined using the following formula:

$$C^* = \sqrt{\frac{2FT}{i}}$$

Example 1 You estimate a cash need for $4,000,000 over a 1-month period in which the cash account is expected to be disbursed at a constant rate. The opportunity interest rate is 6 percent per annum, or 0.5 percent for a 1-month period. The transaction cost each time you borrow or withdraw is $100.

The optimal transaction size (the optimal borrowing or withdrawal lot size) and the number of transactions you should make during the month are:

$$C^* = \sqrt{\frac{2FT}{i}} = \sqrt{\frac{2(100)(4,000,000)}{0.005}} = \$400,000$$

The optimal transaction size is $400,000. The average cash balance is:

$$\frac{C^*}{2} = \frac{\$400,000}{2} = \$200,000$$

The number of transactions required is:

$$\frac{\$4,000,000}{\$400,000} = 10 \text{ transactions during the month.}$$

See Figure 33.1 for a pictorial representation of this example.

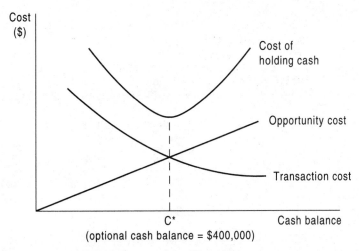

C*
(optional cash balance = $400,000)

Figure 33.1 Pictorial representation of Example 1.

The Miller-Orr Model. You can use a stochastic model for cash management when *uncertainty* exists for cash payments—that is, there is irregularity of cash payments. The Miller-Orr model sets upper and lower limits for cash balances. When the upper limit is reached, a transfer of cash to marketable securities or other suitable investments is made. When the lower limit is reached, a transfer from securities to cash occurs. A transaction will not occur as long as the cash balance falls within the limits.

The Miller-Orr model takes into account the fixed costs of a securities transaction (F), assumed to be the same for buying as well as selling, the daily interest rate on marketable securities (i), and the variance of daily net cash flows (σ^2). A major assumption is the randomness of cash flows. The two control limits in the Miller-Orr model may be specified as d dollars as an upper limit and 0 dollars at the lower limit. When the cash balance reaches the upper level, d less z dollars of securities are bought and the new balance equals zero, z dollars of the securities are sold and the new balance again reaches z. Of course, practically speaking, you should note that the minimum cash balance is established at an amount greater than zero due to delays in transfer as well as to having a safety buffer.

The optimal cash balance z is computed as follows:

$$z = \sqrt{\frac{3F\sigma^2}{4i}}$$

The optimal value for d is computed as $3z$. The average cash balance will approximate $(z + d)/3$.

Example 2 You wish to use the Miller-Orr model. The following information is supplied:

Fixed cost of a securities transaction	$10
Variance of daily net cash flows	$50
Daily interest rate on securities (10%/360)	0.0003

The optimal cash balance, the upper limit of cash needed, and the average cash balance are as follows:

$$z = \sqrt[3]{\frac{(10)(50)}{4(0.0003)}} = \sqrt[3]{\frac{(10)(50)}{0.0012}} = \sqrt[3]{\frac{1,500}{0.0012}}$$

$$= \sqrt[3]{1,250,000} = \$102$$

The optimal cash balance is $102. The upper limit is $306 (3 × $102).

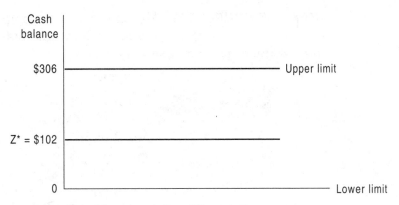

Figure 33.2 Pictorial representation of Example 2.

The average cash balance is

$$\frac{\$102 + \$306}{3} = \$136$$

When the upper limit of $306 is reached, $204 of securities ($306 − $102) will be purchased to bring you to the optimal cash balance of $102. When the lower limit of 0 dollars is reached, $102 of securities will be sold to bring you again to the optimal cash balance of $102. See Fig. 33.2.

HOW IS IT USED AND APPLIED? Cash management models can be used effectively to decide the right amount of cash to keep. You will not want to keep more money than necessary to cover day-to-day operating expenses. However, emergency cash funds are necessary. The models aid in finding the right balance between the cash balance and funds to be placed in short-term investment accounts.

34 Cash Ratios

INTRODUCTION. Cash utilization indicates how well your small business is using its money in running the business, keeping liquid to pay bills and earning a return. Cash availability measures how much money is free for your operating expenses and debt payments. Adequate cash flow is needed not only to stay afloat but also for expansion, purchase of new assets, and to pay vendors.

The need for cash and its utilization depends on the type of small business; a retail store selling high-priced appliances needs more cash to buy expensive inventory than a service-oriented business such as an accounting firm that has no inventory.

HOW IS IT COMPUTED? You may want to compute the following cash ratios to get a handle on how efficient the utilization and adequacy of your cash balance is.

$$\frac{\text{Sales}}{\text{Cash}}$$

$$\frac{\text{Cash flow}}{\text{Total debt}}$$

$$\frac{\text{Cash flow}}{\text{Long-term debt}}$$

$$\frac{\text{Cash + marketable securities}}{\text{Total current sales}}$$

$$\frac{\text{Cash + marketable securities}}{\text{Total current liabilities}}$$

$$\frac{\text{Cash + marketable securities}}{\text{Working capital}}$$

Working capital = current assets − current liabilities

$$\frac{\text{Cash}}{\text{Average monthly payments}} :$$

$$\text{Average monthly payments} = \frac{\text{total payments for the year}}{12}$$

$$\frac{\text{Cash + marketable securities + receivables}}{\text{Year's cash expenses}}$$

Cash flow-to-capital expenditures ratio:

$$\frac{\text{Cash flow from operations}}{\text{Expenditures for plant and equipment}}$$

Example 1 A small business reports the following:

	19X1	19X2
Cash	$ 50,000	$940,000
Sales	800,000	900,000

The sales-to-cash ratio is 16 ($800,000/$50,000) in 19X1 and 22.5 ($900,000/$40,000) in 19X2. It appears that the small business may have a cash deficiency in 19X2 because cash is lower, which implies a possible liquidity problem.

Example 2 Two cash flow ratios are calculated based on the following information for a small business:

	19X5	19X6
Cash flow	$300,000	$ 150,000
Total debt	900,000	1,200,000
Long-term debt	450,000	700,000

The applicable ratios are:

	19X5	19X6
Cash flow to total debt	33.3%	12.5%
Cash flow to long-term debt	66.7%	21.4%

From 19X5 to 19X6, the owner has experienced a significant deterioration in liquidity. The owner may be in a cash squeeze and unable to meet obligations when they fall due.

Example 3 A small business reports the following information:

	19X1	19X2
Cash plus marketable securities	$100,000	$ 90,000
Working capital	300,000	350,000

The relevant ratios are cash plus cash equivalents to working capital = 0.33 for 19X1 and 0.26 for 19X2. The ratios indicate that the business has experienced deteriorating liquidity, since it has less cash and marketable securities available as a liquid base in 19X2.

HOW IS IT USED AND APPLIED? The cash flow-to-total debt ratio indicates a business's ability to satisfy its debts. It is useful in predicting potential bankruptcy. Cash flow to long-term debt appraises the adequacy of available funds to meet noncurrent obligations. Of course, not all the cash flow will be available to pay debt. Some of it will be needed for such things as buying new assets (e.g., property, plant, equipment, inventory).

The ratio of cash plus marketable securities to current liabilities indicates the amount of cash immediately available to satisfy short-term debt. This ratio is much more conservative than the acid test ratio (see Sec. 88). The more your current debt is covered with cash and near-cash assets, the better will be your ability to meet supplier and creditor claims. Further, the ratio provides a "warning sign" of cash deficiencies and helps prevent a crisis situation in which current debt cannot be paid.

A high ratio of cash plus marketable securities to working capital makes it easier to obtain financing at reasonable rates because the liquidity of the small business appears better.

Concern is also directed to how many times a business's immediate liquid resources are sufficient to meet cash expenses. Cash can be improved through the better management of receivables and inventory, encouraging cash sales rather than credit sales, delaying vendor payments, and borrowing money.

The cash flow-to-capital expenditures ratio indicates a business's ability to maintain plant and equipment from cash provided from operations, rather than by borrowing. You are better off obtaining funds internally from the business because there are no financing costs associated.

The purpose of the cash flow adequacy ratio is to determine the degree to which a business has generated sufficient cash flow from operations to cover capital expenditures and net investment in inventories. To remove cyclical and other unstable influences, a 5-year total is used in the computation. A ratio of 1 shows that the business has covered its needs based on attained growth levels without resorting to external financing. If the ratio goes below 1, internally generated cash may be insufficient to maintain current operating growth levels. This ratio may also reflect the effect of inflation on the funds needs of the business.

In evaluating cash, you should also note whether a portion is unavailable for use (restricted). For example, a compensating balance does not constitute "free" cash. (Interest income is not earned.) A compensating balance is a deposit a bank can use to offset an unpaid loan.

Cash held as a time deposit or in a temporary escrow account also is not available funds. An escrow account contains money you temporarily deposit with a neutral third party in conformity with a contract; you have no control over the escrow money until the terms of the agreement have been satisfied. When you sell store furniture and equipment, for example, the buyer might insist that you put escrow money on deposit for 2 months to reimburse the buyer for defects in the furniture and equipment needing repairs.

See Sec. 35, Cash Flow from Operations.

35 Cash Flow from Operations

INTRODUCTION. Cash flow from operations represents the cash earnings of a small business. Utilization of cash flow ratios shows the degree to which net income is backed up by a liquid source of funds. Cash reinvestment into a business indicates the ability of the owner to position himself or herself for future growth.

HOW IS IT COMPUTED? The process of analyzing a small business's cash flow (cash earnings) is as follows:

1. Cash flow from operations is calculated as:

Net income
Add: Noncash expenses (e.g., depreciation, amortization)
Less: Noncash revenue (e.g., amortization of deferred revenue)
Cash flow from operations (cash earnings)

2. This calculation is followed by analyzing the operational cash flow over net income:

$$\frac{\text{Cash flow from operations}}{\text{Net income}}$$

3. A third calculation is derived by stating the cash flow generated from operations less cash payments required to pay debt principal and capital expenditures.

4. The cash reinvestment ratio is calculated as follows:

$$\frac{\text{Cash employed}}{\text{Cash objected}}$$

Cash employed = increase in gross plant and equipment
$$+ \text{ increase in working capital}$$

Cash obtained = income after tax plus depreciation

Example An income statement for a small business and the pertinent cash flow analysis follow:

Sales		$1,000,000
Less: Cost of sales		300,000
Gross margin		$ 700,000
Less: Operating expenses		
Salary	$100,000	
Rent	200,000	
Telephone	50,000	
Depreciation	140,000	
Total operating expenses		490,000
Income before other items		$ 210,000
Other revenue and expense		
Interest expense	$ 70,000	
Amortization of deferred revenue	40,000	
Total revenue and expense		30,000
Net income		$ 180,000

The ratio of cash flow from operations to net income is 1.55, calculated as follows:

Cash flow from operations:	
Net income	$180,000
Add:	
Noncash expenses	
Depreciation	140,000
Less:	
Noncash revenue	
Amortization of deferred revenue	(40,000)
Cash flow from operations	$280,000

$$\frac{\text{Cash flow from operations}}{\text{Net income}} = \frac{\$280,000}{\$180,000} = 1.55$$

HOW IS IT USED AND APPLIED? Earnings are of higher quality if they are backed up by cash, since cash can be used to meet debt payments, buy fixed assets, and so forth.

A high cash reinvestment ratio indicates that more cash is being used in the business. Further, a business with a high percentage of internally generated cash earnings has better liquidity. See Sec. 34, Cash Ratios.

36 Cash Forecasting

INTRODUCTION. Accurate cash forecasting is important for the success of a small business. Cash forecasting is crucial in projecting financial needs, spotting areas of financial strength or weakness, formulating a realistic timetable in which to accomplish goals, and comparing expectations to actual results. Once you know your expected cash position, you can plan expenditures, such as asset acquisition, debt repayment, operating expenses, such as advertising, and wage settlements.

In deciding on the forecasting period to use, consider the nature of your operation. If you have stable sales, a quarterly forecast is suitable. On the other hand, if your sales are unstable, a monthly forecast will help you keep up to date.

The forecasting period also depends on your exposure to economic conditions and the business cycle; for example, if you are subject to 3 months seasonality, a quarterly forecasting period is logical.

HOW IS IT PREPARED? There are two kinds of forecasts: short term and long term. A short-term forecast usually covers 1 year or less, while a long-term forecast covers more than 1 year. A long-term forecast is simply an extension of a short-term forecast.

A short-term forecast is more detailed and reliable than a long-term forecast because the short time span makes projections easier. A short-term forecast tells you whether you can carry on financial and operating activities over the next year and is crucial if you are experiencing cash problems or significant variability in cash. Will you need a short-term loan? When can you repay it? Do you have excess cash to invest? It is crucial for a small business to have a short-term forecast because of the need for tight control over cash.

The steps in constructing a short-term forecast are as follows:

1. Take into account temporary fluctuations in cash flow.
2. Select a representative period to depict cash flows, such as quarterly or monthly.
3. Plan for unusual cash receipts and cash payments.

A new small business should start off with a monthly forecast broken down by week, because control is essential in the early stages. Once the business matures, a quarterly forecast broken down by month is adequate.

The advantages to short-term forecasting are:

Providing the basis for the long-term forecast

Providing a schedule for loan repayments

Timing of borrowing so as to lower interest costs

Timing cash flow to take advantage of cash discounts for early payment to suppliers.

A long-term cash forecast shows major acquisitions of assets, major asset disposals, planned debt financing, and the introduction of new products and/or services. It also provides a basis for judging whether there is sufficient net cash inflows to support growth.

A forecast of cash collections and potential write-offs of customer balances is essential in cash budgeting. The critical step in making such a forecast is estimating the cash collection and bad debt percentages (based on an aging of customer balances) and applying them to sales or accounts receivable balances. Two examples follow.

Example 1 Phil Blake owns a toy store. The accounts receivable balance on June 1 is $35,000, of which $20,000 applies to sales made in April and $15,000 applies to May sales. Past experience indicates that the pattern of collection is as follows: Month of sale, 45 percent; second month, 30 percent; third month, 24 percent; and uncollectible, 1 percent. Credit sales for June are $200,000. Cash collections for June are computed as follows:

April sales ($20,000 3 24%/25%)	$ 19,200
May sales ($15,000 3 30%/55%)	8,182
June sales ($200,000 3 45%)	90,000
Total	$117,382

Example 2 The following information is provided for Milich's Clothing Store:

	September actual	October actual	November estimated
Cash sales	$ 14,000	$12,000	$ 16,000
Credit sales	$100,000	$96,000	$124,000

Previous experience based on aging of receivables shows that collections typically take place in the following pattern:

- No collections are made in the month of sale.
- Seventy percent of the sales of any month are collected in the following month.
- Twenty-five percent of sales are collected in the second following month.
- Five percent of sales are uncollectible.

November's cash receipts are:

Cash receipts:	
Cash sales	$ 16,000
Cash collections	
September sales ($100,000 3 25%)	25,000
October sales ($96,000 3 70%)	67,200
Total cash receipts	$108,200

HOW IT IS USED AND APPLIED? Your cash forecast should cover both the peak and ebb points of sales. For example, a cash forecast for a toy store or gift shop would be erroneous if it did not consider Christmas sales along with projected sales during the slowest part of the year. The seasonality of the business is crucial in making projections.

As a rule of thumb, avoid making large payments (e.g., operating expenses, debt repayment) at the low point in the cash cycle.

37 Accounts Receivable Ratios

INTRODUCTION. Accounts receivable ratios indicate how effectively a business is managing its investment in receivables.

HOW IS IT COMPUTED? The five most useful ratios are the following.

$$1.\ \text{Accounts receivable turnover} = \frac{\text{annual credit sales}}{\text{average accounts receivable}}$$

Accounts receivable turnover indicates how fast the owner is collecting from customers.

$$\text{Average accounts receivable} = \frac{\text{beginning accounts receivable} + \text{ending accounts receivable}}{2}$$

If sales vary greatly during the year, monthly or quarterly sales figures should be used to achieve proper averaging so that the ratio is not distorted. Further, sales should be adjusted for any extraordinary items (e.g., one-time sales that will not be repeated).

2. Average collection period $= \dfrac{365}{\text{accounts receivable turnover}}$

The average collection period indicates how long it takes to collect a receivable.

3. Trend in accounts receivable = accounts receivable (prior year) − accounts receivable (current year)

4. $\dfrac{\text{Accounts receivable}}{\text{Total assets}}$

5. $\dfrac{\text{Accounts receivable}}{\text{Sales}}$

Example A business reports the following data for the years ended December 31, 19X1, and December 31, 19X2:

	19X1	19X2
Sales	$400,000	$500,000
Total assets	600,000	650,000
Accounts receivable	50,000	90,000

On January 1, 19X1, accounts receivable was $45,000.

For this business, three ratios are used to analyze accounts receivables:

	19X1	19X2
1. Accounts receivable turnover	$400,000	$500,000
(sales/average accounts receivable)	47,500	$70,000
	8.42	7.14
2. Collection period (365/turnover)	$\dfrac{365}{8.42}$	$\dfrac{365}{7.14}$
	43.3 days	51.1 days
3. Accounts receivable to total assets	$ 50,000	$ 90,000
	$600,000	$650,000
	8.3%	13.8%

In this example, the realization risk in accounts receivable is higher in 19X2. This is shown by a lower turnover rate, a longer collection period, and a higher ratio of accounts receivable to total assets in that year.

HOW IS IT USED AND APPLIED? Accounts receivable ratios are determined to appraise the degree of risk in accounts receivable. In general, higher accounts receivable turnovers are good signs of successful small businesses since they show that these businesses collect faster from customers and are therefore in a better position to invest funds. An excessively high ratio relative to industry averages, however, may signal that the owner's credit policy is too tight, and the business is not tapping its earnings potential through sales to higher-risk customers. Before modifying credit policy, an owner should weigh the profit potential against the risk inherent in selling to more risk-prone customers.

In terms of the collection period, the longer receivables are outstanding past the anticipated payment date compared to industry norms, the lower is the expectation of collection. In general, a "red flag" is raised when the customer's account is more than 30 days past due. In times of economic hardship, collection periods increase. Appraise separate collection periods by type of customer, product line, and market territory. An aging schedule is also available. In some cases, however, a longer collection period may be warranted, for example, in a business that has extended its credit terms to introduce a new product or to meet heightened competition.

A sharp increase in accounts receivable compared to the prior year may indicate higher realization risk. This could imply that the business is selling to more marginal-credit customers. The owner must examine the trends in accounts receivable to total assets and in accounts receivable to sales to identify unusual increases in receivables.

Accounts receivable ratios are also examined as an indication of a business's *liquidity*. A high turnover ratio and short collection period—indications that a business is able to collect quickly from customers—is considered favorable by creditors because it shows that the business is efficiently managing its cash flow.

To judge the appropriateness of an owner's collection and credit policy, a small business's ratios must be compared with industry averages or ratios of major competitors within the same industry. Trend analysis should be performed, looking at the ratio for the business owner over the years. Are things getting better or worse?

38 Managing Accounts Receivable

INTRODUCTION. In extending credit to retail customers, you should take into account both the amount and the terms, which will influence your sales and the resulting profitability, the collection period, and the number of delinquent or uncollectible accounts. If you set stringent credit terms, you will have lower sales and net income, less money tied up in customer balances, lower bad-debt losses, but adverse customer reaction. If your credit policy is too lax, you will experience higher sales, higher accounts receivable balances, and more bad debts.

Accounts receivable management assists small business owners in determining the opportunity cost associated with holding receivable balances. Key components of this type of analysis are a determination of a business's investment in accounts receivable, and relaxation of credit standards—both aspects of receivable management that have an impact on the owner's bottom line. Each is discussed below.

INVESTMENT IN ACCOUNTS RECEIVABLE. The amount invested in accounts receivable is the cost tied up in the account.

How Is It Computed?

Investment in accounts receivable

$$= \frac{\text{days held}}{360} \times \text{annual credit sales}$$

Investment in accounts receivable

$$= \text{average accounts receivable} \times \text{cost}$$

Example 1 Assume that a small business sells on terms of net 30 days, with accounts that are on average 20 days past due. Annual credit sales are $600,000. The investment in accounts receivable is:

$$\frac{50}{360} \times \$600,000 = \$83,333.28$$

Example 2 Assume that the cost of a product is 30 percent of its selling price, and that the cost of capital is 10 percent of its selling price. Sales average $70,000 per month and accounts are paid 4 months after sale. The small business owner wants to determine his investment in receivables from this product.

Accounts receivable (4 months 3 $70,000)	$280,000
Investment in accounts receivable [$280,000 × (0.30 + 0.10)]	112,000

RELAXATION OF CREDIT STANDARDS. The small business owner will find it useful to evaluate whether to give credit to marginal customers.

How Is It Computed? Compare the earnings on additional sales obtained and the added cost of the receivables. In a situation where a small business has idle capacity, the additional earnings equal the contribution margin on the incremental sales, because fixed costs are constant. The additional cost on the additional receivables is derived from the greater number of uncollectible accounts and the opportunity cost associated with tying up funds in receivables for a longer time period.

$$\text{New average unit cost} = \frac{\text{total cost}}{\text{units}}$$

Additional profitability = additional units
$$\times \text{ contribution margin per unit}$$

Additional bad debts = additional receivables
$$\times \text{ bad debt percentage}$$

Opportunity cost in accounts receivable =
additional investment in accounts receivable × minimum return

Example 3 The following illustrates one owner's analysis of whether he or she should relax credit standards.

Sales price per unit	$120
Variable cost per unit	$80
Fixed cost per unit	$15
Annual credit sales	$600,000
Collection period	1 month
Minimum return	16%

If the owner liberalized the credit policy, the business projected that the following would occur:

- Sales would increase by 40 percent.
- The collection period on total accounts would be 2 months.
- Bad debts on the increased sales would be 5 percent.

Preliminary calculations:

Current units ($600,000/$120)	5,000
Additional units (5,000 × 0.4)	2,000

The new average unit cost was calculated as follows:

	Units	×	Unit cost	=	Total cost
Current units	5,000	×	$95		$475,000
Additional units	2,000	×	$80		160,000
Total	7,000				$635,000

$$\text{New average unit cost} = \frac{\text{total}}{\text{units}} = \frac{\$635,000}{7,000} = \$90.71 \quad \text{(rounded)}$$

Note that, at idle capacity, fixed cost remained constant. Thus, the incremental cost is just the variable cost of $80 per unit, which would cause the new average unit cost to drop.

Advantage of relaxing credit standards
  Additional profitability:

Incremental sales volume	2,000 units
× contribution margin per unit	× $40
(selling price 2 variable cost): $120 2 $80	
Incremental profitability	$80,000

Disadvantage of relaxing credit standards
  Incremental bad debts:

Incremental units × selling price:	$240,000
2,000 × $120	
Bad debt percentage	× .05
Additional bad debts	$12,000

Opportunity cost of funds tied up in accounts receivable
  Average investment in accounts receivable after change in policy:

$$\frac{\text{Credit sales}}{\text{Accounts receivable turnover}} \times \frac{\text{unit cost}}{\text{selling price}} = \qquad \$105,828$$

$$\frac{\$840,000(a)}{6} \times \frac{\$90.91}{\$120}$$

(a) 7,000 units × $120 5 $840,000
Current average investment in accounts receivable:

$$\frac{\$600,000}{12} \times \frac{\$95}{\$120} \qquad\qquad 39,583$$

Additional investment in accounts receivable	$66,245
× minimum return	× 0.16
Opportunity cost of funds tied up	$10,599

Net advantage of relaxation in credit standards

Additional earnings		$80,000
Less: Additional bad debts	$12,000	
Opportunity cost	10,599	22,599
Net savings		$57,401

HOW IS IT USED AND APPLIED? Small business owners need to monitor their investment in receivables and analyze whether offering a discount would hasten collections, resulting in improved earnings. If excessive funds are tied up in accounts receivable, owners risk draining their resources and lowering profitability. Owners must weigh the risks involved in extending credit to marginal customers against the rewards of increased sales. The analysis described above reveals whether these moves improve overall profitability despite the fact that receivable balances are outstanding longer.

Receivable terms should be liberalized when you want to dispose of excessive inventory or obsolete items. Longer receivable terms are suitable for retailers whose products are sold in advance of "demand" seasons (e.g., swimsuits). If products are perishable, short credit terms or even payment on delivery is recommended.

You may have to change your credit policy based on changing circumstances. When times are good, you may give additional credit. However, in bad times, such as in a recession, it is smart to tighten up on granting credit, because higher unemployment rates, salary freezes, and employee givebacks reduce customer's ability to pay their bills. The amount of credit you can safely extend also depends on competitive factors and the incomes of your customers.

Credit policy also varies with the type of business. A vegetable or fruit store will most likely sell only on a *cash basis* because of the perishability of the product. An appliance store will likely include sales on the *installment-payment basis* because of the long life of its product line. A service business may ask for advance payments (retainers) or may bill clients when services are rendered.

Your credit policy should be flexible and tied to the peculiar characteristics of the customer (e.g., age, occupation, income), merchandise or services offered, selling price, cost of the item, profit margin (profit divided by selling price), goals of the business, cash position, liquidity, degree of competition, and shipping arrangements.

Controlling Inventory

39 Inventory Ratios

INTRODUCTION. Inventory ratios reveal the turnover and age of inventory. Knowing whether excess inventory exists is a must to the owner of a small business, because money being tied up in inventory could be invested elsewhere or to pay bills. Excess inventory also involves a high carrying cost for storing goods as well as risk of obsolescence.

HOW IS IT COMPUTED?

1. $$\text{Inventory turnover} = \frac{\text{cost of sales}}{\text{average inventory}}$$

where

$$\text{Average inventory} = \frac{\text{beginning inventory} + \text{ending inventory}}{2}$$

If the inventory amount at year-end is not typical due to cyclicality, a quarterly or monthly average should be used.

2. $$\text{Age of inventory} = \frac{365}{\text{inventory turnover}}$$

3. $$\frac{\text{Sales}}{\text{Inventory}}$$

Example 1 A small business reports the following information for a 2-year period:

	12/31/19X1	12/31/19X2
Inventory	$25,000	$ 40,000
Cost of sales	$150,000	$160,000

The inventory on January 1, 19X1, is $20,000
   The inventory turnover and the number of days inventory is held are computed below.

	19X1	19X2
Inventory turnover	($150,000/$22,500) = 6.67	($160,000/$32,500) = 4.92
Age of inventory	(365/6.67) = 55 days	(365/4.92) = 74 days

Example 2 A small business provides the following information on 2 years' performance:

	19X1	19X2
Sales	$200,000	$290,000
Total inventories	40,000	43,000

The percentage increase in sales is 45 percent, but the advance in total inventories is only 7.5 percent. This analysis shows that the business has good inventory control.

HOW IS IT USED AND APPLIED?   Sound inventory management leads to maximum return at minimum risk. A buildup of inventory may indicate to the owner uncertain future sales. Inventory buildup is indicated when inventory increases at a rate that is much greater than the rate of increase in sales. A low ratio of sales to inventory relative to other businesses in the industry means less efficient utilization of inventory in generating revenue. Further, a decrease in the ratio of sales to inventory means that purchasing of goods has increased faster than sales, or that sales have declined relative to inventory. In general, it is best when the ratio remains fairly constant, even for a growing business.

Inventory turnover is the cycle of using and replacing materials. It is a ratio: the number of "turns" to the investment in a year. If a business sells $100,000 worth of products a year and has an average inventory valued at $50,000, it has two turnovers a year. If the same company produced sales of $100,000 with an average inventory worth $25,000, it would have four turns a year. More turns reduces investment and saves carrying costs as well.

Some businesses use an inventory turnover ratio as an inventory control method. Managers insist on a certain number of turns a year. This control should not be carried very far, however. A high turnover rate means very low inventories, but very low inventories may mean being out of stock more often. High turnover and low inventories at the same time also force frequent and often uneconomical small reorders, which can result in higher unit costs.

Sales volume and reasonable inventory turnover ratios are also related. It is not difficult to obtain more turns when sales volume is high. However, if sales volume decreases to half and inventories are also cut in half in order to keep the turnover ratio constant, there will probably be more stock-outs. This could lead to costly, frequent, and small-quantity reorders, as well as idle production—although, of course, if sales fell this much, idle production might be justified.

The turnover rate should be determined for each major inventory category. A low turnover rate may indicate (1) overstocking, (2) obsolescence, or (3) deficiencies in the product or sales effort. Further, a business with a poor inventory turnover is viewed by suppliers and creditors as possessing greater liquidity risk. In some cases, however, a low rate of turnover is justified, such as when higher inventory levels occur in expectation of rapidly rising prices (e.g., for oil). A high turnover rate may indicate that the business does not keep adequate inventory levels, a situation that could result in lost business if inventory is not on hand. Further, the turnover rate may be unrepresentatively high if a business uses its "natural year-end" to calculate inventory, because the inventory balance at that time of year would be unusually low.

The small business owner can take certain control measures to minimize inventory buildup and their consequent negative effects. These include setting minimum and maximum acceptable turnover rates, evaluating physical counts to spot goods that are not moving, and improving the purchasing process.

40 How Much to Order (Economic Order Quantity) and When to Order (Reorder Point)

INTRODUCTION. One of the most common problems facing managers is inventory planning. This is understandable since inventory usually represents a sizable portion of a business's total assets and, more specifically, on the average, more than 30 percent of total current assets in U.S. industry. Too much money tied up in inventory is a drag on profitability. The purpose of inventory planning is to develop policies which will achieve an optimal investment in inventory. This objective is accomplished by determining the optimal level of inventory necessary to minimize inventory-related costs.

Inventory-related costs fall into three categories:

1. Ordering costs, which includes all costs associated with preparing a purchase order.

2. Carrying (holding) costs, which include storage costs for inventory items plus the cost of money tied up in inventory.

3. Shortage (stock-out) costs, which include costs incurred when an item is out of stock, such as the lost contribution margin on sales plus lost customer goodwill.

Many inventory planning models are available that try to answer the following two questions:

1. How much to order?

2. When to order?

The first question is answered through the *economic order quantity* (EOQ) model. The second question is answered by means of the *reorder-point* (ROP) formula.

HOW IS IT COMPUTED?

Economic Order Quantity. The economic order quantity (EOQ) determines the order quantity that results in the lowest sum of carrying and ordering costs. The EOQ is computed as:

$$EOQ = \sqrt{\frac{2OD}{C}}$$

where C = carrying cost per unit, O = ordering cost per order, and D = annual demand (requirements) in units.

If the carrying cost is expressed as a percentage of average inventory value (say, 12 percent per year to hold inventory), then the denominator value in the EOQ formula is 12 percent times the price of an item.

> **Example 1** Assume that the Buena Park Store buys sets of steel at $40 per set from an outside vendor. It will sell 6400 sets evenly throughout the year. The store desires a 16 percent return on its inventory investment, which is the interest charge on borrowed money. In addition, rent, taxes, etc., for each set in inventory is $1.60 per year. The ordering cost is $100 per order. Thus the carrying cost per set is 16%($40) + $1.60 = $8.00 per year. Therefore,
>
> $$EOQ = \sqrt{\frac{2(6400)(\$100)}{\$8.00}} = \sqrt{160,000} = 400 \text{ sets}$$
>
> $$\text{Total number of orders per year} = \frac{D}{EOQ} = \frac{6400}{400} = 16 \text{ orders}$$

Total inventory costs = carrying cost + ordering cost

$$= C \times \left(\frac{EOQ}{2} \right) + O\left(\frac{D}{EOQ} \right)$$

$$= (\$8.00)\left(\frac{400}{2} \right) + (\$100)\left(\frac{6400}{400} \right)$$

$$= \$1600 + \$1600 = \$3200$$

Based on these calculations, the Buena Park Store should order 400 sets of steel each time it places an order, and it should place an order 16 times during the year. This policy will be most economical, costing the store $3200 per year.

Reorder Point. Reorder point (ROP), which tells when to place a new order, requires knowledge of the *lead time,* which is the time interval between placing an order and receiving delivery. The reorder point can be calculated as follows:

ROP = (average usage per unit of lead time × lead time) + safety stock

First, multiply average daily (or weekly) usage by the lead time in days (or weeks) to yield the lead time demand. Then add safety stock to this to provide for the variation in lead time demand to determine the reorder point. If average usage and lead time are both certain, no safety stock is necessary and can be dropped from the formula.

Example 2 Assume that, for the store in Example 1, lead time is constant at 1 week, and that there are 50 working weeks in a year. Then the reorder point is 128 sets [(6400 sets/50 weeks) × 1 week]. Therefore, when the inventory level drops to 128 sets, a new order should be placed. Suppose, however, that the store is faced with variable usage for its steel and requires a safety stock of 150 additional sets. Then the reorder point is 128 sets plus 150 sets, or 278 sets.

Figure 40.1 shows this inventory system when the order quantity is 400 sets and the reorder point is 128 sets.

HOW IS IT USED AND APPLIED? It is important to realize some strong assumptions underlying the EOQ model:

1. Demand is fixed and constant throughout the year.

2. Lead time is known with certainty.

3. No quantity discounts are taken.

4. No shortages are permitted.

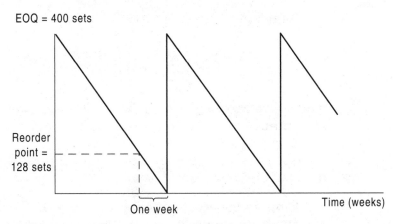

Figure 40.1 Basic inventory system with EOQ and reorder point.

These assumptions may be unrealistic, but the model is still useful in inventory planning for many businesses. In fact, in many situations the assumptions hold or nearly hold. For example, subcontractors who must supply parts on a regular basis to a primary contractor face a constant demand. Even when demand varies, the assumption of uniform usage is valid or nearly valid. Demand for automobiles, for example, varies from week to week over a season, but the weekly fluctuations tend to cancel each other so that seasonal demand can be assumed constant.

Purchasing managers need to know two things: (1) how much to order and (2) when to order. In the face of uncertain reality, managers must determine the safety stock in order to determine the reorder point. Otherwise, they will face the serious consequences of shortages and lost customers.

See also Sec. 43, Allowing for Safety Stock.

41 Calculating Quantity Discounts (EOQ with Quantity Discounts)

INTRODUCTION. The economic order quantity (EOQ) model does not take into account quantity discounts, which is not realistic in many real-world cases. Usually, the more you order, the lower is the unit price you pay. *Quantity discounts* are price reductions for large orders offered to buyers to induce them to buy in large quantities.

HOW IS IT COMPUTED? The buyer's goal is to select the order quantity which will minimize total cost, where total cost is the sum of carrying cost, ordering cost, and product cost:

Total cost = carrying cost + ordering cost + product cost

$$= C \times \left(\frac{Q}{2}\right) + O\left(\frac{D}{Q}\right) + PD$$

where C = carrying cost per unit, O = ordering cost per order, D = annual demand (requirements) in units, P = unit price, and Q = order quantity.

A step-by-step approach to computing EOQ with quantity discounts is summarized below.

1. Compute the economic order quantity (EOQ) when price discounts are ignored and the corresponding costs using the new cost formula given above. Recall that EOQ $= \sqrt{2OD/C}$

2. Compute the costs for those quantities greater than the EOQ at which price reductions occur.

3. Select the value of Q which will result in the lowest total cost.

Example As a continuation of Example 1 in the previous section (Sec. 40), assume further that Buena Park Store has been offered the following price discount schedule:

Order quantity (Q)	Unit price (P)
1–499	$40.00
500–999	39.90
1000 or more	39.80

First, recall from Sec. 40 that the EOQ with no discounts is 400 sets.

$$\text{Total cost} = \$8.00\left(\frac{400}{2}\right) + \$100\left(\frac{6400}{400}\right) + \$40.00\,(6400)$$

$$= \$1600 + \$1600 + \$256{,}000 = \$259{,}200$$

Table 41.1 provides cost information of different order quantities.

We see that the value which minimizes the sum of the carrying cost and the ordering cost but not the purchase cost is EOQ = 400 sets. The farther we move from the point 400, the greater is the sum of the carrying and ordering costs. Thus, 400 is obviously the only candidate for the minimum total cost value within the first price range. $Q = 500$ is the only candidate within the $39.90 price range, and $Q = 1000$ is the only candidate within the $39.80 price bracket. These three quantities are evaluated in Table 41.1. We find that the EOQ with price discounts is 500 sets. Hence, Buena Park Store is justified in going to the first price break, but the extra carrying cost of going to the second

TABLE 41.1   Annual Costs with Varying Order Quantities

	Order quantity		
	400	500	1000
Ordering cost: $100 × (6400/order quantity)	$ 1,600	$ 1,280	$ 640
Carrying cost: $8 × (order quantity/2)	1,600	2,000	4,000
Product cost: unit price × 6400	256,000	255,360	254,720
Total cost	$259,200	$258,640	$259,360

price break more than outweighs the savings in ordering and in the cost of the product itself.

HOW IS IT USED AND APPLIED?   There are favorable and some unfavorable features of buying in large quantities. The advantages are lower unit costs, lower ordering costs, fewer stockouts, and lower transportation costs. On the other hand, there are disadvantages such as higher inventory carrying costs, larger capital requirements, and a higher probability of obsolescence and deterioration.

Whenever quantity (or price) discounts are offered, the purchasing manager must weigh the potential benefits of reduced purchase price and fewer orders that will result from buying in large quantities against the increase in carrying costs caused by higher average inventories. He or she should receive credit for overall savings resulting from quantity buying.

42 Determining Production Run Size

INTRODUCTION.   *Production run size* is an optimum production run quantity which minimizes the sum of carrying and setup costs.

HOW IS IT COMPUTED?   Production run size is computed just as the economic order quantity is, except that the ordering cost in the EOQ formula is replaced by the setup cost. The setup cost is the cost incurred each time a batch is produced. It includes the engineering cost of setting up the production runs or machines, the paperwork cost of processing the work order, and the ordering cost to provide raw materials for the batch.

The economic production run size is computed from

$$Q = \sqrt{\frac{2SD}{C}}$$

where C = carrying cost per unit, S = setup cost per order, D = annual demand (requirements) in units, and Q = production run quantity.

Example ABC Manufacturers has an annual demand for 2000 units of a product which it produces. The cost of setting up for production is $80, and the carrying cost is $2.00 per unit.

The economic production run size is computed as follows:

$$Q = \sqrt{\frac{2(2000)(\$80)}{\$2.00}} = \sqrt{160,000} = 400 \text{ sets}$$

Total production cost = carrying cost + setup cost

$$= C\left(\frac{\text{run size}}{2}\right) + O\left(\frac{D}{\text{run size}}\right)$$

$$= \$2.00\left(\frac{400}{2}\right) + \$80\left(\frac{2000}{400}\right)$$

$$= \$400 + \$400$$

$$= \$800$$

$$\text{Total number of runs per year} = \frac{D}{\text{run size}} = \frac{2000}{400} = 5 \text{ runs}$$

HOW IS IT USED AND APPLIED? Manufacturers need to know the run size that results in the lowest production costs in order to develop a budget for material purchases, labor hiring, and overhead spending. This model is predicated on a constant demand on inventory. When demand (or usage) are not constant, the business must carry extra units of inventory, called safety stock. See Sec. 40, How Much to Order (Economic Order Quantity) and When to Order (Reorder Point), and Sec. 43, Allowing for Safety Stock.

43 Allowing for Safety Stock

INTRODUCTION. When lead time and demand (or usage) are not certain (or are variable), the business must carry extra units of inventory, called *safety stock*, as protection against possible stock-outs. To determine the appropriate level of safety stock, you must consider the service level or stock-out costs.

Service level can be defined as the probability that demand will not exceed supply during the lead time. Thus, a service

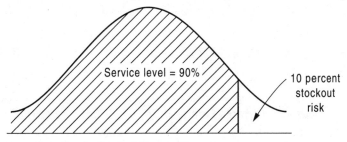

Figure 43.1 Service level of 90 percent.

level of 90 percent implies a probability of 90 percent that usage will not exceed supply during lead time. Figure 43.1 shows a service level of 90 percent.

To determine the optimal level of safety stock, you might also want to measure the costs of not having enough inventory, or stock-out costs.

We will discuss four cases for computing the safety stock. The first three do not recognize stock-out costs; the fourth case does.

HOW IS IT COMPUTED?   Recall from Sec. 40 that, in the case of uncertain usage and/or lead time, the reorder point (ROP) is computed as follows:

ROP = expected usage during lead time + safety stock

= lead time × average usage per unit of time + safety stock

Case 1: Known Maximum Usage Rate, Constant Lead Time.   A simple way to determine the size of safety stock is to deduct average *usage* from the *maximum usage* that can reasonably be expected during a period and then multiply the difference by the lead time.

Example 1   Assume that the economic order-quantity is 500 units, the lead time is 4 weeks, the average weekly usage is 60 units, and the maximum expected weekly usage is 70 units. The owner of a small manufacturing business computes safety stock as follows:

Maximum expected usage	70 units
Average usage	60
Excess	10 units
Lead time	× 4 weeks
Safety stock	40 units

121

ROP = expected usage during lead time + safety stock

= lead time × average usage per unit of time + safety stock

= 4 weeks × 60 + 40

= 240 + 40 = 280 units

Case 2: Variable Usage Rate, Constant Lead Time

ROP = expected usage during lead time + safety stock

$$= \bar{u} \times \text{LT} + z \sqrt{\text{LT}}\, (\sigma_u)$$

where $\bar{u}$ = average usage rate
LT = lead time
σ_u = standard deviation of usage rate
z = standard normal variate (see Table 7 in the Appendix)

Example 2 Norman's Pizza uses large cases of tomatoes at an average rate of 50 cans per day. The usage can be approximated by a normal distribution with a standard deviation of 5 cans per day. Lead time is 4 days. Thus,

$$\bar{u} = 50 \text{ cans per day}$$

$$\text{LT} = 4 \text{ days}$$

$$\sigma_u = 5 \text{ cans}$$

How much safety stock is necessary for a service level of 99 percent? What is the ROP?

For a service level of 99 percent, $z = 2.33$ (from Table 7 in the Appendix). Thus,

$$\text{Safety stock} = 2.33\sqrt{4}(5) = 23.3 \text{ cans}$$

$$\text{ROP} = 50(4) + 23.3 = 223.3 \text{ cans}$$

See Fig. 43.2.

Case 3: Constant Usage Rate, Variable Lead Time

ROP = expected usage during lead time + safety stock

$$= u(\overline{\text{LT}}) + zu(\sigma_{\text{LT}})$$

where u = constant usage rate
$\overline{\text{LT}}$ = average lead time
σ_{LT} = standard deviation of lead time

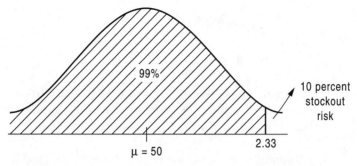

Figure 43.2 Service level of 99 percent.

Example 3 SVL's Hamburger Shop uses 10 gallons of cola per day. The lead time is normally distributed with a mean of 6 days and a standard deviation of 2 days. Thus,

$$u = 10 \text{ gallons per day}$$

$$\overline{LT} = 6 \text{ days}$$

$$\sigma_{LT} = 2 \text{ days}$$

How much safety stock is necessary for a service level of 99 percent? What is the ROP?

For a service level of 99 percent, $z = 2.33$ (from Table 7 in the Appendix). Thus,

$$\text{Safety stock} = 2.33(10)(2) = 46.6 \text{ gallons}$$

$$\text{ROP} = 10(6) + 46.6 = 106.6 \text{ gallons}$$

Case 4: Incorporation of Stock-out Costs. This case specifically recognizes the cost of stock-outs or shortages, which can be quite expensive. Lost sales and disgruntled customers are examples of external costs. Idle machines and disrupted production scheduling are examples of internal costs.

We will illustrate the probability approach to show how the optimal safety stock can be determined in the presence of stock-out costs.

Example 4 Assume that Buena Park Store buys sets of steel at $40 per set from an outside vendor. The store will sell 6400 sets evenly throughout the year. The carrying cost per set is $8.00. If the lead time and demand are certain, then the reorder point is:

ROP = expected usage during lead time + safety stock

= lead time × average usage per unit of time + safety stock

$$= 1 \text{ week} \times \frac{6400}{50 \text{ weeks}} + 0 = (1 \times 128) + 0$$

$$= 128 \text{ sets}$$

If demand (or usage) is not certain, the manager has to make some educated guesses from the past experience to determine the probabilities about the demand.

Example 5 Assume for Example 4 that the total usage over a 1-week period is uncertain but is expected to be as follows:

Total usage	Probability
78	.2
128	.4
178	.2
228	.1
278	.1
	1.00

The stock-out cost is estimated at $12.00 per set. Table 43.1 shows the computation of safety stock. The computation shows that the total costs are minimized at $1200, when a safety stock of 150 sheets is maintained. Therefore, the reorder point is:

$$128 \text{ sets} + 150 \text{ sets} = 278 \text{ sets}$$

HOW IS IT USED AND APPLIED? In reality, managers face either uncertain lead time or uncertain demand, or both. If they have knowledge of the probability distribution and the

TABLE 43.1 Computation of Safety Stock

Safety stock levels in units	Stock-out and probability	Average stock-out in units	Average stock-out costs	No. of orders	Total annual stock-out costs	Carrying costs	Total
0	50 with .2 100 with .1 150 with .1	35*	$420†	16	$6720‡	$ 0	$7140
50	50 with .1 100 with .1	15	180	16	2880	400§	3280
100	50 with .1	5	60	16	960	800	1760
150	0	0	0	16	0	1200	1200

*50(.2) + 100(.1) + 150(.1) = 10 + 10 + 15 = 35 units
†35 units × $12.00 = $420
‡$420 × 16 times = $6720
§50 units × $8.00 = $400

stock-out costs, however, they will be able to determine the optimal safety stock and the resulting order point.

44 Calculating Inventory Dollar Burden

INTRODUCTION. Inventory represents a sizable portion of the total assets of a business and, more specifically, on the average, more than 30 percent total current assets in U.S. industry. Excessive money tied up in inventory is a drag on profitability, which will bring down return on investment.

HOW IS IT COMPUTED? There are three ways to compute and control the inventory dollar burden:

By total carrying and ordering costs

By dollar limits

By time limits

Total Inventory Costs. The inventory dollar consists primarily of the cost of carrying an item in inventory and the cost of ordering items. Opportunity and goodwill costs must also be considered.

$$\text{Carrying costs} = \text{quantity of order} \left(\frac{Q}{2} \right)$$
$$\times \text{ carrying costs of 1 unit } (C)$$

$$\text{Ordering costs} =$$
$$\frac{\text{total quantity used in the period } (D) \times \text{ordering cost } (O)}{\text{order quantity } (Q)}$$

$$\text{Total inventory costs} = \text{carrying costs} + \text{ordering costs}$$

There are also costs that may be harder to quantify, reflecting opportunities and customer goodwill lost due to not carrying enough stock. These should be optimized against the standard cost of carrying excess inventory (safety stock).

Example Assume that a business sells around 100 bottles of glue a month ($S = 100$). The owner orders 500 bottles at a time ($Q = 500$). It costs \$5 per month to keep the glue in inventory based on rent per unit per square foot, insurance, utilities, etc.; these are the unit carrying costs ($C = 5$). The manager also considers obsolete goods and spoilage by multiplying C times the percentage of goods and adding it to the value of C. Therefore, the *carrying costs,* on average, are $Q \times C/2 = 500 \times 5/2 = \$1250$ per month. Paperwork and labor to place and receive an order costs \$25 ($O = 25$). At sales of 100 bottles per month ($D = 100$), *ordering costs* are $OD/Q = (25 \times 100/500) = \$50$. The *total inventory costs* are $\$1250 + \$50 = \$1300$.

Dollar Limits. Most businesses set dollar limits or budgets on the amount they will allow to be invested in each class of materials. Each class has an account in the accounting department showing its investments, and the inventory planning and control manager is responsible for seeing that the amounts stay within the allowed budgets.

This approach is usually applied only to broad classes of materials and not to individual items: It is just too costly to set dollar limits for each item separately. Dollar limits do not tell inventory managers when or how much to reorder; all they do is tell them not to exceed an upper investment limit. The managers have to determine how much of each individual item to provide, while keeping the investment for the item class within the limit.

Time Limits. Time limits are a common way to put dollar limits into effect. To translate dollar limits into time limits, all that is necessary is to divide the dollar limit by the dollar usage per month. A \$20,000 limit is a 2-month limit for an item used at a rate of \$10,000 per month.

While dollar limits can best be used directly to control broad classes of items, time limits can easily be applied to every item. In fact, one single time limit can apply to any number of items at the same time.

Time limits do not determine directly when or how much to order. They merely say, for example, that you should not have more than 30 days' supply on hand. This indirectly sets upper limits on how much should be ordered at one time. To hold the average investment for a class of items down to a month's usage, the inventory controller should never order more than a month's supply of any item on a single order.

For long-lead-time items, time limits control when reorders are released as well as how much is ordered. If it takes 3 months' lead time to receive an item and inventories are limited to 1 month's supply at one time, it will be necessary to place a new order every month for 1 month's needs, but each order will always be for the third month ahead. Thus, there will always be several orders out at the same time. (Items on order do not count in the inventory so far as investment is concerned.)

The inventory "coverage" (the quantity on hand plus the amount on order) is the true available inventory. Assuming reliable lead times, the coverage, in our example, is adequate even though much of it is, for the moment, in the form of open orders rather than stock on hand. The short time limit permitted for stock on hand does not mean that we have to stock out of long-lead-time items.

Time limits are easy to set, easy to change, and easy to operate. And they can be different for different items. If an item's use changes, the time limit can remain unchanged because the reordering quantity can be changed to reflect the new requirements.

A disadvantage of time limits is that they are not often the very best for entire groups of products, although they are usually applied to entire groups. A 30-day limit is probably too much for some items in a group and too little for others. For this reason, both dollar limits and item limits, while commonly used, are not always appropriate.

HOW IS IT USED AND APPLIED?   The calculation of inventory dollar burden is a critical step toward controlling inventory investments.

Dollar limits should be used with discretion when prices or business levels change; otherwise they automatically tighten or loosen the amount allowed to be carried. If, for example, prices rise and the dollar limits are not changed, the inventory manager has to reduce the quantities carried. Similarly, if business improves, dollar limits, if unchanged, hold down the inventories when some increase is really needed to support the larger master production schedule.

45 Using the ABC System for Inventory Control

INTRODUCTION.   *ABC analysis* focuses on the most critical items: gross profitability, sensitive price or demand patterns, and supply excesses or shortages. The ABC method requires the classification of inventory into one of three groups—A, B, or C—according to the potential savings associated with a proper level of inventory control. Class A items, needing close control, are high-dollar-volume items. They may include 80 percent of

TABLE 45.1   ABC Inventory Distribution

Inventory classification	Population (%)	Dollar usage (%)
A	1	80
B	30	15
C	69	5

total inventory cost but only 1 percent of total items stocked. Class B is an intermediate-dollar-volume group—perhaps 15 percent of dollars and 30 percent of items. Class C is the rest— 5 percent of dollars and 69 percent of items. Table 45.1 illustrates an ABC distribution.

HOW IS IT COMPUTED?   To institute the ABC method:

1. Compute annual dollar volume by inventory type anticipated (annual demand times unit cost).

2. Segregate merchandise into components based on annual dollar value.

3. Rank inventory in terms of annual dollar volume, ranging from high to low (e.g., A = top 80 percent, B = next 15 percent, C = last 5 percent).

Tag inventory with the appropriate classification and record the classifications in the inventory records. The following example illustrates.

Example   Garner Auto Supply Co. has arranged its 10 inventory items in order of annual dollar volume. Table 45.2 shows the ordered list,

TABLE 45.2   Inventory Items in Annual-Dollar-Volume Order: Garner Auto Supply Co.

Stock number	Annual demand	Unit cost	Annual dollar volume	Percent
510	35,000	$ 30.50	$1,067,500	53.2
310	1,000	650.00	650,000	32.4
001	2,000	55.00	110,000	5.5
378	20,000	5.00	100,000	5.0
423	4,200	10.00	42,000	2.1
188	500	36.00	18,000	0.9
320	35	275.00	9,625	0.5
115	100	44.00	4,400	0.2
275	400	5.00	2,000	0.1
323	800	1.75	1,400	0.1
			$2,004,925	100.0

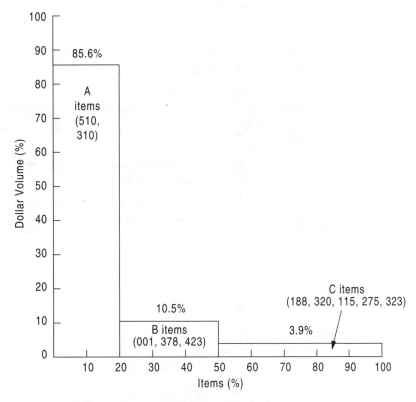

Figure 45.1 ABC classification: Garner Auto Supply Co.

with dollar volume also expressed in percentages. The ordered list is examined in order to arrive at an ABC classification of the items.

Figure 45.1 shows the same 10 items grouped into classes A, B, and C. The two A items account for almost 86 percent—about eight times as much annual dollar volume as the three B items—while the three B items account for about three times as much as the five C items. It is clear that A items should receive major attention, B items moderate attention, and C items little attention.

HOW IS IT USED AND APPLIED? Perpetual inventory records should be maintained for class A items, which require accuracy and frequent, often daily, attention. Class B items are less expensive than A items but are still important and require intermediate control. Class C items include most of the inventory items. Since they are usually less expensive and less used, they require less attention. There is usually a high safety stock level for C items. Blanket purchase orders should exist for A items and only "spot buys" for B and C items.

Examples of inventory controls that may be based on ABC classification are:

Purchasing. A purchase order for a class A item might be signed by the president, one for a class B item by the head of the purchasing department, and one for a class C item by any purchasing agent.

Physical inventory check. Count A items monthly, B items twice a year, and C items annually.

Forecasting. Forecast A items by several methods with resolution by a prediction committee, forecast B items by simple trend projection, and forecast C items by best guess of the responsible purchasing agent.

Safety stock. No safety stock for A items, 1 month's supply for B items, and 3 months' supply for C items.

Buying and Selling Products and Services

46 Sales Ratios

INTRODUCTION. It is tempting to think that if sales numbers are going up, everything is fine. But sales figures must always be considered in the light of other, related factors. You need to know not only the actual amount of sales, but how you are doing in relative terms. Sales ratios are used to measure these relative values.

HOW ARE THEY COMPUTED?

$$\text{Quality of sales} = \frac{\text{cash sales}}{\text{total sales}}$$

Sales dollars differ in quality depending on whether the sale is a cash or a credit sale (credit sales are of less quality because the business does not yet have the use of the money and there is always the risk of noncollection), credit risk, profitability generated, recurring or one-time sale, and costs associated with the sale. Sales are affected by competition, economic environment, product leadership, market position, and so on.

$$\text{Sales growth} = \frac{\text{net sales (current year)} - \text{net sales (prior year)}}{\text{net sales (prior year)}}$$

A decline in sales growth is a negative sign.

Sales growth (adjusted for inflation) =

[(net sales (current year) $\times$ [CPI (prior year)/CPI (current year)])

$-$ net sales (prior year)]/net sales (prior year)

where CPI is the Consumer Price Index.

For example, if the CPI at the end of 19X5 is 128 and it is 134 at the end of 19X6, the 19X6 deflator is 95.5 percent. If 19X6 net sales are $300,000, then deflated net sales are $286,500. If in this case 19X5 sales were $280,000, then sales increased in 19X6 by only $6500 in "real dollars"—not $20,000.

$$\text{Sales per customer} = \frac{\text{net sales}}{\text{average number of customers}}$$

where

Average number of customers =

$$\frac{\text{customers at beginning of year} + \text{customers at end of year}}{2}$$

To take into account the effects of inflation, real dollar sales growth may be computed. Sales growth adjusted for inflation is more meaningful than nominal sales growth because the changes in prices are considered.

Growth in customers =

$$\frac{\text{customers at end of year} - \text{customers at beginning of year}}{\text{customers at beginning of year}}$$

$$\text{Backorders} = \frac{\text{net sales}}{\text{number of transactions}}$$

(Average dollar sales may be based on a quarterly or monthly average.)

Backorders represent future sales because orders have been received but the merchandise is not yet ready. In general, backorders are favorable because they represent guaranteed future business and indicate that the company's products are in high demand. Backorders may increase when marketing efforts (e.g., advertising, sales promotion) are enhanced or when there are good economic times.

$$\text{Order size} = \frac{\text{net sales}}{\text{number of transactions}}$$

The cost and time of handling an order is about the same whether it is for a high or a low dollar amount. Therefore, higher-ticket items result in greater revenue while the cost of processing the orders (e.g., telephone, catalogs) remains constant.

Change in order size (adjusted for inflation)

= (average order size × [CPI (prior year)/CPI (current year)])

− average order size (prior year)

For example, assume that the average order size in 19X8 and 19X9 was $2400 and $2425, respectively. In unadjusted dollars, order size increased by $25. Assuming an inflation rate of 6 percent, the deflated order size is $2280. In constant dollars, the average order size decreased by $120, a negative sign.

The change in order size may be adjusted for inflation to see if there has been a "real" increase or decrease. An increase (after inflation) is a favorable indicator.

Order growth

= [number of transactions (current year)

   − number of transactions (prior year)]/number of

transactions (prior year)

Order response rate =

$$\frac{\text{average number of transactions (3 years)}}{\text{average number of solicitations (3 years)}}$$

A 3-year period gives a representative time period. Alternatively, a 5-year period may be used.

A higher response rate is favorable because it means that customers have been positively influenced by solicitations. Solicitations may be made by mail, telephone, or media advertisement (e.g., newspaper, television, radio).

The business owner is interested in knowing how much is bought by each customer and wants to prompt the customer to purchase more, perhaps by advertising, special promotion, changing the salesperson, or increasing the number of calls.

$$\text{Sales response rate} = \frac{\text{average dollar sales (3 years)}}{\text{average solicitations (3 years)}}$$

$$\text{Customer contact ratio} = \frac{\text{calls to customers}}{\text{total calls}}$$

These ratios indicate the degree to which the business directs its energies to current customers. There is a greater likelihood of making a sale to an existing customer than a new one. It is therefore advantageous to have a strong customer base. In mailing sales literature (promotions, letters, catalogs), telephoning, and visiting, emphasis should be placed on existing customers. The response rate is better because current customers already have a high opinion of the company and are comfortable placing orders, whereas new customers may be unsure.

Example   In 19X7, net sales were $4,000,000 and the number of customers was 1000. In 19X8, net sales were $5,000,000 and the number of customers was 1200.

The growth rate in sales from 19X7 to 19X8 was 25 percent ($1,000,000/$4,000,000), which is outstanding. The sales-per-customer ratio increased from $4000 ($4,000,000/1000) to $4167 ($5,000,000/1200) between 19X8 and 19X9. This is also favorable, because the revenue per account has improved, generating greater profitability to the business.

HOW IS IT USED AND APPLIED?   Sales ratios help the manager evaluate the performance of marketing in generating revenue. A business is growing when it experiences a healthy annual percentage increase in customers that is consistent with its annual percentage increase in sales. An increasing trend of sales per customer is favorable because it means that customers have more confidence in the business or are being influenced by marketing efforts to buy more.

Sales growth indicates that the business is expanding and marketing efforts have been successful. It is best when the growth is *consistently* upward—rising in a roughly straight line—because this means that stable growth is being maintained. It should be noted that growing too fast may present a problem in the long term if that growth is financed exclusively with overburdening debt. In real dollars, positive growth in sales is necessary after adjusting for changes in inflation.

Variability in sales may be unavoidable, depending on the nature of the business. In such a case, average sales over a 5- to 10-year period should be used in ratio computations to eliminate temporary distorting effects. If sales fluctuate greatly, uncertainty makes future predictions difficult.

The owner should try to implement policies to obtain cash at the time of sale, such as by offering a discount or by stipulating in order to take advantage of a special promotion .

If the costs of processing orders increase, selling price has to be increased proportionately to maintain profit levels. If average order size in inflation-adjusted dollars decreases, the business has a problem. The expected order size may influence the owner's decision on which existing products to advertise and which to deemphasize.

An increase in the backorder ratio may mean that additional workers should be hired in receiving, processing, manufacturing, or distribution. It could also mean that present employees are not working efficiently. An increasing ratio may be a sign of possible future customer dissatisfaction for not receiving their orders on time.

Backorders may result in higher costs associated with multiple deliveries, duplicate work, and hours spent keeping track of the backorders and their status.

47 How Good Is the Merchandise?

INTRODUCTION. *Sales returns* are merchandise given back to the seller because of defects. *Sales allowances* are reductions in selling price of goods because of a specific problem (e.g., breakage, defects).

The ratio of sales returns and allowances to sales indicates how much of sales were returned or discounted because of customer dissatisfaction.

HOW IS IT COMPUTED?

$$\frac{\text{Sales returns and allowances}}{\text{Sales}}$$

$$\frac{\text{Net sales}}{\text{Gross sales}}$$

$$\text{Net sales} = \text{gross sales} - \text{sales returns and allowances}$$

A decline in this ratio means a decrease in net sales due to returned merchandise.

Example A small business reports the following information:

	19X5	19X6
Sales returns and allowances	$ 60,000	$ 90,000
Sales	1,000,000	1,200,000

The applicable ratios are

19X5 sales returns and allowances to sales = .06

19X6 sales returns and allowances to sales = .075

The increased sales returns and allowance indicates possible problems with the merchandise. The reasons for the returns must be identified and corrective steps implemented. Are the returns due to defective merchandise, damaged goods, not consistent with advertisements, or not as ordered?

HOW IS IT USED AND APPLIED?   The amount of sales returns and allowances is a good indicator of the quality of the merchandise sold. If returns and allowances are high compared to sales, buyers are not pleased. This will have a negative impact on the reputation of the business's product line. Further, the business may have to incur freight charges for returning the goods.

48 Factoring in Trade Discounts

INTRODUCTION.   Manufacturers and wholesalers of certain types of merchandise frequently give large reductions from the list prices quoted in their catalogs. These reductions are called *trade discounts*. Rather than printing separate catalogs for all classes of potential purchasers (wholesalers, retailers, consumers), the seller gives intermediate or trade buyers (wholesalers, retailers) separate discount sheets that list the discounts. Thus the trade discount is not a true discount but an adjustment of price.

HOW IS IT COMPUTED?   The formula for computing a trade discount is

$$\text{Discount} = \text{list price} \times \text{discount rate}$$

The *net cost* is the price the buyer pays for the item. The *net cost price* is the list price less any discount and may be computed as

$$\text{Net cost price} = \text{list price} - \text{discount (list price} \times \text{discount rate)}$$

Example 1   A television set with a list price of $450 is offered to wholesalers at a 20 percent trade discount. The cost to the wholesalers is computed as follows:

$$\text{Net cost price} = \text{list price} - \text{discount (list price} \times \text{discount rate)}$$

$$= \$450 - (\$450 \times 0.20) = \$450 - \$90 = \$360$$

The trade discount formula may also be stated as the list price multiplied by the complement of the discount rate. The *complement* of the discount rate is the difference between the discount rate and 100 percent. The formula is:

$$\text{Net cost price} = \text{list price} \times$$
$$\text{complement of discount rate } (100\% - \text{discount rate})$$

Example 2 Using the data in Example 1, the price of the television to wholesalers is computed as

$$\text{Net cost price} = \text{list price} \times$$
$$\text{complement of discount rate } (100\% - \text{discount rate})$$

$$= \$450 \times (100\% - 20\%) = \$450 \times 0.80 = \$360$$

Transportation costs, if applicable, are not subject to trade discounts and are added to the net cost price.

HOW IS IT USED AND APPLIED? Trade discounts are an easy way to make changes in prices without printing new catalogs. As prices change, new schedules of discounts may be issued without requiring new catalogs.

49 Calculating Cash Discounts

INTRODUCTION. Cash discounts are offered to encourage buyers to pay their bills quickly. Cash discounts are applied to bills paid within a specified period of time. Hence cash discounts tend to narrow the time gap between the sale of items and receipt of payment.

HOW IS IT COMPUTED? Cash discounts are referred to as *terms* and may appear on a bill as, for example, 2/10, net 30, or 2/10, n/30, where

2 = percentage of discount

10 = number of days within which the buyer may pay in order to qualify for the discount

net 30 = number of days within which payment must be made at the full price

The formula for the discount is:

$$\text{Discount} = \text{list price} \times \text{discount rate}$$

The formula for the net price is:

$$\text{Net price} = \text{list price} - \text{discount}$$

Example 1 An invoice of $300 was received by Mr. Paul, the proprietor of a food store. The invoice was dated March 6, and carries terms of 2/10, n/30. If payment is made by March 16, the discount is $6, and the net cost is $294 computed as follows:

$$\text{Discount} = \text{list price} \times \text{discount rate}$$

$$= \$300 \times 0.02 = \$6$$

$$\text{Net price} = \text{list price} - \text{discount}$$

$$= \$300 - \$6 = \$294$$

If payment is made on March 17, the full $300 must be paid.

Some companies offer various cash discounts, depending on when payment is made. For example, 2/10, 1/20, n/30 means that the company offers a 2 percent discount if the buyer pays within 10 days and a 1 percent discount if the buyer pays after 10 days but within 20 days; the full price amount is due within 30 days.

Example 2 Albee Co. receives an invoice dated September 11 for $7250 with terms of 2/10, 1/20, n/30.

The due date for the 2/10 discount is September 21, and the net cost will be $7105, computed as follows:

Sept. 11 Invoice date
<u> +10</u> Days in discount period
Sept. 21

$$\text{Net cost} = \text{list price} - (\text{list price} \times \text{discount rate})$$

$$= \$7250 - (\$7250 \times 0.02) = \$7250 - \$145 = \$7105$$

The due date for the 1/20 discount is October 1, and the net cost will be $7177.50, computed as follows:

Sept. 11 Invoice date
<u> +20</u> Days in discount period
    31
<u> − 30</u> Number of days in Sept.
Oct.   1

$$\text{Net cost} = \text{list price} - (\text{list price} \times \text{discount rate})$$

$$= \$7250 - (\$7250 \times 0.01) = \$7250 - \$72.50 = \$7177.50$$

The due date for the n/30 discount is October 11, computed as follows:

Sept. 11 Invoice date
<u> +30</u> Days allowed for payment
    41
<u> − 30</u> Number of days in Sept.
Oct. 11

No discount is given for payments made after 20 days, so the full $7250 is due on October 11.

Although in most cases the cash discount period begins with the "invoice" or purchase date, the discount period may also begin either on the date of the receipt of goods (ROG) or on the first date after the end of the month (EOM).

The ROG discount period is used primarily when there is a significant gap between the date of sale and the delivery date. It eliminates the problem of asking a buyer to pay for goods not yet received in order to get a discount.

The EOM discount period is used primarily as a convenience by companies that use traditional end-of-month billing practices.

Example 3 Rex Co. places an order on April 2 for parts which are delivered on April 15, with an invoice for $1250 at terms of 5/20 ROG. To receive the discount, Rex Co. must pay by May 5, computed as follows:

Apr. 15 Date of receipt of goods
+20 Days in discount period
35
−30 Number of days in Apr.
May 5

The net cost will be $1187.50, computed as follows:

$$\text{Net cost} = \text{list price} - (\text{list price} \times \text{discount rate})$$

$$= \$1250 - (\$1250 \times 0.05) = \$1250 - \$62.50 = \$1187.50$$

Example 4 Jethro Co. receives an invoice for $900 dated May 8, with terms of 2/15 EOM.

The terms specify EOM, so payment is due 15 days after the end of the month and Jethro must pay the bill by June 15.

The net cost will be $882, computed as follows:

$$\text{Discount} = \text{list price} \times \text{discount rate}$$

$$= \$900 \times 0.02 = \$18$$

$$\text{Net cost} = \text{list price} - \text{discount}$$

$$= \$900 - \$18 = \$882$$

Example 5 As is shown below, the last date on which a discount can be taken depends on whether the terms stipulate ROG, EOM, or invoice date.

Invoice date	Goods received	Terms	Last day on which discount can be taken
Inv. $500 Oct. 3	Oct. 8	2/10, n/30 ROG	Oct. 18
Inv. $700 Oct. 3	Oct. 8	2/10, n/30 EOM	Nov. 10
Inv. $850 Oct. 3	Oct. 8	2/10, n/30	Oct. 13*

*Calculated from invoice date.

To determine whether the owner should offer a discount for the early payment of accounts receivable, he or she has to compare the return on freed cash from faster collection versus the cost of the discount, where

Return on freed cash =
reduction in average accounts receivable balance × rate of return

Example 6 The following information applies to a small business:

Current annual credit sales	$2,000,000
Collection period	2 months
Terms	net 30
Minimum rate of return	12%

The owner is thinking of offering a 3/10, net 30, discount. She expects 30 percent of the customers to take advantage of the discount. It is anticipated that the collection period will be reduced to 1 month.
The discount is advisable, as shown below.

Advantage of a discount:
  Increased earnings:
    Average accounts receivable
    before a change in
    credit policy $\left(\dfrac{\text{credit sales}}{\text{accounts receivable turnover}} \right) = \dfrac{\$2,000,000}{6}$

$333,333

Average accounts receivable after a $\left(\dfrac{\$2,000,000}{12} \right)$
change in credit policy

$166,667

Reduction in average accounts receivable balance $166,666
  × rate of return   0.12

Return $ 20,000
Disadvantage of a discount:
  Cost of the discount: 0.03 × 0.30 × $2,000,000 $ 18,000
Net advantage of discount $ 2,000

HOW IS IT USED AND APPLIED? A seller may offer a discount for the early payment of cash to improve the company's cash position. The sooner the seller is paid, the sooner he can put the money to work. It is also a good idea for the purchaser to take a discount when offered. The opportunity cost to the buyer of not taking a discount is substantial.

See also Sec. 6, Trade Credit.

50 Single Equivalent Discount and Chain Discount

INTRODUCTION. Rather than give various increasing single discounts to different classes of purchasers, some small businesses use chain discounts. *Chain discounts* are successive discounts on the same item. After initially discounting an item, the second discount is then applied to the discounted price to arrive at the net cost price. These steps have the advantage of appearing to be better than a single discount, as well as emphasizing to the buyer the fact that he or she is receiving more than one discount.

HOW IS IT COMPUTED? Either of two methods may be used to compute the net cost price when chain discounts are involved.

Method 1. Determine the single equivalent discount and then compute the net cost price as shown in Example 2. To compute the equivalent discount, multiply the complements of the discount rates and subtract the result from 100%.

Example 1 The single equivalent discount of a chain discount of 10 percent and 20 percent is computed as follows.

Step 1: $(100\% - 10\%) \times (100\% - 20\%) = 90\% \times 80\%$

Step 2: $0.90 \times 0.80 = 0.72 = 72\%$

Step 3: Single equivalent discount $= 100\% - 72\% = 28\%$

Note that the single equivalent discount permits the seller to compare different chain discounts.

Example 2 A stereo is offered to wholesalers at a list price of $600, less discounts of 25 and 20 percent. The single equivalent discount is computed as follows:

Step 1: $(100\% - 25\%) \times (100\% - 20\%) = 75\% \times 80\%$

Step 2: $0.75 \times 0.80 = 0.60 = 60\%$

Step 3: $100\% - 60\% = 40\%$

$$\text{Net cost price} = \text{list price} - (\text{list price} \times \text{discount rate})$$

$$= \$600 - (\$600 \times 0.40) = \$600 - \$240 = \$360$$

An alternative method is as follows.

Step 1. $\$600 \times 0.25 = \$150$ Price $\times$ first discount rate = first discount

Step 2. $\$600 - \$150 = \$450$ Price $-$ first discount = discounted price

Step 3. $\$450 \times 0.20 = \$90$ Discounted price $\times$ second discount rate = second discount

Step 4. $\$450 - \$90 = \$360$ Discounted price $-$ second discount = net cost price

Method 2. The net cost price can be computed directly by multiplying the list price by the complement of each discount in the series. It does not make any difference in what order the discounts are arranged.

Example 3 Assume the same information as in Example 2 and calculate the net cost price by using method 2.

The complements of the discounts are

$$100\% - 25\% = 75\% = 0.75$$

$$100\% - 20\% = 80\% = 0.80$$

Then

$$\text{Net cost price} = \text{list price} \times \text{complement of each discount}$$

$$= \$600 \times 0.75 \times 0.80 = \$600 \times 0.60 = \$360$$

Example 4 Company A gives a 20 percent discount on all items purchased. Company B gives chain discounts of 15 and 10 percent. If Jane Snell, a small business owner, buys $500 in supplies from Company B, she saves $17.50 by dealing with company B rather than with company A, computed as follows.

Company A	Company B
Discount = list price $\times$ discount rate $= \$500 \times 0.20 = \$100$	Single equivalent discount: 1. $(100\% - 15\%)$ $\times (100\% - 10\%) = 85\% \times 90\%$ 2. $0.85 \times 0.90 = 0.765 = 76.5\%$ 3. $100\% - 76.5\% = 23.5\%$ Discount = list price $\times$ single equivalent discount rate $= \$500 \times 0.235 = \$117.50$

Savings from dealing with company B = $117.50 - $100 = $17.50

Alternative solution:
Difference between the two discounts: $23.5\% - 20\% = 3.5\%$
Savings: $\$500 \times 0.035 = \$17.50$

Example 5 Rick James orders four digital watches which list at $75 each, less discounts of 10 and 5 percent. A shipping charge of $6 is added to the invoice. The cost is $262.50, computed as follows:

Total list price = $75 × 4 = $300

Complements of discounts:

100% − 10% = 90% = 0.90

100% − 5% = 95% = 0.95

Net price = list price × complement of each discount

= $300 × 0.90 × 0.95 = $256.50

Total cost = net price + additional costs

= $256.50 + $6 shipping = $262.50

HOW IS IT USED AND APPLIED? Single equivalent discount and chain discount techniques enable the seller to adjust prices for different classes of purchasers, generate new business, and keep old and established customers. These discount techniques also have the advantage of appearing to be larger than a single discount, as well as emphasizing to the buyer the fact that he or she is receiving more than one discount.

See Sec. 48, Factoring in Trade Discounts; and Sec. 49, Calculating Cash Discounts.

51 Markup Calculations

INTRODUCTION. In order to make a profit, a small business owner must sell his products for more than the product's cost. The difference between the product's cost and the selling price is called the *markup*. Small business owners frequently face decisions on the pricing and relative profitability of their products. Pricing decisions are complex and difficult, and there is no single way of computing a product-cost figure that is universally relevant for all pricing decisions. Three major influences on pricing decisions include customers, competitors, and costs.

HOW IS IT COMPUTED? Often a selling price is based directly on the cost of the item. A markup may be added to cost based on what is typical in the industry. The formula for a markup is:

Selling price = cost + markup

Markup is generally expressed in terms of a percentage:

$$\text{Percent} = \frac{\text{percentage}}{\text{base}} \times 100$$

where percent = markup percent
percentage = markup
base = selling price or cost

By substitution, we have

$$\% \text{ markup} = \frac{\text{markup}}{\text{selling price or cost}} \times 100$$

If the small business owner uses the selling price as the base, the formula is:

$$\% \text{ markup} = \frac{\text{markup}}{\text{selling price}} \times 100$$

The small business owner can also use the percent markup to compute either the cost or the selling price using the following formula:

$$\% \text{ markup} = \frac{\text{markup}}{\text{selling price}} \times 100$$

Example 1 A washing machine selling for $300 costs the seller $200. The markup is $100, computed as follows:

$$\text{Selling price} - \text{cost} = \text{markup}$$

$$\$300 - \$200 = \$100$$

Example 2 A product costs $100 to manufacture and is subject to a 50 percent markup. The selling price is $150, computed as follows:

Cost	$100
Markup (50% × $100)	50
Selling price	$150

Example 3 A book selling for $8 costs the seller $6. The percent markup based on selling price is 25 percent, computed as follows:

$$\text{Markup} = \text{selling price} - \text{cost}$$

$$\$2 = \$8 - \$6$$

$$\% \text{ markup} = \frac{\text{markup}}{\text{selling price}} \times 100$$

$$= \frac{\$2}{\$8} \times 100 = 25\%$$

Example 4   A book has a markup of $2, which is 25 percent of the selling price. The selling price is $8, computed as follows:

$$\% \text{ markup} = \frac{\text{markup}}{\text{selling price}} \times 100$$

$$25\% \text{ markup} = \frac{\$2}{\$8} \times 100$$

$$0.25 \times \text{selling price} = \$2 = \frac{\$2}{0.25} = \$8$$

HOW IS IT USED AND APPLIED?   Cost information is a vital component of all pricing decisions. The estimated time period for sales is also important in determining the price of a product or service. For example, high setup costs for a special-order or short-run product or service must be absorbed by a limited number of sales if the owner is to make a profit. On the other hand, determination of the long-run cost and pricing of a product or service will enable the owner to decide whether or not to produce a product and/or to enter a new market and compete with existing products.

The final selling price for a product or service depends on its cost and the desired markup. The markup used can reflect either the standard used in a particular industry or the amount the small business owner determines is necessary to earn a reasonable rate of profit. The markup percentage may vary among products based on risk, product demand, perishability, volume, seasonality, competition, etc.

If a product is consistently priced below its cost, it will drain off sizable amounts of a business's capital and resources and may eventually lead to insolvency and bankruptcy.

See Sec. 52, Cost as a Basis.

52 Cost as a Basis

INTRODUCTION.   The cost of a manufactured product is the total of direct material, direct labor, and factory overhead. The cost of a product to a retailer is the price paid. On the other hand, the cost of a service is the total of the costs to render it, including salaries and materials.

HOW IS IT COMPUTED?   When cost is used as the basis for markup, it is sometimes referred to as markon. It has the advantage of expressing clearly the fact that the price increase is added directly to the basis (cost).

To calculate the cost from the percent markup and the selling price, we solve the formula for cost as follows:

$$\% \text{ markup} = \frac{\text{markup}}{\text{cost}} \times 100$$

Since markup = selling price − cost, by substitution we have

$$\% \text{ markup} = \frac{\text{selling price} - \text{cost}}{\text{cost}} \times 100$$

$$\frac{\% \text{ markup}}{100} = \frac{\text{selling price}}{\text{cost}} - 1$$

$$\frac{\% \text{ markup}}{100} + 1 = \frac{\text{selling price}}{\text{cost}}$$

$$\text{Cost} = \frac{\text{selling price}}{(\% \text{ markup}/100) + 1}$$

Note that the denominator of this equation [(% markup/100) + 1] is simply 1 plus the percent markup expressed as a decimal.

To calculate selling price from cost and percent markup, we restate the formula as follows:

$$\text{Selling price} - \text{cost} = \text{markup}$$

$$\text{Selling price} = \text{cost} + \text{markup}$$

Since

$$\% \text{ markup} = \frac{\text{markup}}{\text{cost}} \times 100$$

then

$$\frac{\% \text{ markup}}{100} \times \text{cost} = \text{markup}$$

By substitution we have

$$\text{Selling price} = \text{cost} + \left(\frac{\% \text{ markup}}{100} \times \text{cost} \right)$$

Note that % markup/100 is simply the percent expressed as a decimal.

Example 1 A record album that sells for $6 costs $4. The percent markup based on cost is 50 percent, computed as follows:

$$\text{Selling price} - \text{cost} = \text{markup}$$

$$\$6 - \$4 = \$2$$

$$\% \text{ markup} = \frac{\text{markup}}{\text{cost}} \times 100$$

$$= \frac{\$2}{\$4} \times 100 = 50\%$$

Example 2 An item is selling for $72 and has a 20 percent markup on cost. The cost of the item is $60, calculated as follows:

$$\text{Cost} = \frac{\text{selling price}}{(\% \text{ markup}/100) + 1}$$

$$= \frac{\$72}{(20\%/100) + 1}$$

$$= \frac{\$72}{0.20} + 1$$

$$= \frac{\$72}{1.20} = \$60$$

Example 3 If a sweater which costs $10 has a markup of 30 percent on cost, its selling price is $13, computed as follows:

$$\text{Selling price} = \text{cost} + \left(\frac{\% \text{ markup}}{100} \times \text{cost} \right)$$

$$= \$10 + (0.30)(\$10) = \$10 + \$3 = \$13$$

Alternative solution: If we let cost = 100%, then

$$\text{Selling price} = \text{cost} + \text{markup}$$

$$= 100\% + 30\% = 130\% \text{ of cost}$$

$$= 130\% \times \text{cost}$$

$$= 1.3 \times \$10 = \$13$$

HOW IS IT USED AND APPLIED? Markup formulas that are based on the cost of the product or service will result in a realistic selling price. If the cost to manufacture the product or provide the service increases, the retail price will also increase by a proportionate amount. This procedure ensures that the product or service will be sold at a price that will earn the small business owner a reasonable rate of product.

See Sec. 51, Markup Calculations.

53 Commission Computation

INTRODUCTION. When small business owners hire salespeople, they may use one of several compensation techniques. Some receive a salary, others a commission based on the sales they make, and some are paid through a combination of both salary and commission.

HOW IS IT COMPUTED? A commission is a fee paid for a service rendered and is usually expressed as a percentage of the sales revenue received by the business. If the commission is based on a single percentage, it is called straight commission. In variable or sliding-scale commission, two or more percentages are used. A draw, or advance against future commissions, may also be used. By using this method, an employer allows a salesperson to draw a regular amount of money each week to help the employee get through "slow" sales periods. The formula for computing the amount of commission earned is:

Commission rate × sales = commission earned

Example 1 Suppose that an employee of Drake Stationary Store works on a 25 percent commission basis. The commission rate multiplied by the sales in dollars equals the amount of commission earned. Thus the commission on $800 of sales is $200, computed as follows:

Commission rate × sales = commission earned

25% × $800 = $200

Example 2 An employer pays 25 percent commission on sales up to $1000 and 10 percent on the amount of sales above $1000. The commission on $1400 of sales is $290, computed as follows:

Commission rate × sales = commission earned

0.25 × $1000 = $250
0.10 × $400* = $\underline{\quad 40}$
Total earned = $\underline{\underline{\$290}}$

*The amount above $1000 is $400 ($1400 − $1000).

Example 3 An employee of Olden Sales draws $200 at the beginning of a week and earns a commission of $240 by the end of the week. The employee collects a commission of $40 at the end of the week, computed as follows:

$$\text{Commission} - \text{draw} = \text{difference paid to employee}$$

$$\$240 - \$200 = \$40$$

Example 4 Belle Music pays its salespeople the following commissions on all sales:

2 percent on the first $1000 in sales

5 percent on the next $1000 in sales

8 percent on any sales over $2000

Commissions are paid monthly. Determine to the nearest cent the commissions earned by the following employees:

Employee	Sales			Commissions
P. Latch	2% ×	$1000	=	$ 20.00
	5% ×	569.80	=	28.49
	Total	$1569.80	=	$ 48.49
E. Marks	2% ×	$1000	=	$ 20.00
	5% ×	1000	=	50.00
	8% ×	1486	=	118.88
	Total	$3486		$188.88

HOW IS IT USED AND APPLIED? Paying a salesperson a commission based on his or her results is an effective and equitable method of rewarding an employee's performance. Under this system, ambitious and successful salespeople are rewarded with high compensation for their efforts. At the same time, a practice of allowing employees a draw gives them a salary during periods of slow sales. The draw can also be used to monitor employee performance. Under this procedure, employees who fail to earn their draw for a stated period of time can be terminated for low productivity.

54 Cost-Volume-Profit Analysis

INTRODUCTION. A company would not want to sell a product or render a service unless it is at least breaking even. To break even on your products or services, you must be able to calculate the sales volume needed to cover your costs, and how to use this information to your benefit. You must also be familiar with how your costs react to changes in volume, and how a price change affects your profits. Further, you must know what effect expense reductions will have. Breakeven analysis aids in profit planning!

Breakeven formulas are useful to all small businesses in determining the point at which a business can begin to turn a profit. The three most common breakeven formulas, described below, determine the breakeven point, the margin of safety, and the cash breakeven point.

1. BREAKEVEN POINT

Introduction. The breakeven point is the sales volume at which total revenue equals total costs, resulting in zero profit—that is, the minimum sales necessary to avoid a loss.

By knowing the breakeven point, you know which products and/or services to emphasize and which to deemphasize (perhaps even to drop). The knowledge allows you to improve operating results and facilities planning, because you know how much you must sell of a new item even before you introduce it.

How Is It Computed? Breakeven is that point where total sales are exactly the same as total costs:

$$\text{Sales} = \text{variable costs} + \text{fixed costs}$$

Fixed costs remain constant regardless of activity (such as rent and insurance), whereas *variable costs* vary with activity (such as materials, direct labor, and the cost of merchandise for retailers and wholesalers).

To determine the dollar sales to make a certain desired before-tax profit, use this breakeven formula:

$$\text{Sales} = \text{variable costs} + \text{fixed costs} + \text{desired profit}$$

The guidelines for breaking even are:

- An increase in selling price lowers breakeven sales.
- An increase in variable cost increases breakeven sales.
- An increase in fixed cost increases breakeven sales.

Example 1 If the selling price is $25, variable cost (VC) per unit is $10, and fixed costs (FC) are $15,000, you will break even when you sell 1000 units (U).

$$S = VC + FC$$

$$\$25U = \$10U + \$15,000$$

$$\$15U = \$15,000$$

$$U = 1,000$$

$$\text{Total sales} = 1,000 \text{ units} \times \$25 = \$25,000$$

If the desired profit is $3000, the unit sales needed are:

$$S = VC + FC + P$$

$$\$25U = \$10U + \$15,000 + \$3,000$$

$$\$15U = \$18,000$$

$$U = 1,200$$

Example 2 A product has a fixed cost of $400,000 and a variable cost of 80 percent of sales. The breakeven sales figure is:

$$S = FC + VC$$

$$1S = \$400,000 + 0.8S$$

$$0.2S = \$400,000$$

$$S = \$2,000,000$$

If the selling price per unit is $50, breakeven units are 40,000 ($2,000,000/$50). If desired profit is $60,000, the sales required to generate that profit (P) are:

$$S = FC + VC + P$$

$$1S = \$400,000 + 0.8S + \$60,000$$

$$0.2S = \$460,000$$

$$S = \$2,300,000$$

Example 3 You sell 600,000 units of a product. The variable cost is $4 per unit. Fixed cost totals $800,000. The selling price per unit needed to break even is:

$$S = FC + VC$$

$$600,000SP = \$800,000 + \$4(600,000)$$

$$600,000SP = \$3,200,000$$

$$SP = \$5.33$$

Example 4 The following data apply to a product: selling price $50, variable cost $30, fixed cost $200,000, after-tax profit $100,000, and tax rate 20 percent.

How many units have to be sold to generate the after-tax profit?

$$S = FC + VC + P$$

$$\$50U = \$200{,}000 + \$30U + \$125{,}000^*$$

$$\$20U = \$325{,}000$$

$$U = 16{,}250 \text{ units}$$

*$0.80 \times$ before-tax profit = after-tax profit:

$$0.80 \text{ before-tax profit} = \$100{,}000$$

$$\text{before-tax profit} = \frac{\$100{,}000}{0.80} = \$125{,}000$$

Example 5 The following information is provided for a product: selling price $60, variable cost $20, sales volume 40,000 units, fixed cost $250,000, and tax rate 40 percent. What is the after-tax profit?

$$S = FC + VC + P$$

$$(\$60 \times 40{,}000) = \$250{,}000 + (\$20 \times 40{,}000) + P$$

$$\$1{,}350{,}000 = P$$

$$\text{After-tax profit} = \$1{,}350{,}000 \times 0.60 = \$810{,}000$$

Example 6 Assume the following:

Sales volume	10,000 units
Selling price	$50
Variable cost	$10
Fixed cost	$150,000
After-tax profit	$80,000
Tax rate	40%

How much will be available to spend on advertising (A)?

$$S = FC + VC + P + A$$

$$\$50 \times 10{,}000 = \$150{,}000 + \$10 \times 10{,}000 + \$133{,}333^* + A$$

$$\$116{,}667 = A$$

*$80,000 = 0.6 \times$ before-tax profit

$$\frac{\$80{,}000}{0.6} = \text{before-tax profit}$$

$$\$133{,}333 = \text{before-tax profit}$$

Example 7 You are considering producing a product that you presently purchase externally for $0.15 per unit. The fixed cost is $13,000 and the variable cost per unit is $0.06. The number of units you need to sell so that the annual cost of your machine equals the outside acquisition cost is:

$$\$0.15U = \$13{,}000 + \$0.06U$$

$$0.09U = \$13,000$$

$$U = 144{,}444 \text{ units}$$

Sales Mix. Breakeven analysis involves more complex calculations when two or more products are manufactured and sold. Different selling prices and different variable costs cause different contribution margins. As a result, breakeven points change based on the proportions of the products sold. This is referred to as *sales mix*. You have to predetermine the sales mix and then calculate a weighted-average contribution margin. There is an assumption that sales mix does not change over the prescribed time period. Holding other things constant, a shift from a low-margin product or service to a high-margin one will increase earnings.

Example 8 You produce products L and M. The following information is relevant:

		L	M
Selling price		$25	$40
Variable cost		15	24
Contribution margin		$10	$16
Sales mix		40%	60%
Fixed cost	$60,000		

The weighted-average contribution margin per unit is

$$(\$10 \times 0.4) + (\$16 \times 0.6) = \$13.60$$

Breakeven units are:

$$\frac{\text{Fixed cost}}{\text{Contribution margin}} = \frac{\$60{,}000}{\$13.60} = 4{,}412 \text{ units} \quad \text{(rounded)}$$

The 4,412 units are allocated as follows:

Product L: 4,412 × 0.4 = 1,765
Product M: 4,412 × 0.6 = 2,647
                          4,412

2. MARGIN OF SAFETY

Introduction. The margin of safety is the amount by which sales revenue may drop before losses begin.

How Is It Computed?

$$\text{Margin of safety} = \frac{\text{expected sales} - \text{breakeven sales}}{\text{expected sales}}$$

The lower the ratio, the more risk there is of reaching the breakeven point.

Example 9 If projected sales are $30,000 with breakeven sales of $25,000, the projected margin of safety is:

$$\frac{\$30,000 - \$25,000}{\$25,000} = 20\%$$

3. CASH BREAKEVEN POINT

Introduction. The cash breakeven point is the sales volume that will cover all cash expenses during a period. Note that not all fixed operating costs involve cash payment (e.g., depreciation expense).

How Is It Computed?

Cash breakeven point = sales = variable costs
+ fixed cash costs

The cash breakeven point is lower than the usual breakeven point because noncash charges are subtracted from fixed costs.

Example 10 Assume the same facts as in Example 1, except that the fixed costs of $15,000 include depreciation of $1,500. The cash breakeven point units are:

$$S = VC + FC$$
$$\$25U = \$10U + \$13,500$$
$$\$15U = \$13,500$$
$$U = 900$$

HOW IS IT USED AND APPLIED? Cost-volume-profit analysis relates to the way in which profit and costs change with a change in volume. A relatively small percentage reduction in sales can cause a major decline in earnings. It is therefore important for the owner to keep sales at or exceeding planned levels, and above the breakeven point. Cost-volume-profit analysis examines the impact on earnings of changes in such factors as variable cost, fixed cost, selling price, volume, and product mix. It thus aids in the planning process. Do a breakeven analysis to determine whether or not the breakeven point can be achieved.

Breakeven analysis is used for many purposes, including to determine:

- The sales volume required to break even
- The sales volume necessary to earn a desired profit
- The improvement in revenue required to "get out of the red"
- The effect that changes in selling price, variable cost, fixed cost, and output have on profit
- The selling price that should be charged
- The desired variable cost per unit or fixed costs

The applications of breakeven analysis are many, including introducing a new product or service, modernizing facilities, starting a new business, and evaluating production and administrative activities.

Breakeven analysis is used to organize thinking on important broad aspects of any small business—for example, determining the breakeven occupancy rate for an inexpensive motel or the breakeven passenger load rate for a small chartered bus service.

The margin of safety is a measure of operating risk. The larger the ratio, the safer is the situation due to the reduction in risk in reaching the breakeven point.

The cash breakeven point is used when a small business has a minimum of cash available, or when the opportunity cost of holding excess cash is high.

Breakeven analysis is important when beginning a new activity, such as starting a new line of business, expanding an existing business, or introducing a new product or service.

Sales mix analysis is vital to the overall success of the business. It is needed at all managerial levels. Top managers may have to make important strategic decisions involving mergers, buyouts, acquisitions, and divestitures as part of diversification. Business owners may have to decide on which segments (e.g., product lines, services, divisions, sales territories, departments, salespersons, etc.) to keep, drop, or add.

The managers of retail stores such as Thrifty and Save-On must constantly check their product mix. For example, the retailer may have to decide which products to replace with high-margin vacation products before the summer season begins.

Examples of questions that are commonly answered by breakeven formulas include the following:

- What is the financial feasibility of a proposed investment?
- Have the business's breakeven possibilities been improving or deteriorating?
- Will advertising generate sufficient sales to justify the cost of a campaign?
- Would introduction of a new product add or detract from profitability?
- What will be the impact of labor negotiations?
- Would modernization of production facilities pay for itself?
- What bid price should be offered on a contract?
- Should the contract with a vendor or customer be renegotiated?

See Sec. 124, Averages (Means): Simple and Weighted.

55 Contribution Margin Analysis

INTRODUCTION. Contribution margin is the difference between sales and the variable costs of the product or service— that is, the amount of money available to cover fixed costs and generate profit.

HOW IS IT COMPUTED? There are two ways to calculate the contribution margin. The easiest method assumes that variable costs include both variable manufacturing costs and variable operating expenses. A sample calculation of contribution margin is thus:

Sales	$1,000,000
Less: Variable costs	600,000
Contribution margin	$ 400,000

Often, the contribution margin computation is shown in more detail as:

Sales	$1,000,000
Less: Variable manufacturing costs	350,000
Manufacturing contribution margin	$ 650,000
Less: Variable operating expenses	250,000
Contribution margin	$ 400,000
Less: Fixed costs	100,000
Net income	$ 300,000

Further analysis is provided by determining the *contribution margin ratio:*

$$\text{Contribution margin ratio} = \frac{\text{contribution margin}}{\text{sales}}$$

Example 1 Sales are $15,000, variable costs are $6,100, and fixed costs are $4,000. The contribution margin is

Sales	$15,000
Less: Variable costs	6,100
Equals: Contribution margin	$ 8,900

The contribution margin of $8,900 is the amount available to cover fixed costs.

Example 2 Ten thousand units have been sold at $30 per unit. Variable cost per unit is $18, and fixed costs total $100,000. Therefore, fixed cost per unit is ($100,000/10,000) = $10. Assume that idle capacity exists. A prospective customer is willing to buy 100 units at a price of only $20 per unit.

The order should be accepted, even though the offering price is below the normal selling price, because is results in additional profit of $200, computed as follows:

Sales (100 × $20)	$2000
Less: Variable costs (100 × $18)	1800
Contribution margin	$ 200
Less: Fixed costs	0
Net income	$ 200

The analytical implication here is that a small business can sell an item below the normal selling price when idle capacity exists, provided there is a contribution margin, because these sales will help to cover fixed costs or add to profits. Even if fixed costs were to go up—say, by $50 for this example—it is still financially attractive to accept this order, because a profit of $150 ($200 − $50) would still result. Note that the contribution margin calculation requires the segregation of fixed and variable costs, which is also needed in breakeven analysis.

Contribution margin analysis can be used to ascertain the best way of utilizing capacity.

Example 3 You can produce an intermediate product that can either be sold at this stage or processed further and sold as a finished product. The following information is available:

	Intermediate product	Finished product
Selling price	$400	$600
Variable cost	160	250

Total fixed cost is $700,000, and 50,000 hours of capacity are interchangeable between the products. Unlimited demand exists for both products. Four hours are required to make the intermediate product, and 6 hours are needed to produce the finished product.

Contribution margin per hour is calculated as follows.

	Intermediate product	Finished product
Selling price	$400	$600
Less: Variable cost	160	250
Contribution margin	$240	$350
Hours per ton	4	6
Contribution margin per hour	$ 60	$58.33

You should sell only the intermediate product because it results in the highest contribution margin per hour. Fixed costs are not considered because they are constant regardless of which product is manufactured.

Example 4 You desire a markup of 30 percent over cost on a product. The following information is relevant:

Direct material	$ 6,000
Direct labor	15,000
Overhead	5,000
Total cost	$26,000
Markup on cost (30%)	7,800
Selling price	$33,800

Total direct labor the year is $2,000,000. Total overhead for the period equals 50 percent of direct labor. The overhead is segregated between 40 percent fixed and 60 percent variable. A customer offers to purchase the item for $30,000. Idle capacity exists. You should accept the incremental order because additional earnings occur:

Selling price		$30,000
Less: Variable costs		
Direct material	$ 6,000	
Direct labor	15,000	
Variable overhead ($15,000 × 30%)*	4,500	25,500
Contribution margin		$4,500
Less: Fixed costs		0
Net income		$4,500

*Total overhead 0.50 × $2,000,000 = $1,000,000.

Variable overhead = 0.30 × direct labor, calculated as follows:

$$\frac{\text{Variable overhead}}{\text{Direct labor}} = \frac{0.60 \times \$1{,}000{,}000}{\$2{,}000{,}000} = \frac{\$600{,}000}{\$2{,}000{,}000} = 30\%$$

Contribution margin analysis aids in establishing a bid price on a contract to produce a product or perform a service.

Example 5 You receive an order for 20,000 units. You wish to know the lowest bid price that will result in a $40,000 increase in profit. The current income statement follows.

Sales (100,000 units × $25)		$2,500,000
Less: Cost of sales		
Direct material	$240,000	
Direct labor	400,000	
Variable overhead ($400,000 × 0.30)	120,000	
Fixed overhead	200,000	960,000
Gross margin		$1,540,000
Less: Selling and administrative expenses		
Variable (includes freight costs of $0.70 per unit)	$120,000	
Fixed	60,000	180,000
Net income		$1,360,000

If the contract is awarded, cost behavior for the incremental order is the same except that:

- Freight costs will be paid by the customer.
- Special tools costing $10,000 will be required solely for this order. The tools are not reusable.
- Direct labor time for each unit of the order will be 10 percent longer.

Preliminary computations are as follows.

	Per-unit cost
Direct material ($240,000/100,000)	$2.40
Direct labor ($400,000/100,000)	4.00
Variable selling and administrative expense ($120,000/100,000)	1.20

A forecasted income statement appears below.

Forecasted Income Statement

	Current	Projected	Explanation
Units	100,000	120,000	
Sales	$2,500,000	$2,722,400	Calculated last: Note (a)
Cost of sales:			
Direct material	$ 240,000	$ 288,000	($2.40 × 120,000)
Direct labor	400,000	488,000	[$400,000 + (20,000 × $4.40)]: Note (b)

Forecasted Income Statement (*Continued*)

	Current	Projected	Explanation
Variable overhead	120,000	146,400	($488,000 × 0.30)
Fixed overhead	200,000	210,000	
Total	$ 960,000	$1,132,400	
Selling and administrative expenses:			
Variable	$ 120,000	$ 130,000	($120,000 + 20,000 × $0.50): Note (*c*)
Fixed	60,000	60,000	
Total	$ 180,000	$ 190,000	
Net income	$1,360,000	$1,400,000	Note (*d*)

Net income + selling and administrative expenses + cost of sales = sales
(*a*) $1,400,000 + $190,000   + $1,132,400 = $2,722,400
(*b*) $4 × 1.10 = $4.40
(*c*) $1.20 − $0.70 = $0.50
(*d*) $1,360,000 + $40,000 = $1,400,000

The contract price for the 20,000 units should be $222,400 ($2,722,400 − $2,500,000), or $11.12 per unit ($222,400/20,000). The contract price per unit of $11.12 is below the $25 current selling price per unit. Remember that total fixed cost is the same, excluding the $10,000 payment for the special tool.

Contribution margin analysis aids in assisting how to obtain the same net income as last year, regardless of a decline in sales volume.

Example 6 In 19X1, sales volume was 100,000 units, selling price was $12.50, variable cost per unit was $7.50, and fixed cost was $250,000.

In 19X2, sales volume is anticipated to total 75,000 units. In consequence, fixed costs have been reduced by $40,000. On 6/1/X2, 20,000 units have already been sold. You wish to determine the contribution margin that must be earned on the remaining units for 19X2.

The 19X1 net income is:

$$S = FC + VC + P$$

$$\$12.50 \times 100,000 = \$250,000 + \$7.50 \times 100,000 + P$$

$$\$250,000 = P$$

The contribution margin to be earned in 19X2 is:

Total fixed cost ($250,000 − $40,000)	$210,000
Net income	250,000
Contribution margin required for year	$460,000

Contribution margin already earned:
  (Selling price − variable cost) × units
    ($12.50 − $7.50) × 20,000   100,000
Contribution margin remaining $360,000

Contribution margin per unit required

$$= \frac{\text{contribution margin remaining}}{\text{units remaining}}$$

$$= \frac{\$360,000}{55,000} = \$6.55$$

The decision whether to drop an old product line or add a new one has to take into account qualitative and quantitative variables. However, any ultimate decision must be based mostly on the effect the decision has on earnings.

Example 7 A small business has three major products: A, B, and F. The owner is thinking of dropping the B line because it is being sold at a loss, as indicated below. The profitability of the products follows:

	A	B	F	Total
Sales	$20,000	$30,000	$50,000	$100,000
Less: Variable costs	12,000	16,000	24,000	52,000
Contribution margin	$ 8,000	$14,000	$26,000	$ 48,000
Less: Fixed costs				
Direct	$ 4,000	$13,000	$ 8,000	$ 25,000
Allocated	2,000	3,000	5,000	10,000
Total	$ 6,000	$16,000	$13,000	$ 35,000
Net income	$ 2,000	($2,000)	$13,000	$ 13,000

Direct fixed costs are identified directly with each of the product lines. Allocated fixed costs are common fixed costs allocated to the product lines using some base such as square footage. Common fixed costs usually continue regardless of the decision and cannot be saved by dropping the product line to which it is distributed.

If product B is dropped, the following effect on net income occurs:

Sales foregone		$30,000
Gains:		
Elimination of variable costs	$16,000	
Elimination of direct fixed costs	13,000	29,000
Decrease in profit		($1,000)

By eliminating product B, the business loses $1000. Hence, the B product line should be retained. One danger in allocating common fixed costs is that such allocations can make a product line appear less profitable than it is. Because of the allocation, the B product line shows a loss of $2000, but it contributes $1000 ($14,000 − $13,000) to meeting the common fixed costs.

HOW IS IT USED AND APPLIED?   Contribution margin analysis is valuable in owner decision making with respect to pricing strategy and which products to push. When performing manufacturing and selling functions, the owner is faced with the problem of choosing among alternative courses of action. Typical questions to be answered include: Which products are profitable? Where should I sell the products? What prices should I charge for products and services? How should I make the products? Contribution margin helps to evaluate alternatives arising from production, special advertising, and so on.

Often business is sought during the slack season, when it may be financially beneficial to bid on extra business at a competitive price that covers all variable costs and makes some contributions to fixed costs plus profits. A knowledge of your variable and fixed costs is necessary to make an accurate bid price determination.

The applications of contribution margin include analysis of performance and whether to:

- Accept or reject a special order in cases when idle capacity exists
- Keep, drop, or add a product line
- Make or buy a certain part

A short-term special order for a product at a lower price than customary may be received. Normally, such an order may be rejected because it will not generate a reasonable profit. However, in poor economic times, the order may be accepted if the additional revenue obtained exceeds the additional costs. The order should be accepted as long as there is a contribution margin.

If contribution margin analysis is used to determine the best utilization of capacity, the alternative with the highest contribution margin per unit is selected, assuming that interchangeable capacity exists. The emphasis on products with higher contribution margins maximizes the business's total net income, even though total sales may decrease. This is not true, however, where there are constraining factors and scarce resources. A *constraining factor* is one that restricts or limits the production or sale of a given product. The constraining factor may be machine hours, labor hours, or cubic feet of warehouse space. In the presence of constraining factors, maximizing total profits depends on obtaining the highest contribution margin per unit of the factor (rather than the highest contribution margin per unit of product output).

This analysis can also be used to appraise proposals and programs. Contribution margin analysis can be used to determine the price on a contract or order for a product or service based on the desired profit.

Contribution margin analysis is valuable in evaluating the performance of a small business. A high contribution margin ratio is preferred, since it shows a greater contribution to profits for each sales dollar generated.

56 How Does Product Demand React to a Price Change?

INTRODUCTION. One of the most important ways of gauging demand is the determination of elasticity, which tells how sensitive quantity demand is to a change in a factor influencing demand. The principal factors in demand elasticity are:

1. The price of the good or service (in the case of price elasticity)

2. Income (in the case of income elasticity)

3. The price of a substitute product (in the case of cross-elasticity)

4. Advertising (in the case of promotional elasticity)

Only price elasticity is discussed here, since other elasticity considerations are similar with respect to their computations and implications.

The owner should also determine the degree of correlation that exists between products. This is important because products that are closely related results in greater risk to the business than if the products were inversely related. Diversification in the product line lowers risk. The correlation between products is revealed through a correlation matrix determined by a computer program.

HOW IS IT COMPUTED? Price elasticity, denoted by e_p, is the ratio of a percentage change in quantity demanded (Q) to a percentage change in price (p):

$$e_p = \frac{dQ/Q}{dp/p} = \left(\frac{dQ}{dp}\right)\left(\frac{p}{Q}\right)$$

where dQ/dp is the slope of the demand function $Q = Q(p)$. The price elasticity of demand is classified into three categories:

If $e_p > 1$, demand is elastic.

If $e_p = 1$, demand is unitary.

If $e_p < 1$, demand is inelastic.

Example 1 The two major products of a hardware store are A and B. Relevant data regarding product elasticity follows:

	A	B
Selling price	$20	$15
Unit sales	20,000	24,000

If the selling price of product A is increased to $22, it is estimated that sales volume will decrease by 900 units. If the selling price of product B is increased to $18, sales volume is projected to decrease by 5000 units.

$$\text{Product demand elasticity} = \frac{\text{percentage change in quantity}}{\text{percentage change in price}}$$

Product A has inelastic demand:

$$\frac{900/20,000}{\$2/\$20} = \frac{0.045}{0.10} = 0.45$$

Product B has elastic demand:

$$\frac{5,000/24,000}{\$3/\$15} = \frac{0.208}{0.20} = 1.04$$

Example 2 The correlation matrix for a small business's product line follows:

Product	A	B	C	D	E
A	1.0	0.13	− 0.03	− 0.01	− 0.07
B	0.13	1.0	− 0.02	− 0.07	0.00
C	− 0.03	− 0.02	1.0	0.01	0.60
D	− 0.01	− 0.07	0.01	1.0	− 0.90
E	− 0.07	0.00	0.60	− 0.90	1.0

There is perfect correlation for the same product. For example, product A is correlated exactly to itself (1.0).

There is high positive correlation between products E and C (0.60). These products are very related to each other, indicating risk.

There is low negative correlation between products A and C (− 0.03).

There is no correlation between products B and E (0.00).

Risk is less when significant negative correlation exists, such as between products E and D (−0.9).

HOW IS IT USED AND APPLIED?   Economists have established the following relationships between price elasticity (e_p) and total revenue (TR), which can aid a small business in setting its price:

Price	$e_p > 1$	$e_p = 1$	$e_p < 1$
Price rises	TR falls	No change	TR rises
Price falls	TR rises	No change	TR falls

Small businesses need to be aware of the elasticity of their own demand curves when they set product prices. For example, a profit-maximizing business would never choose to lower its price in an inelastic situation: Such a price decrease would only decrease total revenue and at the same time increase costs, since output would rise. The result would be a significant decrease in earnings. In fact, when costs are rising and demand is inelastic, the small business would have no difficulty passing on the increases by raising the price to the customer.

When there are many substitutes and demand is elastic, increasing prices may lead to a reduction in total revenue rather than an increase. The result may be lower profits rather than higher ones.

Similarly, small business managers are sometimes surprised by the lack of success of price reductions, though this merely reflects the fact that demand is relatively inelastic. In such a case, they may have to rely on other marketing efforts such as advertising and sales promotion in order to increase market share.

Small business owners must ascertain how competitive their products are in the marketplace in order to determine the products' market share. The examination of elasticity aids them in setting prices. Various elasticity measures allow small business managers to see how effective each of the demand determinants (i.e., advertising, price change, and external factors) is going to be. In this way marketing resources may be utilized more profitably and efficiently.

A negative situation exists when products are positively correlated and have elastic demands. In this case, the owner should try to restructure the product line to make it negatively correlated or at least not correlated to reduce risk. Further, an attempt should be made to make product demand inelastic or unitary to reduce price risk. It is best to have a diversified product line consisting of negatively correlated items to enhance stability under various economic conditions. This arises because revenue obtained from one product increases at the same time that revenue obtained from another decreases.

The small business owner is better off if total sales consists of a high percentage of proprietary products (ratio of proprietary product sales to total net sales). These are products customers consider to be difficult or impossible to buy elsewhere. Examples are patented and specialty products: There is a high propensity to buy these products.

Putting Money to Work

57 Figuring the Risk-Return Trade-off

INTRODUCTION. Integral to many business decisions is the concept of a risk-return trade-off. In fact, all financial decisions involve some sort of risk-return trade-off. The greater the risk associated with any financial decision, the greater is the return expected from it and vice versa. For example, in managing working capital, the less inventory you keep, the higher will be the expected return (since less of your current assets is tied up), but also the greater will be the risk of running out of merchandise and thus losing potential revenue from sales.

HOW IS IT COMPUTED?

Example Companies A and B are identical in every respect but one: Company B has invested $20,000 in T-bills, which have been financed with equity. Assume a 50 percent tax rate. The balance sheets and earnings of the two companies are shown in Table 57.1.

Note that Company A has a current ratio of 1.73 and earns 13.16 percent return on its total assets. Company B, on the other hand, has a higher liquidity as expressed by its current ratio of 2.4, but earns only 12.09 percent.

TABLE 57.1

	Company A	Company B
Cash	$ 2,000	$ 2,000
Marketable securities	—	20,000
Other current assets	50,000	50,000
Fixed assets	100,000	100,000
Total	$152,000	$172,000
Current liabilities	$ 30,000	$ 30,000
Long-term debt	50,000	50,000
Owner's equity	72,000	92,000
Total	$152,000	$172,000
Net income	$ 20,000	$ 20,800*
Current ratio	$\dfrac{\$52,000}{\$30,000} = 1.73$	$\dfrac{\$72,000}{\$30,000} = 2.4$
Return on total assets (ROA)	$\dfrac{\$20,000}{\$152,000} = 13.16\%$	$\dfrac{\$20,800}{\$172,000} = 12.09\%$

*During the year Company B held $20,000 in T-bills, which earned an 8% return or $1,600 for the year, or $800 after taxes.

HOW IS IT USED AND APPLIED? The proper assessment and balance of the various risk-return trade-offs is part of creating a sound financial and investment plan.

As a means of increasing liquidity, the business may choose to invest additional monies in cash or/and marketable securities such as T-bills and commercial papers. Such action involves a trade-off, since such assets are likely to earn little return.

58 Opportunity Cost

INTRODUCTION. Opportunity cost is the revenue forfeited by rejecting one use of time or facilities in favor of another alternative.

HOW IS IT COMPUTED?

Opportunity cost = annual return rate foregone
$$\times \text{ fraction of year} \times \text{capital invested}$$

Example A small business owner has money tied up in receivables because of a collection problem. The funds tied up for a 3-month period were $400,000. The business earns 10 percent per annum. The opportunity cost is:

$$\$400,000 \times 10\% \times \frac{3}{12} = \$10,000$$

HOW IS IT COMPUTED AND APPLIED? The owner uses opportunity cost analysis when selecting among alternatives in making decisions. The opportunity cost is a consideration in whether, for instance, to increase production, liberalize credit policy, or produce a different product. Its importance in decision making is that the best outcome can be sought, since this analysis considers what it would cost if the best available alternative is not taken. The opportunity cost approach is used to solve short-term, nonroutine decision problems.

59 How Many Years Does It Take to Get Your Money Back (Payback Period)?

INTRODUCTION. The payback period is the number of years it takes to recover an initial investment. Analyzing the payback period of an investment assists in evaluating a project's risk and liquidity.

HOW IS IT COMPUTED?

1. Payback Period

$$\text{Payback period} = \frac{\text{initial investment}}{\text{annual cash inflow}}$$

2. Discounted Payback Period

$$\text{Discounted payback period} = \frac{\text{initial cash outlay}}{\text{discounted annual cash inflows}}$$

The discounted payback period takes into account the time value of money. It is calculated by adding the present value of each year's cash inflows until they equal the initial investment. The payback period will be longer using the discounted method, because money is worth less over time.

3. Payback Reciprocal

$$\text{Payback reciprocal} = \frac{1}{\text{payback period}}$$

The payback reciprocal is the reciprocal of the payback time. It gives a quick but accurate estimate of the internal rate of return (IRR) on an investment when the project life is more than twice the payback period and the cash inflows are uniform during every period.

Example 1 A small business is considering offering a new product, which will initially cost $250,000. Expected cash inflows are $80,000 for the next 5 years. The owner wants her money back in 4 years. The payback analysis is as follows:

$$\text{Payback period} = \frac{\text{initial investment}}{\text{annual cash inflow}} = \frac{\$250,000}{\$80,000} = 3.125$$

Because the payback period (3.125) is less than the cutoff payback period (4), the owner should offer the new product.

Example 2 A business invests $40,000 and receives the following cash inflows:

Year 1 $15,000
Year 2 $20,000
Year 3 $28,000

$$\$35,000 + \frac{\$5,000}{\$28,000}$$

$35,000 is recovered after 2 years, with the balance of $5,000 being recovered after 0.18 of the third year.

$$2 \text{ years} + 0.18 = 2.18 \text{ years}$$

$$\text{Payback period} = 2.18 \text{ years}$$

To determine the payback period when there are unequal cash inflows each year, add up the annual cash inflows that equal the initial cash outlay. The answer is the length of time it takes to recover the initial investment.

Example 3 Assume the same facts as in Example 2 and a cost of financing of 10 percent. Then

$$\text{Discounted payback} = \frac{\text{initial cash outlay}}{\text{discounted annual cash inflows}}$$

Year 1		Year 2		Year 3
$15,000	+	$20,000	+	$28,000
× 0.9091*		× 0.8264*		× 0.7513*
$13,637	+	$16,528	+	$21,036

*The factors are from Table 3 (Present Value of $1) in the Appendix.

$$\$13,637 + \$16,528 = \$30,165$$

$$\$30,165 + \frac{\$9,835}{\$21,036}$$

$$(\$9,835 = \$40,000 - \$30,165)$$

$$2 \text{ years} + 0.47 = 2.47 \text{ years}$$

Example 4 A business owner is considering three projects, each involving an initial investment of $6000. Each project is anticipated to result in annual cash inflows of $1500.

$$\text{Payback period} = .\frac{\$6000}{\$1500} = 4 \text{ years}$$

$$\text{Payback reciprocal} = \frac{1}{4} = 25\%$$

The owner is earning approximately 25 percent on his money.

HOW IS IT USED AND APPLIED? The payback period is one method that can be used to select among alternative proposals. A shorter payback period is desirable because it indicates less risk, improved liquidity, and a faster rate of return. A benefit of payback is that it permits small businesses that have a cash problem to evaluate the turnover of scarce resources in order to recover invested funds more quickly.

Some believe that payback should not be used in unstable, uncertain industries subject to rapid technological change because the future is so unpredictable that there is no point in guessing what cash flows will be more than 2 years into the future.

Advantages of payback are that it is easy to use and understand, handles investment risk effectively, and can be used as a supplement to other techniques since it does indicate risk.

Deficiencies of payback analysis are that it ignores the time value of money, does not consider cash flows received after the payback period, and does not measure profitability.

60 How Do You Calculate Future Values? How Money Grows

INTRODUCTION. A dollar now is worth more than a dollar to be received later. This statement sums up an important principle: Money has a time value. The rationale of this principle is not that inflation might make the dollar received at a later time worth less in buying power. The reason is that you could invest the dollar now and have more than a dollar at the specified later date.

Future value (also called *compounding*) is the value of an investment (or a series of investments) at a future date based on a rate of interest being paid at stated time intervals. Future value includes not only the earned rate of interest, but also the compounding effect of earning interest on the interest already accrued. Interest may be compounded at various intervals, such as daily. The more often the compounding, the higher is the future value.

HOW IS IT COMPUTED? For the discussion of the concepts of compounding and time value, let us define:

F_n = future value = the amount of money at the end of year n

P = principal

i = annual interest rate

n = number of years

Then

$$F_1 = \text{amount of money at the end of year 1}$$

$$= \text{principal and interest} = P + iP = P(1 + i)$$

$$F_2 = \text{amount of money at the end of year 2}$$

$$= F_1(1 + i) = P(1 + i)(1 + i) = P(1 + i)^2$$

The future value of an investment compounded annually at rate i for n years is

$$F_n = P(1 + i)^n = P \times T_1(i,n)$$

where $T_1(i,n)$ is the compound amount of $1 and can be found in Table 1 in the Appendix.

Example 1 You put $1000 in a savings account earning 8 percent interest compounded annually. How much money will you have in the account at the end of 4 years?

$$F_n = P(1 + i)^n = P \times T_1(i,n)$$

$$F_4 = \$1000(1 + 0.08)^4 = \$1000T_1(8\%, 4 \text{ years})$$

From Table 1, the T_1 for 4 years at 8 percent is 1.361. Therefore,

$$F_4 = \$1000(1.361) = \$1361$$

Example 2 You invest a large sum of money in the stock of ABC Corporation. The company currently pays a $3 dividend per share. The dividend is expected to increase by 20 percent per year for the next 3 years. You wish to project the dividends for years 1 through 3.

$$F_n = P(1 + i)^n = P \times T_1(i,n)$$

$$F_1 = \$3(1 + 0.2)^1 = \$3T_1(20\%,1) = \$3(1.200) = \$3.60$$

$$F_2 = \$3(1 + 0.2)^2 = \$3T_1(20\%,2) = \$3(1.440) = \$4.32$$

$$F_3 = \$3(1 + 0.2)^3 = \$3T_1(20\%,3) = \$3(1.728) = \$5.18$$

Intrayear Compounding. Interest is often compounded more frequently than once a year. Banks, for example, compound interest quarterly, daily, or even continuously. If interest is compounded m times a year, then the general formula for solving the future value becomes:

$$F_n = P\left(1 + \frac{i}{m}\right)^{n \times m} = P \times T_1\left(\frac{1+i}{m, n \times m}\right)$$

The formula reflects more frequent compounding ($n \times m$) at a smaller interest rate per period (i/m). For example, for semiannual compounding ($m = 2$), the above formula becomes:

$$F_n = P\left(1 + \frac{i}{2}\right)^{n \times 2} = P \times T_1\left(1 + \frac{i}{2, n \times 2}\right)$$

Example 3 You deposit $10,000 in an account offering an annual interest rate of 20 percent. You will keep the money on deposit for 5 years. The interest rate is compounded quarterly. The accumulated amount at the end of the fifth year is calculated as follows:

$$F_n = P\left(1 + \frac{i}{m}\right)^{n \times m} = P \times T_1\left(\frac{i}{m, n \times m}\right)$$

where $P = \$10,000$

$$\frac{i}{m} = \frac{20\%}{4} = 5\%$$

$$n \times m = 5 \times 4 = 20$$

Therefore,

$$F_5 = \$10,000(1 + 0.05)^{20} = \$10,000T_1(5\%,20) = \$10,000(2.653) = \$26,530$$

Example 4 Assume that $P = \$1000$, $i = 8$ percent, and $n = 2$ years. Then for:

Annual compounding

($m = 1$):

$$F_2 = \$1000(1 + 0.08)^2 = \$1000T_1(8\%,2)$$
$$= \$1000(1.166)$$
$$= \$1166.00$$

Semiannual compounding

($m = 2$):

$$F_2 = \$1000[1 + (0.08/2)]^{2 \times 2}$$
$$= \$1000(1 + 0.04)^4 = \$1000T_1(4\%,4)$$
$$= \$1000(1.170)$$
$$= \$1170.00$$

Quarterly compounding $F_2 = \$1000[1 + (0.08/4)]^{2\times4}$

$(m = 4)$: $= \$1000(1 + 0.02)^8 = \$1000T_1(2\%,8)$

        $= \$1000(1.172)$

        $= \$1172.00$

As the examples show, the more frequently interest is compounded, the greater is the amount accumulated. This is true for any interest for any period of time.

Future Value of an Annuity. Two types of annuities are discussed here: the *ordinary annuity,* when the payment is made at the end of the year; and the *annuity due,* when the payment is made at the beginning of the year. In addition, the discussion examines the future difference in value between these two annuities.

Ordinary annuity. An *annuity* is defined as a series of payments (or receipts) of a fixed amount for a specified number of periods. Each payment is assumed to occur at the end of the period. The future value of an annuity is a compound annuity which involves depositing or investing an equal sum of money at the end of each year for a certain number of years and allowing it to grow.

Let S_n = the future value of an n-year annuity, and let $A =$ the amount of the annuity. Then we can write:

$$S_n = A(1 + i)^{n-1} + A(1 + i)^{n-2} + \cdots + A(1 + i)^0$$

$$= A[(1 + i)^{n-1} + (1 + i)^{n-2} + \cdots + (1 + i)^0]$$

$$= A \sum_{t=0}^{n-1} (1 + i)^t = A\left[\frac{(1 + i)n - 1}{i}\right] = A \times T_2(i,n)$$

where $T_2(i,n)$ represents the future value of an annuity of $1 for n years compounded at i percent and can be found in Table 2 in the Appendix.

Example 5   You wish to determine how much money you will have in a savings account at the end of 6 years if you deposit $1000 at the end of each year for the next 6 years. The annual interest rate is 8 percent. The T_2 (8%, 6 years) is given in Table 2 as 7.336. Therefore,

$$S_6 = \$1000T_2(8\%,6) = \$1000(7.336) = \$7336$$

Example 6   You deposit $30,000 semiannually into a fund for 10 years. The annual interest rate is 8 percent. The amount accumulated at the end of the tenth year is calculated as follows:

$$S_n = A \times T_2(i,n)$$

where A = \$30,000
$\quad i$ = 8%/2 = 4%
$\quad n$ = 10 × 2 = 20

Therefore,

$$S_n = \$30,000 T_2(4\%,20)$$

$$= \$30,000(29.778) = \$893,340$$

Annuity due. The formula for computing the future value of an annuity due must take into consideration one additional year of compounding, since the payment comes at the beginning of the year. Therefore, the future value formula must be modified to take this into consideration by compounding it for one more year. Generally speaking, an annuity due is preferable over an ordinary annuity, since an amount equivalent to an additional year of compounding is received.

CAN A COMPUTER HELP? Financial calculators marketed by several manufacturers (e.g., Hewlett-Packard, Sharp, Texas Instruments) have a "future (compound) value" function. Future value is also incorporated as a built-in function in spreadsheet programs such as Lotus 1-2-3. For example, Lotus 1-2-3 has a routine @FV (*payments,interest,term*), which calculates the future value of an investment, based on a series of equal payments. To calculate the future value of an annuity due, use the formula @FV (*payments,interest,term*)* (1 + *interest*).

HOW IS IT USED AND APPLIED? The time value of money is a critical consideration in financial and investment decisions. For example, compound interest calculations are needed to determine future sums of money resulting from an investment.

1. Future value calculations of a single investment are widely used to determine what a sum of money invested at interest rate i will be worth in n years. This calculation is used every time a decision must be made about a long-term investment, whether the investment is in government bonds, a savings account, or any other interest-bearing financial instrument. Future value computation can also be used to determine a growth rate, how many years it will take to reach a financial goal, and what interest rate is being charged on a loan.

2. Future value determination based on periodic equal payments will give the accumulated amount in a fund such as a retirement account, a sinking fund, or a bank account. The computation enables a distinction between the accumulated principal and interest, and a determination of the equal annual cash payment, interest rate, or number of periods.

The future annuity computation reveals what equal annual payments will be worth at a future date. For example, an individual might want to calculate how much income is generated after 30 years of depositing $2000 a year into an IRA account, or the annual deposit necessary to generate $1 million after 20 years. Future value computations are also extremely important when determining how much will be accumulated in a pension fund within a certain period of time at a certain interest rate at specified compounding intervals.

61 Determining Annual Deposits (Sinking Funds)

INTRODUCTION. A small business owner might wish to find the annual deposit (or payment) that is necessary to accumulate a future sum.

HOW IS IT COMPUTED? To find this future amount (or *sinking fund*), we can use the formula for finding the future value of an annuity:

$$S_n = A \times T_2(i,n)$$

Solving for A, we obtain:

$$\text{Annual deposit amount} = A = \frac{S_n}{T_2}(i,n)$$

Example 1 You wish to determine the equal annual end-of-year deposits required to accumulate $5000 in your retirement fund at the end of 5 years. The interest rate is 10 percent. The annual deposit is:

$$S_5 = \$5000$$

$$T_2(10\%, 5 \text{ years}) = 6.105 \qquad \text{(from Table 2)}$$

$$A = \frac{\$5000}{6.105} = \$819$$

In other words, if you deposit $819 at the end of each year for 5 years at 10 percent interest, you will have accumulated $5000 at the end of the fifth year.

Example 2   You need a sinking fund for the retirement of a bond 30 years from now. The interest rate is 10 percent. The annual year-end contribution needed to accumulate $1,000,000 is

$$S_{30} = \$1,000,000$$

$$T_2(10\%, 30 \text{ years}) = 164.49$$

$$A = \frac{\$1,000,000}{164.49} = \$6,079.40$$

HOW IS IT USED AND APPLIED?   This computation is used to determine the amount of annual deposits for a retirement fund, a sinking fund to retire debt, or a fund to be used to buy business assets.

62 Determining Number of Periods Required

INTRODUCTION.   You might want to know how long it will take for your money to double or how long it will take to reach your monetary goal.

HOW IS IT COMPUTED?

Case 1: Single-Deposit Investment.   The number of years it will take to reach a certain future sum can be computed as follows:

$$F_n = P \times T_1(i,n)$$

Solving for T_1, we obtain:

$$T_1(i,n) = \frac{F_n}{P}$$

where F_n = future value in period n, and P = a present sum of money or base-period value.

Example 1   At an interest rate of 12 percent, you want to know how long it will take for your money to double. The value is computed as follows:

$$F_n = \$2.00 \text{ and } P = \$1.00$$

Therefore,

$$T_1(12,n) = \frac{\$2.00}{\$1.00} = 2$$

From Table 1 in the Appendix, a T_1 of 2 at 12 percent is at n = almost 6 years. It will take almost 6 years.

Example 2   You want to have $250,000. You have $30,000 to invest. The interest rate is 12 percent. The number of years it will take to reach your goal is computed below:

$$\text{Factor} = \frac{\$250,000}{\$30,000} = 8.333$$

From Table 1, n is approximately 18.5 years.

Case 2: Equal Periodic Deposits.   The number of years it will take for equal periodic deposits to reach a certain future sum can be computed as follows:

$$F_n = P \times T_2(i,n)$$

Solving for T_2, we obtain:

$$T_2(i,n) = \frac{F_n}{P}$$

where F_n = future value in period n, and P = a present sum of money or base-period value.

Example 3   You want $500,000 in the future. The interest rate is 10 percent. You can deposit $80,000 each year. The number of years it will take to accomplish this objective is computed below:

$$\text{Factor} = \frac{\$500,000}{\$80,000} = 6.25$$

From Table 2, we see that n is approximately 5 years.

CAN A COMPUTER HELP?   More exact answers can be obtained using computer software. For example, Lotus 1-2-3 has a routine @CTERM (*payment,interest,future-value*), which calculates the number of compounding periods for a single-deposit investment. It also has @TERM (*payments,interest,future-value*), which calculates how long it will take for equal periodic payments to reach a specific amount at a given interest rate. Furthermore, many financial calculators contain preprogrammed formulas and perform many present-value and future-value applications. They include Radio Shack, Hewlett-Packard, Sharp, and Texas Instruments models.

HOW IS IT USED AND APPLIED?   When you have an investment goal, such as for capacity expansion, a retirement fund, or a sinking fund, you can determine how long it will take for you to reach your monetary goal.

63 Rules of 69 and 72

INTRODUCTION.   The *rule of 72* is a rule-of-thumb method used to determine how many years it takes to double investment money. The *rule of 69,* which is very similar to the rule of 72, also states how long it takes an amount of money invested at r percent per period to double.

HOW IS IT COMPUTED?   Using the rule of 72, dividing the number 72 by the fixed rate of return gives the number of years it takes for annual earnings from the investment to double. That is,

$$\frac{72}{r} \text{ (in percent)}$$

Using the rule of 69,

$$\frac{69}{r} \text{ (in percent)} + 0.35 \text{ years}$$

Example   A small business owner bought a piece of property yielding an annual return of 25 percent. This investment will double in less than 3 years, because

$$\frac{72}{25} = 2.88 \text{ years}$$

Alternatively, using the rule of 69,

$$\frac{69}{25} + 0.35 = 2.76 + 0.35 = 3.11 \text{ years}$$

HOW IS IT USED AND APPLIED?   These are simply handy rules of thumb to determine how long it takes to double money on an investment. Both methods may be used in conjunction. Without looking up the present value and future value in tables or using a financial calculator, it is easy to see the number of years it will take to do this.

64 Computing Interest Rate

INTRODUCTION. You might want to know about the interest rate you are charged on a loan or the interest rate you must earn on your annual deposits to reach your investment goal.

HOW IS IT COMPUTED?

Case 1: Single-Deposit Loan. The interest rate you are charged on a loan can be computed as follows:

$$F_n = P \times T_1(i,n)$$

Solving for T_1, we obtain

$$T_1(i,n) = \frac{F_n}{P}$$

where F_n = future value in period n, and P = a present sum of money or base-period value.

> **Example 1** You agree to pay back $3000 in 6 years on a $2000 loan made today. You are being charged an interest rate of 7 percent, calculated as follows:
>
> $$T_1(i,6) = \frac{\$3000}{\$2000} = 1.5$$
>
> From Table 1 in the Appendix, a T_1 of 1.5 at 6 years is at 7 percent.

Case 2: Equal Periodic Deposits. The interest rate you must earn on your annual deposits to reach your investment goal can be computed as follows:

$$F_n = P \times T_2(i,n)$$

Solving for T_2, we obtain

$$T_2(i,n) = \frac{F_n}{P}$$

where F_n = future value in period n, and P = a present sum of money or base-period value.

> **Example 2** You want to have $500,000 accumulated in a pension plan after 9 years. You deposit $30,000 per year. The interest rate you must earn is computed below.

$$\text{Factor} = \frac{\$500,000}{\$30,000} = 16.667$$

From Table 2, the interest rate is approximately 15 percent.

CAN A COMPUTER HELP?   More exact answers can be obtained using computer software. For example, Lotus 1-2-3 has a routine @RATE (*future-value,present-value,term*), which calculates the interest rate you are charged on a loan. Furthermore, many financial calculators include preprogrammed formulas and perform many present-value and future-value applications. They include Radio Shack, Hewlett-Packard, Sharp, and Texas Instruments models.

HOW IS IT USED AND APPLIED?   The information is useful when you need to calculate the compound rate of an investment or the interest rate you are being charged on a loan. The businessperson can compare the interest rate he comes up with to the interest rate the financial institution is quoting to see if the two agree.

65 How to Calculate After-Tax Cash Flows

INTRODUCTION.   Income taxes make a difference in many capital budgeting decisions. The project which is attractive on a before-tax basis may have to be rejected on an after-tax basis. Income taxes typically affect both the amount and the timing of cash flows.

HOW IS IT COMPUTED?   Let us define:

$$S = \text{sales}$$

$$E = \text{cash operating expenses}$$

$$d = \text{depreciation}$$

$$t = \text{tax rate}$$

Then, before-tax cash inflows (or cash savings) = $S - E$, and net income = $S - E - d$.

   Since net income, not cash inflows, is subject to tax, after-tax cash inflows are not usually the same as after-tax net income. By definition,

After-tax cash inflows = before-tax cash inflows − taxes

$$= (S - E) - (S - E - d)(t)$$

Rearranging gives the short-cut formula

After-tax cash inflows $= (S - E)(1 - t) + (d)(t)$

$$= (S - E - d)(1 - t) + d$$

As can be seen, the deductibility of depreciation from sales in arriving at taxable net income reduces income tax payments and thus serves as a *tax shield*.

Tax shield = tax savings on depreciation $= (d)(t)$

Example 1 Assume that:

$S = \$12,000$

$E = \$10,000$

$d = \$500$ per year using the straight-line method

$t = 30\%$

Then:

After-tax cash inflow $= (\$12,000 - \$10,000)(1 - 0.3) + (\$500)(0.3)$

$$= (\$2,000)(0.7) + (\$500)(0.3)$$

$$= \$1,400 + \$150$$

$$= \$1,550$$

Tax shield = tax savings on depreciation $= (d)(t)$

$$= (\$500)(0.3) = \$150$$

Since the tax shield is dt, the higher the depreciation deduction, the higher will be the tax savings on depreciation. Therefore, an accelerated depreciation method (such as double-declining balance) produces higher tax savings than the straight-line method. Accelerated methods produce higher present values for the tax savings, which may make a given investment more attractive.

HOW IS IT USED AND APPLIED?   In making a capital investment decision, after-tax cash flow data must be used before net-present-value analysis can be implemented. See Sec. 66, What Is Present Value? How Much Is Money Worth Now?

Example 2   Green Machine Tools estimates that it can save $2500 a year in cash operating costs for the next 10 years if it buys a special purpose machine at a cost of $10,000. No residual value is expected.

Depreciation is by the straight-line method. Assume that the income tax rate is 30 percent, and the after-tax cost of capital (minimum required rate of return) is 10 percent. Should the company buy the machine?

To answer the question, after-tax cash savings must be calculated first. Straight-line depreciation is $10,000/10 = $1000 per year. Thus:

$$\text{After-tax cash savings} = (S - E)(1 - t) + (d)(t)$$
$$= \$2500(1 - 0.3) + \$1000(0.3)$$
$$= \$1750 + \$300 = \$2050$$

To see if this machine should be purchased, the net present value (NPV), which is present value (PV) minus initial investment (I), can be calculated.

$$PV = \$2,050 \ T_4(10\%, 10 \text{ years}) = \$2,050(6.145) = \$12,597.25$$

where T_4 is the present value of an annuity of $1 and is found in the Appendix. Thus:

$$NPV = PV - I = \$12,597.25 - \$10,000 = \$2,597.25$$

Since the NPV is positive, the machine should be bought.

66 What Is Present Value? How Much Is Money Worth Now?

INTRODUCTION. Present value is a method for determining the current value of money based on a future yield; it is also called *discounting*. The concept of present value assumes that money received or paid out in the future is not worth as much as money today. Investing a discrete value of money necessarily implies an opportunity cost. Thus, given some future value, what is the equivalent value of the money today, or its present value? In connection with present-value calculations, the interest rate i is called the *discount rate*. The discount rate we use is more commonly called the *cost of capital*, which is the minimum rate of return required by the business.

HOW IS IT COMPUTED? Recall from Sec. 64, Computing Interest Rate, that

$$F_n = P(1 + i)^n$$

Therefore,

$$P = \frac{F_n}{(1 + i)n} = F_n \left[\frac{1}{(1 + i)n} \right] = F_n \times T_3(i, n)$$

where $T_3(i,n)$ represents the present value of $1 and is given in Table 3 in the Appendix.

Example 1 You have been given an opportunity to receive $20,000 6 years from now by investing in a joint venture with another business. If you can earn 10 percent on your investments, what is the most you should pay for this opportunity? To answer this question, you must compute the present value of $20,000 to be received 6 years from now at a 10 percent discount rate. F_6 is $20,000, i is 10 percent, and n is 6 years. $T_3(10\%,6)$, from Table 3, is 0.565.

$$P = \$20,000\left[\frac{1}{(1 + 0.1)^6}\right] = \$20,000\ T_3(10\%,6) = \$20,000(0.565)$$

$$= \$11,300$$

This means that you can earn 10 percent on your investment, and you would be indifferent to receiving $11,300 now or $20,000 6 years from today since the amounts are time equivalent. In other words, you could invest $11,300 today at 10 percent and have $20,000 in 6 years.

Present Value of Mixed Streams of Cash Flows. The present value of a series of mixed payments (or receipts) is the sum of the present value of each individual payment. We know that the present value of each individual payment is the payment times the appropriate T_3 value.

Example 2 You are thinking of starting a new product line that will cost $32,000 initially. Your annual projected cash inflows are:

Year 1 $10,000
Year 2   20,000
Year 3   5,000

If you must earn a minimum of 10 percent on your investment, should you undertake this new product line?

The present value of this series of mixed streams of cash inflows is calculated as follows:

Year	Cash inflows	$\times$	$T_3(10\%,n)$	Present value
1	$10,000		0.909	$ 9,090
2	20,000		0.826	16,520
3	5,000		0.751	3,755
				$29,365

Since the present value of your projected cash inflows is less than the initial investment, you should not undertake this project.

Present Value of an Annuity. Interest received from bonds, pension funds, and insurance obligations all involve annuities. To compare these financial instruments, we need to know the present value of each. The present value of an annuity (P_n) can be found by using the following equation:

$$P_n = A\left[\frac{1}{(1+i)^1}\right] + A\left[\frac{1}{(1+i)^2}\right] + \cdots + A\left[\frac{1}{(1+i)^n}\right]$$

$$= A\left[\frac{1}{(1+i)^1} + \frac{1}{(1+i)^2} + \cdots + \frac{1}{(1+i)^n}\right]$$

$$= A\sum_{t=1}^{n} = \frac{1}{(1+i)^t}\left[1 - \frac{1}{(1+i)}\right] = A \times T_4(i,n)$$

where $T_4(i,n)$ represents the present value of an annuity of $1 discounted at i percent for n years and is found in Table 4 in the Appendix.

Example 3 Assume that the cash inflows in Example 2 form an annuity of $10,000 for 3 years. Then the present value is

$$P_n = A \times T_4(i,n)$$

$$P_3 = \$10,000T_4(10\%, 3 \text{ years}) = \$10,000(2.487) = \$24,870$$

CAN A COMPUTER HELP? Computer software can be extremely helpful in making present-value calculations. For example, @PV (*payments,interest,term*) of Lotus 1-2-3 determines the present value of an investment, based on a series of equal payments, discounted at a periodic interest rate over the number of periods. To calculate the present value of an annuity due, use the following formula: @PV (*payments,interest,term*) * (1 + *interest*). Financial calculators can do this too.

HOW IS IT USED AND APPLIED?

1. The present-value information is useful in comparing different types of investments, for example, comparing a single-payment investment from a pension fund with a series of periodic payments.

2. Present-value analysis is used to assess the financial attractiveness of investments. This important technique is used in making capital budgeting decisions to select the optimum alternative long-term investment opportunity. It helps to

identify where money should be placed, whether leasing or buying is the best option, whether a business should be kept or sold, whether a new product should be introduced, or whether old equipment should be replaced with new equipment.

3. Present-value tables can also be used to make financial decisions when there are competing choices such as which machine to buy or which product to make.

4. The present value of an annuity is used to determine the equal annual payment, interest rate, and length of time. Present-value-of-annuity computations enable selection of mutually exclusive proposals or projects, revealing which alternative is most financially advantageous. It can be applied to situations involving loans, leases, capital expansion, product-line selection, and so forth.

5. Annuities and their current worth are important in analyzing pension plans, insurance policies, and investments. Present value enables determination of the price to pay for an investment, such as a bond that pays semiannual interest. Discounting applications also reveal the interest rate that is being charged on a loan, and the number of years necessary to pay off that loan.

67 Calculating Loan Payments

INTRODUCTION. A loan may be paid off in periodic equal installments and include varying portions of principal and interest during its term. Examples include auto loans, mortgage loans, and most commercial loans. The longer the loan period, the higher is the interest cost.

HOW IS IT COMPUTED? There are two ways to find the periodic amortized amount:

1. Divide the principal loan amount (A) by T_4, which is a Table 4 factor (Present Value of an Annuity of $1); that is,

$$\text{Amount of loan} = A = \frac{P}{T_4}$$

2. Use a handy table such as Table 5 (a table of monthly installment loan payments) in the Appendix. The table pro-

vides the monthly payment required to retire a $1000 installment loan for a selected annual interest rate and term.

Example 1 Assume that a business borrows $2000 to be repaid in 3 equal installments at the end of each of the next 3 years. The bank charges 12 percent interest. The amount of each payment is

$$P = \$2000$$

$$T_4(12\%, 3 \text{ years}) = 2.402$$

Therefore,

$$A = \frac{\$2000}{2.402} = \$832.64$$

Example 2 A retailer takes out a $15,000, 12%, 48-month loan. He wants to determine the monthly installment loan payment.

Using Table 5, he needs to follow these three steps:

Step 1. Divide the loan amount by $1000.

$$\frac{\$15,000}{\$1,000} = 15$$

Step 2. Find the payment factor from Table 5 for a specific interest rate and loan maturity. The Table 5 payment factor for 12 percent and 48 months is $26.34.

Step 3. Multiply the factor obtained in step 2 by the amount from step 1.

$$\$26.34 \times 15 = \$395.10$$

The monthly installment loan payment is $395.10.

CAN A COMPUTER HELP? Spreadsheet programs can be used in making loan calculations. For example, Lotus 1-2-3 has a function @PMT (*principal,interest,term*), which calculates the payment on a loan at a given interest rate for a specified number of payments. Many financial calculators have similar features. *Note:* @PMT assumes that payments occur at the end of each payment period (an ordinary annuity).

If you make payments at the beginning of each period (an annuity due), you must use the formula @PMT (*principal,interest,term*)/(1 + *interest*).

Once we compute the periodic loan amount, we can develop a *loan amortization schedule.* Each loan payment consists partly of interest and partly of principal. The interest component of the payment is greatest in the first period (because the principal balance is the highest) and subsequently declines, whereas the principal portion is smallest in the first period (because of the high interest) and increases thereafter, as shown in the following example.

Example 3 Using the same data as in Example 1, we set up the following amortization schedule:

Year	Payment	Interest	Repayment of principal	Remaining balance
0				$2000.00
1	$832.64	$240.00*	$592.64†	1407.36
2	832.64	168.88	663.76	743.60
3	832.64	89.23	743.41‡	

*Interest is computed by multiplying the loan balance at the beginning of the year by the interest rate. Therefore, interest in year 1 is $2000(0.12) = $240; in year 2 interest is $1407.36(0.12) = $168.88; and in year 3 interest is $743.60(0.12) = $89.23. All figures are rounded.

†The reduction in principal equals the payment less the interest portion ($832.64 − $240.00 = $592.64).

‡Not exact because of accumulated rounding errors.

Borrowers want to know not only the amount of the periodic payment, but also and perhaps more important, how much they can save in total interest if they prepay the loan.

HOW IS IT USED AND APPLIED? Business owners and managers must be able to calculate the periodic payment amount, and break it down into principal-reduction and interest portions. They have to check the accuracy of bank calculations.

68 Ranking Proposals and Projects

INTRODUCTION. The *ranking* (profitability) index is used to differentiate the net present values of competing proposals. It compares the initial cash investment to the discounted value of future net cash inflows. The index is used to rank projects in order of their attractiveness.

HOW IS IT COMPUTED?

$$\text{Profitability index} = \frac{\text{present value of cash inflows}}{\text{present value of cash outflows}}$$

Rule of thumb: Accept a proposal with a profitability index equal to or greater than 1. If the index is less than 1, the business is losing money on the proposal.

Warning: A higher profitability index does not always coincide with the project with the higher net present value. Thus, it eliminates the distortive effect of size because it looks at a percentage rather than a total dollar amount.

Example 1 Assume that the following information is provided about two proposals being considered by the owner of Desk Mate Stores:

	Proposal A	Proposal B
Initial investment	$100,000	$10,000
Present value of cash inflows	500,000	90,000

The net present value of proposal A is $400,000 and that of proposal B is $80,000. There is a budget constraint of $90,000. Based on net present value, proposal A appears better than proposal B; however, this would be an incorrect conclusion, because a budget constraint exists. The profitability index should be used in evaluating proposals when budget constraints exist. In this case, proposal B's profitability index of 9 far surpasses proposal A's index of 5. The net result is that proposal B should be selected over proposal A.

Example 2 A *contingent proposal* is one that requires acceptance of another, related proposal. Hence, the proposals depend on each other and must be analyzed together, and a profitability index should be computed for the group, as indicated below.

Project	Investment	Present value	Profitability	Index ranking
A	$ 70,000	$112,000	1.6	1
B	100,000	145,000	1.45	2
C	110,000	126,500	1.15	5
D	60,000	79,000	1.32	3
E	40,000	38,000	0.95	6
F	80,000	95,000	1.19	4

The budget constraint is $250,000. Projects A, B, and D should be selected, as indicated by the following calculations.

Project	Investment	Present value
A	$ 70,000	$112,000
B	100,000	145,000
D	60,000	79,000
	$230,000	$336,000

where net present value = $336,000 − $230,000 = $106,000

Proposal	Present value of cash outflow	Present value of cash inflow
A	$160,000	$210,000
B	60,000	40,000
Total	$220,000	$250,000

The combined profitability index is:

$$\text{Profitability index} = \frac{\$250,000}{\$220,000} = 1.14$$

HOW IS IT USED AND APPLIED? The ranking (profitability) index is used to rank competing proposals to determine a priority order. It allows you to rank proposals of different dollar magnitude on a comparative basis.

A business establishes an upper limit to its capital budget based on budgetary constraints. *Special note:* With capital rationing, the project with the highest-ranking index rather than the highest net present value should be selected for investment.

See Sec. 66, What Is Present Value? How Much Is Money Worth Now?

69 Determining Rate of Return (Internal Rate of Return, Time-Adjusted Rate of Return)

INTRODUCTION. The *internal rate of return* (IRR) is the return earned on a business proposal—that is, the discount rate equating the present value of cash inflows to the initial investment. The internal rate of return assumes that cash inflows are reinvested at the internal rate. It is used to determine whether to make capital expenditures.

INTERNAL RATE OF RETURN WITH UNEQUAL CASH INFLOWS

How Is It Computed? This computation uses the trial-and-error method while working through the present-value tables (see the Appendix). Step by step, the IRR is computed as follows:

1. Compute net present value at the cost of capital, denoted r_1.
2. See if net present value is positive or negative.

3a. If net present value is positive, use a higher rate (r_2) than r_1.

3b. If net present value is negative, use a lower rate (r_2) than r_1.

3c. The exact internal rate of return at which net present value equals zero is sometimes between the two rates.

4. Compute net present value using r_2.

5. Perform interpolation for the exact rate.

The internal rate of return may easily be calculated on a financial calculator.

Example 1 An owner expects to receive the annual net cash inflows (cash receipts less cash payments) below from her business after investing $100,000 in it. She wants to know what return rate she will earn.

Year	Cash inflow
1	$50,000
2	30,000
3	20,000
4	40,000

Using trial and error, the interest rate is calculated as follows:

Year	At 16%	Present value	At 18%	Present value
1	0.862	$ 43,100	0.847	$ 42,350
2	0.743	22,290	0.718	21,540
3	0.641	12,820	0.609	12,180
4	0.552	22,080	0.516	20,640
		$100,290		$ 96,710
Investment		−100,000		− 100,000
Net present value		$ 290		− $ 3,290

The internal rate of return on this project is a little more than 16 percent, because at that rate the net present value of the investment is approximately zero.

Note: Personal computers and calculators can be used to make successive approximations.

INTERNAL RATE OF RETURN WITH EQUAL CASH INFLOWS

How Is It Computed?   The internal rate of return with equal cash inflows is computed first by determining a factor (which happens to be the same as the payback period) and then looking up the rate of return in a table of the present value of an annuity of $1 (see Table 4 of the Appendix).

Example 2 Assume that $100,000 is invested in a proposal that will produce annual cash inflows of $15,000 for the next 20 years. Then

$$\frac{\$100,000}{\$15,000} = 6.6667$$

Consult the present value of an annuity of $1 table (see Table 4 in the Appendix). Looking across 20 years, find the factor closest to 6.6667, that is, 6.6231, in the 14 percent column.

Example 3 Assume the following investment:

Initial investment	$12,950
Estimated life	10 years
Annual cash inflows	$3,000
Cost of financing	12%

The internal rate of return, including the interpolation to achieve the exact rate, is found as follows.

$$\text{Present value of annuity factor} = \frac{\$12,950}{\$3,000} = 4.317$$

The value of 4.317 is somewhere between 18 and 20 percent in the 10-year line of the present value of an annuity of $1 table. Using interpolation,

Present value of annuity factor		
18%	4.494	4.494
IRR		4.317
20%	4.192	
	0.302	0.177

Therefore,

$$\text{IRR} = 18\% + \frac{0.177}{0.302} (20\% - 18\%)$$

$$= 18\% + 0.586(2\%) = 18\% + 1.17\% = 19.17\%$$

Because the internal rate of return (19.17 percent) exceeds the cost of capital (12 percent), this analysis concludes that the project should be accepted.

HOW IS IT USED AND APPLIED?   The internal rate of return shows how good the expected return on a capital investment is. If the IRR is greater than the cost of capital, the project should be accepted.

The advantages of using the IRR method are that it does consider the time value of money and, therefore, is more exact and realistic than the accounting rate of return method. Accounting rate of return equals income earned divided by the total investment.

The shortcomings of this method are that (1) it is time-consuming to compute, especially when cash inflows are not even (although most business calculators have a program for calculating IRR), and (2) it fails to recognize the varying sizes of investment in competing projects and their respective dollar profitabilities.

70 Capitalization Rate

INTRODUCTION. *Capitalization rate*, also called *cap rate* or *income yield*, is a widely used method of determining the rate of return on a real estate investment.

HOW IS IT COMPUTED? The capitalization rate is found by dividing the net operating income (NOI) for the first year by the total investment.

> **Example** Assume that net operating income is $18,618 and the purchase price is $219,000. Then the cap rate is
>
> $$\frac{\$18,618}{\$219,000} = 8.5\%$$
>
> If the market rate (average return earned on comparable property) is 10 percent, the fair market value of similar property is $18,618/10 percent = $186,180. The property may be overpriced.

HOW IS IT USED AND APPLIED? The capitalization rate, when applied to the earnings of an investment, determines its appraisal or market value. The higher the cap rate, the lower is the perceived risk to the investor and the lower should be the asking price. Whether a piece of property is overpriced or not depends on the rates for similar properties in the marketplace.

There are two limitations to use of the cap rate: (1) It is based on only the first year's NOI; and (2) it ignores return through appreciation in property value.

The cap rate assists real estate investors who are interested in buying income-producing property in ascertaining the value of that property. A small business owner might use the cap rate to determine the appraised value of a property to see if it qualifies for a loan.

71 Gross Income Multiplier

INTRODUCTION. The *gross income multiplier* is one method of determining the price of income-producing property to a small business. Other methods are the net income multiplier (see Sec. 72) and the capitalization rate (see Sec. 70). This rule-of-thumb valuation, or pricing formula, is also used for acquiring other small businesses.

HOW IS IT COMPUTED? The gross income multiplier is obtained by dividing the asking price (or market value) of the property by the current gross rental income.

Example Assume that current gross rental income is $23,600 and the asking price is $219,000. The gross income multiplier is

$$\frac{\$219,000}{\$23,600} = 9.28$$

A property in a similar neighborhood may be valued at "eight times annual gross." Thus, if its annual gross rental income amounts to $23,600, the value is taken as $8 \times \$23,600 = \$188,800$, which means that the property with the asking price of $219,000 may be overvalued.

HOW IS IT USED AND APPLIED? The gross income multiplier is used to determine the value of a property. Applications of this approach in other industry sectors include the following:

1. In the publishing industry, new, fast-growing magazines are worth 5 to 10 times before-tax annual earnings.
2. Radio stations sell for 7.5 times earnings or cash flows.
3. Insurance agencies sell for 150 percent of annual commissions.
4. Automobile repair garages sell for three times average monthly receipts.

Real estate agencies may use this approach to determine an approximate market value for a property. This approach should be used with caution, however, since different properties have different operating expenses that must be taken into account in determining value.

This rule-of-thumb pricing formula can be used for purchasing other small businesses; however, reliance on this technique alone can result in gross oversimplification of the market value of a property.

See Sec. 142, Determining How Much Your Small Business Is Worth.

72 Net Income Multiplier

INTRODUCTION. The *net income multiplier* (NIM) is a method of determining the price of income-producing property. The other methods are the gross income multiplier (see Sec. 71) and the capitalization rate (see Sec. 70).

HOW IS IT COMPUTED?

$$\text{NIM} = \frac{\text{purchase price}}{\text{net operating income (NOI)}}$$

where NOI is gross income less allowances for vacancies and operating expenses, depreciation and debt payments.

> **Example** Assume that NOI = $18,618 and the asking price is $219,000. The net income multiplier is calculated as follows:
>
> $$\frac{\$219,000}{\$18,618} = 11.76$$

HOW IS IT USED AND APPLIED? A property in a similar neighborhood may be valued at "10 times annual net." Thus, if its annual gross rental income amounts to $18,618, the value is taken as 10 × $18,618 = $186,180, which means that the property with an asking price of $219,000 may be overvalued.

Real estate professionals can use this approach to determine an approximate market value for a property. This approach is better than the gross income multiplier, since it takes into account vacancies and operating expenses.

Scheduling, Planning, and Efficiency Measures

73 How Are Your Assets Operating?

INTRODUCTION. The *operating assets ratio* analyzes the percentage of a small business's assets that are used to generate revenue.

HOW IS IT COMPUTED?

$$\text{Operating assets ratio} = \frac{\text{operating assets}}{\text{total assets}}$$

Operating assets are those used in the business to manufacture products such as equipment and machinery.

Example A small business reports the following data for 19X3 and 19X4:

	19X3	19X4
Operating assets	$ 300,000	$ 560,000
Total assets	$1,100,000	1,400,000
Operating assets to total assets	27%	40%

The business has experienced an increase in productive assets. This should lead to more efficient operations, greater use of facilities, and improved profitability.

HOW IS IT USED AND APPLIED? The operating assets ratio isolates those assets that are actively used in *current* operations. Nonoperating assets reduce profits and return on investment, because there is no benefit to current operations—they neither generate sales nor reduce costs. Nonoperating assets are a "drain" on the small business and may require financing.

74 Repairs and Maintenance Ratios

INTRODUCTION. Repairs and maintenance need to be performed so that plant and equipment are in good working order. *Repair and maintenance ratios* demonstrate the level of investment that a small business makes in these kinds of activities.

HOW IS IT COMPUTED? There are two common repair and maintenance ratios by which a business's commitment can be measured:

1. Repairs and maintenance to fixed assets:

$$\frac{\text{Repairs and maintenance}}{\text{Fixed assets}}$$

2. Repairs and maintenance to sales:

$$\frac{\text{Repairs and maintenance}}{\text{Sales}}$$

Example   A small business provides 2 years of data relative to its fixed assets:

	19X5	19X6
Fixed assets	$200,000	$175,000
Repairs and maintenance	7,800	4,100
Replacement cost	400,000	430,000

Replacement cost is the cost to replace the existing fixed asset with a new one.

There is now less maintenance of facilities, as indicated by the lower ratio of repairs to fixed assets—from 3.9 percent ($7,800/$200,000) in 19X5 to 2.3 percent ($4,100/$175,000) in 19X6, the substantially higher replacement cost relative to historical cost of the fixed assets, and the reduction in property, plant, and equipment from 19X5 to 19X6.

HOW IS IT USED AND APPLIED?   Failure to perform adequate maintenance on productive assets and failure to replace obsolete fixed assets with new and more efficient equipment will cause manufacturing and operating problems. By understanding the implications of these repair and maintenance ratios, the owner will be able to investigate possible problems, thus reducing the risk that these failures may have a long-term negative effect on the business.

75 Maintenance and Repair Index

INTRODUCTION.   The *maintenance and repair index* reveals how much maintenance and repair time was needed for each direct hour of labor. The ratio is best used to compare groups of similar machinery.

Maintenance and repair index

$$= \frac{\text{maintenance and repair hours}}{\text{total direct labor hours}}$$

Example Harry Cohen is evaluating the condition of machinery in his manufacturing business. He wants to evaluate the following information:

	19X8	19X9
Maintenance and repair hours	500	1,500
Total direct labor hours	30,000	28,000
Maintenance and repair hours to total direct labor	1.7%	5.4%

The analysis shows that the increase in the ratio from 19X8 to 19X9 is unfavorable. It indicates that more maintenance and repairs are being required, which indicates that the small business is sustaining more problems with its machinery.

HOW IS IT USED AND APPLIED? The extent of repairs necessary compared to direct labor input may reflect the quality of manufacturing equipment. An increasing trend in the percentage may reveal that the business has had to cope with an increasing number of machinery malfunctions.

76 Utilization of Space

INTRODUCTION. A business should use its space fully, not waste it. Floor space should generate sufficient revenue to justify the cost. If this is not the case, the space is not profitable and perhaps the location should be abandoned or the company moved elsewhere. Business activity is compared to space as a measure of effective utilization and efficiency.

There should be sound planning to assure that employees have just enough space in which to do their jobs effectively and safely, and which is healthy (e.g., enough air), and psychologically pleasing (e.g., sufficient lighting).

Parking lot space should be sufficient to accommodate customers and employees. However, the space should not be excessive because of the high cost associated with land.

Because real estate costs are significant for owned property, it is important to generate adequate earnings to cover the cost.

For rented property, rental charges are typically significant. Rents may be tied to a price index and/or vary with sales. Rents are typically higher in newer locations than in older ones because of the higher cost of construction. Further, rents in urban areas are higher than in rural areas because urban land is more expensive. The ratio of rent expense to sales indicates how well space is being used in the manufacturing process.

HOW IS IT COMPUTED?   There are several ways to calculate the efficiency of space use, using sales, production, profitability, customer base, staff level, and rentals.

$$\text{Revenue per square foot} = \frac{\text{net sales}}{\text{square feet of space}}$$

$$\text{Production per square foot} = \frac{\text{total units produced}}{\text{square feet of space}}$$

$$\text{Profit per square foot} = \frac{\text{net income}}{\text{square feet of space}}$$

$$\text{Customer space} = \frac{\text{number of customers}}{\text{square feet of space}}$$

$$\text{Employee space} = \frac{\text{square feet of space}}{\text{number of employees}}$$

$$\text{Parking lot space} = \frac{\text{square feet of parking lot space}}{\text{number of customers}}$$

$$\text{Rent per square foot} = \frac{\text{rent expense}}{\text{square feet of space}}$$

$$\text{Rent expense ratio} = \frac{\text{rent expense}}{\text{net sales}}$$

Expenses per square foot for owned property

$$= \frac{\text{expenses of owning property}}{\text{square feet of space}}$$

where expenses of owning property include insurance, real estate taxes, depreciation, maintenance, and utilities.

Example A small business owner uses the following information to appraise how well space in his business is being used:

	19X6	19X7
Sales	$3,000,000	$4,000,000
Net income	1,000,000	1,500,000
Units produced	200,000	250,000
Square feet	100,000	100,000

The relevant ratios are:

	19X6	19X7
Revenue per square foot	$30	$40
Profit per square foot	10	15
Production per square foot	2.0	2.5

The ratios show better utilization of space in generating revenue, profit, and production volume in 19X7. The business has experienced an improved level of efficiency over the period 19X6–19X7.

HOW IS IT USED AND APPLIED? A decline in the ratios of (1) net sales to space and (2) number of customers to space are negative indicators, because they show improper space planning and usage. Perhaps the business is losing accounts or the space is just too large. These ratios will differ significantly among various types of businesses. For example, a business with a few small accounts that requires a large showroom will have a low ratio. However, a mail-order business with many customers and high-priced merchandise operating out of a small office will have a high ratio.

Space ratios can be used to determine whether square footage should be expanded or contracted. Further, if rental charges for space occupied are excessive, the lease should be modified at its expiration or the company moved to a new location.

The profit return on space is also important to consider when deciding whether to expand or relocate. In indicates whether the space used historically generated acceptable profit levels.

A determination should be made as to whether plant space is being utilized effectively in production. An attempt should be made to keep rental costs down without sacrificing units produced.

The sales-to-space ratio should be examined to determine whether the space used is providing an adequate return in the form of revenue generation. This is particularly true when leasing is very expensive. An example is a retail store in a fashionable neighborhood. High-rent locations may be suitable for high-priced items but not low-priced ones. In the latter case, the revenue obtained may be inadequate to cover the significant rental payments.

The rent-to-space ratio of a business may be compared to other competitors to determine the management of space. In evaluating the space of a new location, consideration should be given to geographic location to meet customer needs, security, public transportation, and zoning requirements.

If the ratio of rent expense to sales is decreasing, this may indicate business growth. There is efficient utilization of physical facilities.

The business should establish space standards by job description. For example, executives may have private rooms, whereas factory workers may have small workstations.

77 Efficiency Measurements

INTRODUCTION. It is important to gauge the efficiency and effectiveness of your small business so as to maximize profitability. Are your capital assets and operations efficient in carrying on the daily activities of the business? Have sales and earnings grown consistently over the years?

HOW IS IT COMPUTED? Three common measures of efficiency involve profit margin, return on total assets, and return on physical plant:

$$\text{Profit margin} = \frac{\text{net income}}{\text{sales}}$$

$$\text{Return on total assets} = \frac{\text{net income}}{\text{total assets}}$$

$$\text{Return on property, plant, and equipment} = \frac{\text{net income}}{\text{productive assets}}$$

Example A small business experienced the following for the period 19X3 to 19X4:

	19X3	19X4
Sales	$600,000	$900,000
Total assets	300,000	310,000
Net income	60,000	200,000

An analysis of the data reveals the following:

$$\text{Increase in sales} = \frac{\$300,000}{\$600,000} = 50\%$$

$$\text{Increase in profit} = \frac{\$140,000}{\$60,000} = 233\%$$

	19X3	19X4
Profit margin	$\dfrac{\$60,000}{\$600,000} = 10\%$	$\dfrac{\$200,000}{\$900,000} = 22.2\%$
Return on assets	$\dfrac{\$60,000}{\$300,000} = 20\%$	$\dfrac{\$200,000}{\$310,000} = 64.5\%$

Worker efficiency has improved sharply, since sales generated per employee increased from $1200 per employee ($60,000/50) to $3333 per employee ($200,000/60). These are all very positive efficiency and productive trends.

HOW IS IT USED AND APPLIED? Compare profitability to sales and assets to ascertain the success of the small business. Cost controls and/or better manufacturing procedures may be needed to bolster profits.

There are other ways to determine how efficient your business is; which of these measures you use depends a great deal on your industry. You may wish to look at several.

- Input/output relationship—What was put in the product or service in terms of time and cost and what was gotten out in terms of quantity, quality, and revenue. Was the effort expended worth the results attained?

- New products.

- New customer accounts.

- Manufacturing costs to units produced.
- Production volume to labor hours.
- Reduced equipment downtime.
- Trends in sales and profit.
- The number of years of profitable operations.
- Trends in production volume.
- Trends in market share.

See Sec. 137, Employee Efficiency.

78 Direct Costs-to-Sales Ratios

INTRODUCTION. Direct costs include direct materials, direct labor, direct factory overhead, and other costs such as direct travel and computer usage. Direct costs relate *directly* to the product or service. Direct cost ratios are commonly used in analyzing operating costs. Indirect costs, on the other hand, are difficult to trace directly to specific revenue.

HOW IS IT COMPUTED? There are several ratios to relate costs to sales, such as looking at direct material, direct labor, overhead, and travel.

$$\text{Direct material to sales} = \frac{\text{direct material}}{\text{sales}}$$

$$\text{Direct labor to sales} = \frac{\text{direct labor}}{\text{sales}}$$

$$\text{Direct factory overhead to sales} = \frac{\text{direct factory overhead}}{\text{sales}}$$

Other indirect costs to sales include:

$$\text{Direct travel to sales} = \frac{\text{direct travel}}{\text{sales}}$$

$$\text{Computer usage to sales} = \frac{\text{computer usage}}{\text{sales}}$$

and so on.

Example The following information is provided for a small business:

	19X1	19X2
Direct labor	$1,100,000	$1,200,000
Direct factory overhead	$1,150,000	$1,340,000
Sales	$1,000,000	$1,200,000

The relevant ratios are:

	19X1	19X2
Direct labor to sales	10%	16.7%
Factory overhead to sales	15	28.3

The increase in production costs compared to sales over the year indicates less efficiency and productivity in the manufacturing process than in the past. Cost excesses have taken place, which might indicate inadequate supervision and planning.

HOW IS IT USED AND APPLIED? The production manager should analyze the ratios of production cost elements to sales. The reasons for changes in the ratios should be identified as a basis on which to estimate and plan production. If production costs increase significantly as a percentage of sales, it is a negative indication with regard to the business's manufacturing operations. In this case, the owner should ask if cost control was lacking, and if so, who was at fault. The owner must identify whether the problem is internal (e.g., poor supervision) or external (e.g., general economic problems) and take corrective steps.

If, for example, analysis reveals that delivery charges have skyrocketed compared to sales, investigation should determine whether the reason is poor traffic routing and planning or increased fuel costs.

Preparing Financial Statements and Charts

79 Balance Sheet Basics

INTRODUCTION. The *balance sheet* presents the assets, liabilities, and owner's capital of a small business and enables the owner to evaluate its financial condition. The balance sheet is cumulative and thereby differs from the income statement, which shows the profit earned for a given time interval only.

The balance sheet lists the type and amount of each asset, liability, and capital account (if partners) as of the last day of the reporting period. This listing is necessary so that the proprietor knows the specific items that he or she owns (i.e., cash, inventory, equipment), what is owed (accounts payable, loans payable), and the amount of ending equity in the business (capital). The equity at the end of the period consists of the capital investments made plus the profits earned less any withdrawals.

The balance sheet is classified into major groups of assets and liabilities in order to facilitate analysis of the financial health of the business.

Assets may be broken down into the following categories.

Current assets are those assets which are expected to be converted into cash within 1 year. Examples are cash, accounts receivable, and inventory.

Fixed assets are assets employed in the production of goods or services and having a life greater than 1 year. They have tangible physical substance and include land, building, machinery, and automobiles. Unlike inventory, these assets are not being held for sale in the normal course of business.

Intangible assets are assets with a long-term life that *lack* physical substance, such as a right granted by the government (patent) or by another company (franchise or license). An example is the right acquired by paying a fee to open a fast-food franchise.

High-risk assets may involve future write-offs. An example of a high-risk asset is obsolete inventory, receivables from financially troubled customers, rental equipment not actually being leased, and undesirable real estate.

Liabilities may be classed as either current or noncurrent. One year is the demarcation line.

HOW IS IT COMPUTED?

$$\text{Assets} - \text{liabilities} = \text{capital}$$

A SMALL BUSINESS
Balance Sheet
December 31, 19XX

Current Assets
  Cash
  Receivables
  Inventory
  Office Supplies
Fixed Assets
  Automobiles
  Less: Accumulated Depreciation
  Equipment
  Less: Accumulated Depreciation
Intangible Assets
  Franchise Fees
Total Assets

Current Liabilities
  Accrued Expenses Payable
  Accounts Payable
  Short-term Loans Payable
Noncurrent Liabilities
  Mortgage Payable
  Long-term Loans Payable

Total Liabilities

Owner's Equity
  Mr. A, Capital
Total Liabilities and Capital

$$\text{Realization risk in assets} = \frac{\text{high risk assets}}{\text{total assets}}$$

Example 1

CHARLENE DRAKE
Balance Sheet
October 31, 19XX

Assets			
Cash			$10,000
Accounts Receivable			20,500
Office Supplies			10,500
Office Equipment			30,000
Total Assets			$71,000
Liabilities and Capital			
Liabilities			
Accounts Payable			$30,000
Capital			
Balance, Oct. 1, 19XX		$35,600	
Net Income for Oct.	$5,800		
Less: Withdrawals	400		
Increase in Capital		5,400	
Total Capital			41,000
Total Liabilities and Capital			$71,000

Example 2

JOHN WESTON
Classified Balance Sheet
December 31, 19XX

Assets
  Current Assets

Cash	$ 3,000	
Accounts Receivable	6,000	
Inventory	5,000	
Office Supplies	1,000	
Total Current Assets		$15,000

Long-Term Investments

Investment in X Company Stock		2,000

Property, Plant, and Equipment

Land	$20,000	
Building	30,000	
Machinery	7,000	
Delivery Truck	5,000	
Total Property, Plant, and Equipment		62,000

Intangible Assets

Patents		$ 3,000

Deferred Charges

Deferred Moving Costs		1,000
Total Assets		$83,000

Liabilities and Capital
  Current Liabilities

Accounts Payable	$8,000	
Notes Payable (9 months)	4,000	
Accrued Liabilities	2,000	
Total Current Liabilities		$14,000

Noncurrent Liabilities

Mortgage Payable		30,000
Total Liabilities		$44,000
Capital, Dec. 31		39,000
Total Liabilities and Capital		$83,000

HOW IS IT USED AND APPLIED?   The balance sheet is useful to the owner of a small business for evaluation and control purposes, because it indicates what resources the business has and what it owes. For example, an analysis of the balance sheet can help the owner to determine whether there are sufficient resources to pay debt.

The balance sheet position will tell the owner whether it will be easy or difficult to obtain credit based on the business's financial position.

The owner is interested in the quality of the assets in terms of the amount and timing of the realization into cash. Asset quality is affected by economic conditions and the nature of business operations.

In evaluating the financial well-being of the business, the owner should compare the balance sheet numbers to those of competing small businesses and industry averages. In addition, he or she should look at the trend in balance sheet accounts (e.g., cash, inventory) over the years to identify potential problems.

80 Profit and Loss Statement

INTRODUCTION. The income statement reports the revenue less the expenses of a business. If total revenue exceeds total expenses, there is a profit. The profit will increase the owner's equity in the business. In the opposite case, there is a loss.

Revenue is the increase in capital arising from the sale of merchandise (as by a retail business) or the performance of services (as by an engineer).

Expenses decrease capital and result from performing those functions necessary to generate revenue. The amount of an expense is equal to the cost of the inventory sold, the value of the services rendered (e.g., salaries expense), or the expenditures necessary for conducting business operations (e.g., rent expense) during the period. *Selling expenses* are those incurred to obtain the sale (e.g., advertising, salesperson salaries) and in distributing the merchandise to the customer (e.g., freight paid on a shipment). *General and administrative expenses* apply to the costs of running the business as a whole and do not relate to the selling function. Examples are office salaries and depreciation on office furniture.

Other revenue (expense) relates to incidental sources of revenue and expense of a *nonoperating* nature. These revenue or expense sources do not apply to the major activities of the business. They are typically of a financial nature. Examples are interest income and interest expense.

HOW IS IT COMPUTED?

A SERVICE BUSINESS
Income Statement
For the Year Ended December 31, 19XX

Revenue (professional fees earned, commission income)
Less: Expenses
Net Income

A business that has inventory (retail store, manufacturer, wholesaler) shows the following income statement:

A RETAIL STORE
Income Statement
For the Year Ended December 31, 19XX

Sales
Less: Cost of Goods (Merchandise) Sold
    Beginning Inventory + Purchases (or Cost of Goods Manufactured) =
    Cost of Goods Available − Ending Inventory
Cost of Goods Sold
Gross Profit
Less: Operating Expenses
    Selling Expenses
    General and Administrative Expenses
Net Income

Example 1 Charlene Drake is a self-employed engineer. For the month of October 19XX, she earned income of $10,000 from services rendered. Her business expenses were: telephone, $1000; electricity, $500; rent, $2000; secretarial salary, $300; and office supplies used, $400. Her income statement for the period is as follows:

CHARLENE DRAKE
Income Statement
For the Month Ended October 31, 19XX

Revenue from Professional Services		$10,000
Less: Operating Expenses		
Telephone	$1,000	
Electricity	500	
Rent	2,000	
Secretarial Salary	300	
Office Supplies	400	
Total Operating Expenses		4,200
Net Income		$ 5,800

Example 2

JOHN WESTON
Classified Income Statement
For the Year Ended December 31, 19XX

Revenue			
Gross Sales		$40,000	
Less: Sales Returns and Allowances	$1,000		
Sales Discounts	500	1,500	
Net Sales			$38,500
Cost of Goods Sold			
Inventory, Jan. 1		$ 1,000	
Add: Purchases		15,000	
Cost of Goods Available for Sale		$16,000	
Less: Inventory, Dec. 31		5,000	
Cost of Goods Sold			11,000
Gross Profit			$27,500

Operating Expenses			
Selling Expenses			
Advertising	$3,000		
Salespeople's Salaries	2,000		
Travel and Entertainment	1,000		
Depreciation on Delivery Truck	500	$ 6,500	
General and Administrative Expenses			
Officers' Salaries	$5,000		
Rent	2,000		
Insurance	1,000	8,000	
Total Operating Expenses			$14,500
Operating Income			$13,000
Other Expenses (net)			
Interest Expense		$ 2,000	
Less: Interest Income	$ 500		
Dividend Income	1,000	1,500	
Other Expenses (net)			500
Net Income			$12,500

HOW IS IT USED AND APPLIED? The income statement provides a detailed listing of the sources and amounts of revenues and expenses. This breakdown allows the owner to determine trends in revenue and expense items. For example, if revenue is decreasing, the owner will want to know why and how sales can be improved. The owner will want to know if a given expense item (e.g., telephone) is disproportionately large so that he or she can determine the reasons why and possibly control that expense item.

An analysis of the income statement indicates the current and future earning power of the business. The owner is interested in the effect of decisions on profitability.

The income statement shows whether the small business is making money for the period. It indicates whether revenue is sufficient to meet expenses. It reveals whether costs are excessive and need to be reduced. It also reveals the productivity of the business.

Income statements covering different time periods are easily compared; the comparison over time of revenue sources, expense items, and the relationship between them might reveal areas requiring attention and corrective action. For example, if service revenue or sales have declined sharply over the past several months, action is needed to reverse this trend.

If profit relative to sales is down, it may indicate the failure to control costs.

The owner should compare labor growth to sales: Labor costs may be disproportionate to operational activity.

The owner uses the income statement to evaluate past performance, which, to some extent, is indicative of success in the future.

81 Ratios, Proportions, and Percentages

INTRODUCTION. As a small business owner, you have to make sense out of the numbers in the financial statements prepared for your business. Therefore, the numbers must be put in a meaningful context.

A *ratio* compares two or more numbers (quantities, costs). Further, a cost can be allocated according to a ratio.

A *proportion* occurs when two ratios are equal, such as 2:1 = 4:2.

The term *percent* (%) means per 100. Therefore, 60 percent is the same as 60/100 (or 0.60 or 6/10 or 3/5).

HOW IS IT COMPUTED? A ratio may be expressed as:

$$\frac{a}{b}$$

A percentage of an item to the total may be computed as follows:

$$\frac{\text{Item amount}}{\text{Total}}$$

A proportion expresses the equality of two ratios:

$$\frac{a}{b} = \frac{c}{d}$$

In a *direct proportion,* as one ratio increases (decreases), so does the other. In an *inverse proportion,* as one ratio increases, the other decreases, and vice versa.

A *percentage* is obtained by multiplying a number (called the *base*) by a percent (called the *rate*):

$$\text{Percentage} = \text{rate} \times \text{base}$$

or

$$\text{Rate} = \frac{\text{percentage}}{\text{base}}$$

or

$$\text{Base} = \frac{\text{percentage}}{\text{rate}}$$

Example 1 If profit is $60,000, and sales are $1,200,000, the profit margin is 5 percent.

Example 2 To allocate $200,000 of profit to three partners in the ratio of 5:4:1,

$$\frac{5}{10} \times \$200,000 = \qquad \$100,000$$
$$\frac{4}{10} \times \$200,000 = \qquad 80,000$$
$$\frac{1}{10} \times \$200,000 = \qquad \underline{20,000}$$
$$\qquad\qquad\qquad\qquad \underline{\$200,000}$$

When one term in a proportion is missing, cross-multiplication will find it.

Example 3 A new owner of a small business wants to determine how much profit should be earned relative to the amount invested. To do so, he will compare it against an existing competitor. The competitor reports a profit of $100,000 on a total investment of $200,000. The new owner invests $40,000. The expected profit is $20,000, as computed below:

$$x{:}40 = 100{:}200$$

$$\frac{x}{40} = \frac{100}{200}$$

$$200x = 400$$

$$x = 20$$

Example 4 For the first 3 months of the year, advertising costs were $5000, while sales volume was $100,000. The owner of the business wants to know the relationship between advertising and sales.

$$\$5,000{:}\$100,000 = 5{:}100 = 1{:}20$$

Example 5 A construction job requires 8 workers for 6 days. The owner wants to know how many workers will be needed to complete the job in 2 fewer days.

$$\frac{x}{8} = \frac{6}{4}$$

$$4x = 48$$

$$x = 12 \text{ workers}$$

Example 6 Phil invests $60,000 and Bill invests $20,000 in their partnership. It is agreed that profits will be shared in the same proportion as the capital investment. If Phil's share of the profit is $15,000, then Bill receives

$$\frac{\$60,000}{\$20,000} = \frac{\$15,000}{x}$$

$$\frac{3}{1} = \frac{\$15,000}{x}$$

$$3x = \$15,000$$

$$x = \$5,000$$

Example 7   A business owner wants to know what her income was last year if she was in the 40 percent tax bracket and paid $25,000 in taxes.

$$\text{Base} = \frac{\text{percentage}}{\text{rate}} = \frac{\$25,000}{0.40} = \$62,500$$

Another useful calculation is:

New quantity = original quantity + increase (or − decrease)

Example 8   A small business had inventory on 1/1/19X2 of 650 units. In the first quarter of the year, the inventory increased by 10 percent. The inventory on 3/31/19X2 was:

$$\text{New quantity} = \text{original quantity} + \text{increase}$$

$$= 650 + 65 = 715$$

Example 9   The price of a product, including an 8 percent sales tax, was $25. The price of the product itself is determined as follows:

$$\text{New quantity} = \text{original quantity} + \text{increase}$$

$$\$25 = x + 8\%x$$

$$\$25 = 1.08x$$

$$\frac{\$25}{1.08} = x$$

$$\$23.15 = x$$

Example 10   After a 20 percent discount, the selling price of a product is $80. The regular price is found as:

$$\text{New quantity} = \text{original quantity} - \text{decrease}$$

$$\$80 = x - 0.20x$$

$$\$80 = 0.80x$$

$$\frac{\$80}{0.80} = x$$

$$\$100 = x$$

The discount is:

$$\$100 - \$80 = \$20$$

To obtain the equivalent before-tax rate of return on a tax-free investment, we use the following formula:

$$\frac{\text{Tax-free rate of return}}{1 - \text{tax rate}}$$

Example 11 The equivalent before-tax rate of return of earning 4 percent on a tax-free bond assuming a 30 percent tax bracket is:

$$\frac{0.04}{1 - t} = \frac{0.04}{1 - 0.03} = \frac{0.04}{0.7} = 5.7\%$$

HOW IS IT USED AND APPLIED? A comparison of numbers in the form of a ratio is more enlightening than either of the numbers individually. For example, the profit of a business can be compared to the total assets in the business and to sales to obtain rates of return. Ratios can be compared to those of similar businesses to determine relative position. Percentages make it easier to determine the importance of each item (e.g., costs, product revenue) in relation to the total (e.g., total costs, total product revenue) and to each other. Percentages are also useful in determining the percentage change in an item over time. For example, a 60 percent increase in sales over a 1-year period is a very favorable sign.

The business owner may use proportions in connection with producing products. In other words, a mix of products may be manufactured to result in a combination generating the highest overall profit for the business.

82 Charts and Graphs

INTRODUCTION. A small business manager can use charts and graphs to show visually important information in an interesting way. Charts may be used to indicate sales dollars or units, costs, profits, or number of employees.

There are three types of graphs. A *line graph* shows change over time. A *bar graph* compares related information and may present relative importance. A *circle (pie) graph* presents a unit's contribution to the whole. The graph should be accompanied by an explanation. For example, a comment may be made about the trend and the reasons for changes in direction.

HOW IS IT PREPARED? The chart or graph should be at the proper place within a report or presentation. There should be a balance between visual presentation and narrative discussion.

To condense the information on a graph so it is clear, legends and footnotes may be used below the graph. The title should appear above the graph. If the graph needs an explanation of a part(s), it should be annotated with small notes on the side of it.

A line graph is shown in Fig. 82.1, a bar graph in Fig. 82.2, and a circle graph in Fig. 82.3.

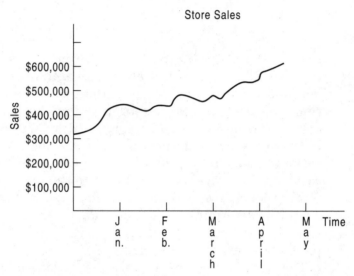

Figure 82.1 A line graph.

Figure 82.2 A bar graph.

Total Sales by Geographic Area

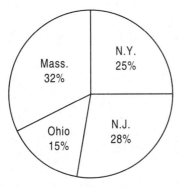

Figure 82.3 A circle graph.

Example 1 A chart may appear as follows:

Summary of Employees		
Category	19X7	19X6
Increases		
Clerical	23	20
Operations	<u>18</u>	<u>16</u>
Total	<u>41</u>	<u>36</u>
Sales	$600,000	$400,000

The chart indicates that there was a 13.9 percent (5/46) increase in staff due to increased work load. The higher labor cost was well worth it, because of the significant increase in sales revenue (50 percent) generated from new business.

HOW IS IT USED AND APPLIED? Charts and graphs may be used by the small business manager to show financial and non- financial information in an understandable manner, especially to those who are not familiar with the business. Further, presenting a group of complex numbers and calculations may bore and confuse readers. Visual presentations may be able to communicate mathematical information in digestible form. Visual discussions may be helpful in staff meetings, presentations to lenders and investors, and when courting potential customers.

Analyses of sales, production, and advertising are types of trend data that work well in graphic form. They can be shown as both budgeted and actual figures, and may be given by month and year.

How Healthy Is the Business?

83 Comparing Accounts over the Years (Horizontal Analysis)

INTRODUCTION. *Horizontal analysis* is a time series analysis of financial statements covering more than one accounting period. Horizontal analysis looks at the percentage change in an account over time. It shows direction. Vertical analysis is covered in the next section.

HOW IS IT COMPUTED?

$$\text{Percentage change} = \frac{\text{dollar change}}{\text{base year amount}} = \frac{\text{year 2} - \text{year 1}}{\text{year 1}}$$

Example Horizontal analysis across two years yields the following outcome: If sales in 19X8 and 19X9 were $100,000 and $300,000, respectively, the increase is $200,000/$100,000 = 200 percent.

HOW IS IT USED AND APPLIED? By examining the magnitude and direction of a financial statement item, an owner can evaluate the reasonableness of the trend. A five-year period of analysis is recommended.

Trend analysis identifies areas of wide divergence, and alerts owners to the need for further evaluation. For example, a large increase in sales returns and allowances coupled with a decrease in sales would be a cause for concern. An owner might compare these results with those of competitors to investigate whether the problem is industrywide, or particular to the business.

The trend may be distorted for a one-time unusual item, and therefore the financial figures should be adjusted to exclude the extraordinary item. Examples are a one-time substantial gain from the sale of land held for 50 years, and a one-time government contract.

See Sec. 84, Comparing Accounts within the Current Year.

84 Comparing Accounts within the Current Year

INTRODUCTION. In *common size (vertical)* analysis of financial statements, an item is used as a base value and all other accounts in the financial statement are compared to this base value.

HOW IS IT COMPUTED? On the balance sheet, total assets equal 100 percent. In vertical analysis, each asset is stated as a percentage of total assets. Similarly, total liabilities and stockholders' equity are assigned 100 percent, with a given liability or equity account stated as a percentage of total liabilities and stockholders' equity.

On the income statement, 100 percent is assigned to net sales, with all revenue and expense accounts then related to it.

The following examples illustrate vertical analysis of financial statement data for Tie City.

Example 1

Net sales	$300,000	100%
Less: Cost of sales	60,000	20
Gross profit	$240,000	80%
Less: Operating expenses	150,000	50
Net income	$ 90,000	30%

Example 2

Current assets	$200,000	25%
Noncurrent assets	600,000	75
Total assets	$800,000	100%

HOW IS IT USED AND APPLIED? Common size percentages can be compared from one period to another to identify areas that require improvements in performance.

Vertical analysis tends to exhibit the internal structure of the small business, indicating the relation of each income statement account to revenue. It shows clearly the mix of assets that produces the income and the mix of sources of capital, regardless of whether they are provided by current or long-term liabilities or by owners' capital.

The vertical percentages of a particular small business should be compared to those of competing businesses or to industry percentages so that relative position may be ascertained.

As in horizontal analysis, vertical analysis is not an end in itself. The owner must be prepared to probe deeper into the areas that the analysis indicates may have possible problems.

See Sec. 83, Comparing Accounts over the Years (Horizontal Analysis).

85 How to Use Index Numbers

INTRODUCTION.   An *index number* is a percentage by which an amount in a given year is expressed as a ratio to a base-year figure. Index numbers can be used for quantity, price, and value. Index numbers can be used to make clearer relationships among financial figures. In an *index-number trend series*, an index is assigned to a base year and values for other years are computed by reference to the base year.

HOW IS IT COMPUTED?   A base year that is most representative (typical, normal) of the business's operations is selected and assigned an index of 100. All index numbers are computed with regard to the base year. When there is a very long time period under examination (e.g., 10 years), the base year may be based on an average of a few years (e.g., 3 years).

$$\text{Index} = \frac{\text{current year amount}}{\text{base-year amount}}$$

Caution: As with the computation of year-to-year percentage changes, certain fluctuations in a series, such as changes from negative to positive amounts, cannot be expressed by means of index numbers.

An index number for production cost might be based on price per unit in a typical year. For example, if the price per unit was $20 in the first year (selected as the base year), the owner would just multiply the units produced in each year by the base price per unit to derive a constant-dollar amount of production.

There are several types of indexes and several ways to compute them. They include single, composite, value, Paasche, and link indices.

A *single index number* is used to compare individual products, while an *aggregate (composite) index number* applies to a group of products.

$$\text{Single index} = \frac{p_n \text{ or } q_n}{p_0 \text{ or } q_0}$$

where p_n = price of the product in a given year
p_0 = price of the product in the base year
q_n = quantity of the product in a given year
q_0 = quantity of the product in the base year

Note: Quantity may be expressed in terms of either units produced or units sold.

A *value index* is the price of the product multiplied by the units sold (or produced).

$$\text{Value index} = \frac{p_n q_n}{p_0 q_0}$$

To be useful, a composite index should be *weighted* based on the quantities of the product involved. For example, a price index of 120 for product X in a given year means that it was 20 percent higher in price than that in the base year—a single index. A price index of 140 percent for products A–Z is a composite index because it applies to a *basket* (more than one) of products.

Laspeyres' composite index weights the prices by the quantities of the *base year.* It is expressed as:

$$I(\text{L}) = \frac{\Sigma p_n q_0}{\Sigma p_0 q_0}$$

where Σ = sum

Paasche's index, unlike the Laspeyres' index, uses the *current year's* quantities as the weights. It is expressed as:

$$I(\text{P}) = \frac{\Sigma p_n q_n}{\Sigma p_0 q_n}$$

A *link relative index* always uses as the base the immediately preceding year. The index number is a percentage comparison to the prior year, which is beneficial when making year-to-year comparisons. However, this index formulation is *not* useful in deriving long-run comparisons.

If the owner wants to change the base to a more recent year to make it more up to date, than the original index should be divided by the index of the newly prescribed base year:

$$\text{Index (shifted)} = \frac{\text{original index}}{\text{old index of new base year}}$$

Example 1   The base year is 19X1 and sales for that year are $600,000. An index number of 100 is assigned to 19X1. Sales for 19X2 and 19X3 are $660,000 and $500,000, respectively. The appropriate index numbers are:

$$19\text{X2:} \qquad \frac{\$660,000}{\$600,000} = 110$$

$$19X3: \quad \frac{\$500,000}{\$600,000} = 83$$

An owner who sees this type of sharp decline in sales in 19X3 should study the causes and identify responsible parties.

Example 2 The price of a product in the base year was $25; today the price is $30. The price index is:

$$\frac{p_n}{p_0} = \frac{\$30}{\$25} = 120\%$$

Example 3 The quantity for a product sold in 19X5 was 60,000, while in 19X0 (the base year) it was 40,000. The index is:

$$\frac{q_n}{q_0} = \frac{60,000}{40,000} = 150\%$$

Example 4 In 19X8, product X had a selling price of $10 and 30,000 units were sold; in 19X2 (the base year), the selling price was $7 and 25,000 units were sold.

$$\text{Simple value index} = \frac{p_n q_n}{p_0 q_0} = \frac{\$10 \times 30,000}{\$7 \times 25,000} = \frac{\$300,000}{\$175,000} = 171\%$$

Example 5 A small business presents the following information for its products:

	Average price		Quantities	
Product	19X2 (p_0)	19X8 (p_n)	19X2 (q_0)	19X8 (q_n)
A	$1.00	$1.10	8000	9000
B	1.20	1.40	5000	7000
C	0.80	0.90	5600	5400

The Laspeyres' composite index for 19X8 for the three products using 19X2 as the base year is:

$$I(L) = \frac{\Sigma p_n q_0}{\Sigma p_0 q_0} = \frac{\$20,840}{\$18,480} = 112.8\%$$

Product	$p_n q_0$	$p_0 q_0$
A	$ 8,800	$ 8,000
B	7,000	6,000
C	5,040	4,480
Total	$20,840	$18,480

Example 6 Assume the same information as in Example 5 except that we now compute Paasche's composite index as follows:

$$I(P) = \frac{\Sigma p_n q_n}{\Sigma p_0 q_n} = \frac{\$24{,}560}{\$21{,}720} = 113.1\%$$

Product	$p_n q_n$	$p_0 q_n$
A	$ 9,900	$ 9,000
B	9,800	8,400
C	4,860	4,320
Total	$24,560	$21,720

Example 7 A value index is to be shifted from 19X0 to 19X6. The 19X0 index was 100. The old index of 19X6 was 134. The new value index for 19X0 is:

$$\frac{100}{134} = 74.6\%$$

HOW IS IT USED AND APPLIED? Index numbers are useful in measuring and clarifying important financial data. Sales, production, and costs may be expressed in index numbers. When comparing accounts covering more than 3 years, the year-to-year method of comparison may become too cumbersome. Often the best way to examine a long-term trend is through the use of index numbers. The owner can identify any financial statement accounts or items that seem to be out of line. This includes production volume, sales volume, prices, and costs. If the trend is illogical or signals a problem, the item should be investigated. Where possible, corrective action should be taken.

86 Growth Rate

INTRODUCTION. *Growth* rate is the percentage change in earnings, sales, or total assets, compared to a base-year amount. It is also the compounded annual rate of growth in earnings.

HOW IS IT COMPUTED? The compound annual rate of growth can be computed as

$$F_n = P \cdot \text{FVIF}(i,n)$$

where $\quad F_n$ = future value in period n

$\quad P$ = present sum of money or base-period value

$\quad \mathrm{FVIF}(i,n)$ = future value factor at a specified interest rate for a stated number of periods; $= F_n/P$

The growth rate can be calculated using financial calculators and/or spreadsheet software.

Example Assume that a business has earnings of \$250,000 in 19X1, and 10 years later the earnings have increased to \$370,000. The compound annual rate of growth in earnings is computed as follows:

$$F_{10} = \$370{,}000 \quad \text{and} \quad P = \$250{,}000$$

Therefore,

$$\mathrm{FVIF}(i,10) = \frac{\$370{,}000}{\$250{,}000} = 1.48$$

From Table 1 in the Appendix, the FVIF of 1.48 at 10 years is at $i = 4$ percent. The compound annual rate of growth is therefore 4 percent.

HOW IS IT USED AND APPLIED? The growth rate is used in many ways. Owners need to know the rate of growth in earnings in order to determine how they are doing financially. Performance is best measured over a 5-year period.

CAN A COMPUTER HELP? Lotus 1-2-3 has a routine @RATE *(future-value, present-value, term)* for this calculation. Other spreadsheet programs have similar routines. Also many financial calculators include preprogrammed formulas and perform many present-value and future-value applications. They include Radio Shack, Hewlett-Packard, Sharp, and Texas Instrument models.

87 Current Ratio

INTRODUCTION. Current assets have a life of 1 year or less and include such items as cash, accounts receivable, and inventory. The *current ratio*, which is subject to seasonal variability, is used to measure the ability of a small business to pay its short-term bills out of current assets. Because it shows the margin of safety to cover any possible shrinkage in the value of current assets, it is an indicator of liquidity. The current ratio conveys the extent to which current assets are available to cover every \$1 of short-term debt.

HOW IS IT COMPUTED?

$$\text{Current ratio} = \frac{\text{current assets}}{\text{current liabilities}}$$

In general, the current ratio for a small business should be at least 2:1. The adequacy of the current ratio depends on the particular industry under examination. For a full understanding of the implications, a comparison must be made to competing small businesses.

Example A small business reports the following balance sheet information for 19X1 and 19X2:

	19X1	19X2
Current assets	$110,000	$120,000
Current liabilities	70,000	55,400
Current ratio	1.57	2.17

The trend in the ratio has improved during the year, indicating better liquidity in 19X2 than in 19X1. For example, in 19X2, for each $1 owed to short-term creditors, there is $2.17 in current assets to cover it.

HOW IS IT USED AND APPLIED? The current ratio measures the reserve of liquid funds in excess of current obligations that is available as a safety margin against uncertainty and against the random contingencies to which the flow of funds within a business is subject. Random shocks, such as strikes, extraordinary losses, and other uncertainties, can temporarily and unexpectedly stop or reduce the inflow of funds.

If the current ratio increases significantly but the quick ratio (see Sec. 88) remains constant, there may be an inventory buildup. A very high current ratio could mean that the owner is not aggressive in putting current assets to work in generating high returns. For example, cash could be invested in plant assets.

A high current ratio is needed when a business has difficulty borrowing on short notice.

A sharp decline in the current ratio indicates a deterioration in a business's liquidity, which may mean that the business will be unable to pay current debt when due. Liquidity means the readiness and speed with which current assets can be converted to cash.

A lower current ratio may mean that the owner will have greater difficulty borrowing short-term funds.

88 Quick (Acid Test) Ratio

INTRODUCTION. The *quick ratio* is a stringent test of liquidity that compares the most liquid current (quick) assets to current debt.

HOW IS IT COMPUTED?

Quick ratio

$$= \frac{\text{cash} + \text{marketable securities} + \text{accounts receivable}}{\text{current liabilities}}$$

Inventory is not included in the quick ratio because it takes a while for inventory to be converted into cash, and there is the possibility of obsolescence. Further, prepaid expenses are not included in this analysis because they cannot be converted into cash and hence are not capable of paying current liabilities.

The acid test ratio should generally be at least 1:1, but determining what is an acceptable ratio depends on the nature of the specific industry in which the small business functions. Comparisons to competing businesses and trends over time should also be made.

Example Following is balance sheet information for a small business for 19X1 and 19X2:

	19X1	19X2
Quick assets	$160,000	$150,000
Current liabilities	140,000	155,000

The acid test ratios are 1.14 for 19X1 and 0.97 for 19X2. The reduction in the ratio means less liquidity. For example, in 19X2, for each $1 in current debt, only $0.97 in quick assets are available to cover it.

HOW IS IT USED AND APPLIED? A lower quick ratio may mean that the business will have greater difficulty borrowing short-term funds. A very low ratio may signal that the owner will be unable to make his or her short-term debt payments.

89 Operating Cycle

INTRODUCTION. The *operating cycle* is the number of days taken to translate cash to inventory to accounts receivable and back to cash.

$$Cash \rightarrow Inventory \rightarrow Accounts\ receivable \rightarrow Cash$$

HOW IS IT COMPUTED?

Operating cycle = age of inventory
+ collection period on accounts receivable

Example Assume that inventory is held for 85 days, while it takes 45 days to collect from accounts receivable. The operating cycle is:

Operating cycle = 85 days + 45 days = 130 days

HOW IS IT USED AND APPLIED? The small business owner is interested in the operating cycle because it tells how long cash is tied up in inventory and receivables. A shorter operating cycle is preferred, since the freed cash can be invested for a return or used to pay bills. A shorter period also means less risk of inventory obsolescence and customer uncollectibility.

See Sec. 37, Accounts Receivable Ratios, and Sec. 39, Inventory Ratios.

90 Are Your Defensive Assets Sufficient?

INTRODUCTION. The *defensive interval* ratio is a liquidity measure that shows the small business's ability to meet its current obligations.

HOW IS IT COMPUTED?

Defensive interval ratio =
$$\frac{defensive\ assets}{projected\ daily\ operational - noncash\ charges}$$

where

Defensive assets = cash + marketable securities + receivables

Projected daily operational expenditures
$$= \text{(cost of sales + operating expenses}$$
$$+ \text{ other ordinary cash expenses)}/360$$

Example A small business has cash of $30,000, marketable securities of $38,000, receivables of $46,000, projected daily expenditures of $450,000, and noncash charges of $20,000. The defensive interval ratio is:

$$\frac{\$114,000}{(\$450,000 - \$20,000)/360} = \frac{\$114,000.00}{\$1,194.44} = 95 \text{ days} \quad \text{(rounded)}$$

This analysis shows that defensive assets can cover projected daily expenditures by 95 days.

HOW IS IT USED AND APPLIED? The defensive interval ratio indicates the time period during which the business can operate on its liquid assets without needing revenues from the next period's sources. It shows near-term liquidity as a basis for paying expenses.

91 Working Capital

INTRODUCTION. *Working capital* compares current assets to current liabilities, and indicates the liquid reserve available to meet contingencies and uncertainties. A high working capital balance is needed if the business is unable to borrow on short notice. Working capital must be compared to other financial statement elements, such as sales and total assets. A business owner can change the level of working capital to enhance profitability.

HOW IS IT COMPUTED? Several types of calculations are commonly used to evaluate working capital. They compare working capital to a balance sheet or income statement item as an indicator of liquidity.

1. Working capital = current assets − current liabilities

2. $\dfrac{\text{Working capital}}{\text{Sales}}$

3. $\dfrac{\text{Working capital}}{\text{Total assets}}$

4. Working capital provided from operations:

Net Income
Plus: Nonworking capital expenses (e.g., depreciation)
Minus: Nonworking capital revenue (e.g., amortization of deferred revenue)
Equals: Working capital provided from operations

5. $\dfrac{\text{Working capital provided from operations}}{\text{Net income}}$

6. $\dfrac{\text{Working capital provided from operations}}{\text{Total liabilities}}$

7. $\dfrac{\text{Net income}}{\text{Working capital (beginning of year)}}$

8. $\dfrac{\text{Cash}}{\text{Working capital}}$

Example A small business reports the following information:

Working capital provided from operations	$100,000
Net income	300,000
Current assets	900,000
Current liabilities	500,000
Noncurrent liabilities	600,000

The industry averages of other small businesses are:

Working capital provided from operations to total liabilities	30.5%
Working capital to net income	50.0%
Working capital	$1,100,000

The applicable ratios for the small business are:

Working capital	$400,000
Working capital provided from operations to total liabilities	9.1%
Working capital provided from operations to net income	33.3%

The analysis reveals that working capital generated from operations is inadequate to pay total debt—an outcome that indicates poor liquidity. Additionally, the business has less profits backed up by liquid funds than other businesses in the industry. Overall, the business's working capital is deficient relative to the industry averages.

HOW IS IT USED AND APPLIED? The owner should watch the level of working capital closely, because loan agreements often include stipulations regarding the maintenance of minimum working capital levels.

To identify changes in the composition of working capital, the owner should determine the trend in the percentage of each current asset to total current assets. A shift from cash to inventory, for example, indicates less liquidity.

The working capital-to-sales ratio tells whether the business is using its liquid balance optimally, and how frequently working capital is turned over during the year. Is the business controlling working capital to produce sales? A low ratio indicates the small business's ability to generate revenue from liquid funds. When sales increase, inventories also increase to meet sales demand. Accounts receivable and accounts payable also increase. The ratio indicates the relationship between purchasing and selling. A high ratio indicates cash availability for operations, but this may tie up cash and provide little return. A low ratio may make the business owner susceptible to adverse economic conditions. A problem situation occurs when sales volume increases significantly but accounts receivable are deteriorating in quality.

A high ratio of working capital provided by operations to net income is favorable, since a liquidity rating is higher when profits are backed up by liquid funds.

The ratio of working capital provided from operations to total liabilities indicates the extent to which internally generated working capital flow is available to pay obligations.

However, keep in mind that working capital is still *not* cash. You should not rely too much on working capital in an emergency. Cash is needed to pay liabilities and expenses. A high ratio of cash to working capital is desirable.

92 Liquidity Index

INTRODUCTION. The liquidity index is the number of days that current assets are removed from cash.

HOW IS IT COMPUTED?

Current asset amount × days removed from cash = total

$$\text{Index} = \frac{\text{total}}{\text{amount}} = \text{number of days}$$

Example The liquidity index for a typical small business may be computed as:

Current asset	Amount	×	Days removed from cash	=	Total
Cash	$ 20,000	×	0	=	0
Accounts receivable	50,000	×	30	=	$1,500,000
Inventory	80,000	×	50	=	4,000,000
Total	$150,000				$5,500,000

$$\text{Index} = \frac{\$5,500,000}{\$150,000} = 36.7 \text{ days}$$

HOW IS IT USED AND APPLIED? The liquidity index is used by the owner to determine a business's liquidity. The index reveals how many days it would take to convert the current assets to cash. A business with poor liquidity is viewed negatively by lenders, since it may not be able to meet its debt payments when due. The owner should be concerned with deficient liquidity, since the business may fail to operate because of insufficient funds. When liquidity difficulties exist, the owner must take corrective action.

93 Assessing Asset Utilization (Turnover)

INTRODUCTION. *Asset utilization*, or *turnover*, indicates how well business assets are utilized to generate revenue. It is a measure of efficiency and performance. A declining trend in asset utilization means that assets are not contributing adequately to production.

HOW IS IT COMPUTED? Several types of calculations are commonly used to analyze asset utilization. Each involves an examination of the ratio of sales to some other aspect of a business's assets.

1. Total asset turnover

$$\frac{\text{Sales}}{\text{Total assets}}$$

2. Sales to specific assets

$$\text{Sales to cash:} \quad \frac{\text{Sales}}{\text{Cash}}$$

Accounts receivable ratio: $\dfrac{\text{Sales}}{\text{Accounts receivable}}$

Inventory ratio: $\dfrac{\text{Sales}}{\text{Inventory}}$

Sales to working capital: $\dfrac{\text{Sales}}{\text{Working capital}}$

Fixed asset turnover: $\dfrac{\text{Sales}}{\text{Fixed assets}}$

Operating revenue to operating property:

$$\dfrac{\text{Total operating revenues}}{\text{Operating property}}$$

Sales to other assets: $\dfrac{\text{Sales}}{\text{Other assets}}$

Higher ratios reflect favorably on the business's ability to employ assets effectively.

Example Implications of the use of the total asset turnover ratio are illustrated by comparing the performance of two small businesses:

	Small Business A	Small Business B
Sales	$ 1,000,000	$20,000,000
Total assets	10,000,000	10,000,000
Turnover of assets	0.1 times	2 times

This analysis shows that for business A, each dollar invested in assets supports only $0.10 in sales, whereas business B obtains $2 of sales for each dollar invested in assets. The appropriate question that should be prompted by this analysis is to ask why business A's turnover is so low. Are there excess assets that generate little or no return? Are there idle assets that business A should dispose of? Are the assets inefficiently or uneconomically utilized?

The conclusion of this analysis is that business A can achieve more immediate and significant improvements by concentrating on improving turnover—by increasing sales, reducing its investment, or both.

HOW IS IT USED AND APPLIED? Owners understand that assets should not be held by a business unless they contribute to sales or profitability; thus, utilization of many of these turnover ratios is critical to understanding the productivity of assets. Higher ratios of asset utilization are better because they indicate that assets are more productive in producing a return. A high ratio also implies the sales are being generated at low cost. A high ratio for one industry, however, may be considered a low ratio for another. On the other hand, a low fixed asset turnover may mean that the investment in plant and equipment is excessive relative to the value of output produced. In such a case, the owner might consider consolidating operations, perhaps by selling some assets and investing the proceeds for a higher return or using the fixed assets to expand into a more financially lucrative area. A low ratio may also indicate inadequate sales.

In certain special situations, such as developmental businesses, the meaning of asset turnover may have to be modified because most assets are committed to the development of future potential. Similarly, if abnormal supply situations exist or if strikes occur, these factors affect capital utilization and require separate evaluation and interpretation.

The following provides some guidance to interpreting high and low ratios:

- A high ratio of sales to cash may be caused by a cash shortage that could eventually result in a liquidity crisis if the owner has no other ready sources of funds. A low turnover may also indicate the holding of idle cash balances, resulting in less return being earned. Cash accumulated for specific purposes or contingencies may result in a temporary drop in the turnover ratio.

- A low ratio of sales to receivables may indicate overextension of credit, and collection problems. A high ratio may point to an overly stringent credit policy.

- A low ratio of sales to inventory may indicate overstocking, slow-moving goods, overestimation of sales, or a lack of balance in inventory. A temporary problem, such as a strike at a major customer, may also be responsible. A high turnover may represent underinvestment in inventory, which can cause deficient customer service and lost sales.

- A low ratio of sales to fixed assets may signal inefficient or obsolete equipment, excess capacity, or interruptions in the supply of raw materials.

- A low ratio of operating revenue to operating property means that the business is less productive in utilizing operating property.

94 Fixed-Asset Ratios

INTRODUCTION. *Fixed-asset ratios* compare fixed assets to debt and capital. Fixed assets are assets that possess physical substance and a life in excess of 1 year. Fixed assets are bought for use in the operation of the business, such as building, machinery, and equipment. The ratio is favorable when the proceeds from and return on fixed assets substantially exceeds debt, because sufficient money will be available from the fixed assets to pay off that debt.

HOW IS IT COMPUTED? Several different kinds of fixed asset ratios are used to measure different aspects of the business. Fixed assets may be compared to total assets, debt, and owners' equity.

1. Fixed assets to short-term debt:

$$\frac{\text{Fixed assets}}{\text{Short-term debt}}$$

2. Fixed asset mix:

$$\frac{\text{Fixed assets}}{\text{Total assets}}$$

3. Fixed assets to owner's equity:

$$\frac{\text{Fixed assets}}{\text{Owner's equity}}$$

4. Funded capital ratio:

$$\frac{\text{Long-term debt} \times \text{owner's equity}}{\text{Fixed assets}}$$

Example The following information applies to a small business:

	19X1	19X2
Fixed assets	$700,000	$1,000,000
Short-term debt	300,000	400,000

The relevant ratios are:

	19X1	19X2
Fixed assets to short-term debt	2.33	2.5

There are more fixed assets compared to short-term debt in 19X2, which is a good sign.

HOW IS IT USED AND APPLIED?   A business with high short-term debt may be unable to pay current obligations if most of its money is tied up in long-term assets. Financing fixed assets with current debt is a precarious financing strategy; rather, assets should be financed with liabilities of similar maturity.

A high ratio of fixed assets to total assets means a lot of money tied up in noncurrent, illiquid property, plant, and equipment. This means less flexibility in adjusting to changes in sales and market position. A possible way to lower this ratio and improve flexibility is to sell ineffective fixed assets and either subcontract the work or rent the property, plant, and equipment. However, the difference in cost between owning the fixed assets and renting them (or subcontracting) must also be considered.

A higher ratio of fixed assets to owner's equity may indicate a buildup in inactive fixed assets, resulting in excessive costs—such as for insurance, taxes, maintenance, and storage—which will raise the breakeven point.

The funded capital ratio shows the degree to which fixed assets are financed by long-term commitments of creditors.

A high ratio of sales to floor space for machinery indicates the efficient utilization of space.

See Sec. 93, Assessing Asset Utilization (Turnover).

95 Noncurrent Assets to Noncurrent Liabilities

INTRODUCTION.   A noncurrent asset or liability has a life of 1 year or more. Examples of noncurrent assets are building, equipment, furniture, and auto. Examples of noncurrent liabilities are mortgages payable and bonds payable. The ratio of noncurrent assets to noncurrent liabilities looks primarily at the relationship between property, plant, and equipment and long-term debt.

HOW IS IT COMPUTED?

$$\frac{\text{Noncurrent assets}}{\text{Noncurrent liabilities}}$$

Example A small business has the following balance sheet information for 19X1 and 19X2:

	19X1	19X2
Property, plant, and equipment	$800,000	$700,000
Long-term liabilities	400,000	500,000

The ratio of noncurrent assets to noncurrent liabilities is 2 for 19X1 and 1.4 for 19X2. The trend in the ratio has dropped from 19X1 to 19X2, pointing to a possible solvency problem.

HOW IS IT USED AND APPLIED? A decline in the coverage of long-term debt by noncurrent assets may trigger an alarm, because fewer long-term assets are available to cover debt when it is due.

Long-term debt will eventually be paid out of long-term assets; hence, a high ratio indicates protection.

A lower ratio of noncurrent assets to noncurrent liabilities means that it may be more difficult to borrow funds and, even if you can, you will probably be charged a higher interest rate.

96 Accounts Payable Ratios

INTRODUCTION. Accounts payable ratios tell how long it takes a small business to pay its suppliers. Accounts payable ratios indicate whether the business is in a good position to obtain short-term, unsecured (no collateral) credit in the form of cost-free funds (no interest is charged by the supplier).

Although accounts payable is considered current debt, it is typically renewed automatically as long as payments are being made. Credit terms are usually good because the supplier is anxious for the customer's business.

HOW IS IT COMPUTED? Three accounts payable ratios are commonly used by small businesses.

1. Sales to accounts payable:

$$\frac{\text{Sales}}{\text{Accounts payable}}$$

2. Accounts payable to average daily purchases (also called "days purchases in accounts payable"):

$$\frac{\text{Accounts payable}}{\text{Purchase/360 days}}$$

3. Accounts payable to total assets:

$$\frac{\text{Accounts payable}}{\text{Total assets}}$$

If accounts payable fluctuate widely, an average rather than the year-end balance should be used.

Example Assume the following information for two time periods:

	Year 1	Year 2
Accounts payable	$ 50,000	$ 40,000
Purchases	800,000	750,000
Sales	2,000,000	1,300,000

The relevant ratios for each of the years are:

	Year 1	Year 2
Sales to accounts payable	$\dfrac{\$2,000,000}{\$50,000} = 40$	$\dfrac{\$1,300,000}{\$40,000} = 32.5$
Days purchases in accounts payable	$\dfrac{\$50,000}{\$800,000/360} = 22.50$	$\dfrac{\$40,000}{\$750,000/360} = 19.20$

The lower of the two sales-to-accounts payable ratios indicates the business's improved ability in year 2 to obtain short-term credit in the form of cost-free funds.

The decrease in the days purchases in accounts payable is a favorable sign because it shows that the owner is able to repay creditors more quickly in year 2 than in year 1.

HOW IS IT USED AND APPLIED? The accounts payable ratios involve a trade-off between retaining operating cash and the credit rating of the business.

Owners use accounts payable ratios as indicators of a business's financial strength. For example, if trade credit declines, as indicated by an increase in the ratio of sales to accounts payable, creditors may have less faith in the business's financial health.

The days in accounts payable determines the average number of days that it takes for the owner to pay short-term creditors. This ratio is used to measure the degree to which accounts payable represents current rather than overdue obligations. The owner should make a comparison to the terms of purchase. If vendor terms are 60 days and the payment period is 50 days, the owner is paying bills too early. The payments should be delayed so interest can be earned.

A decline in the payment period may indicate that the business is taking advantage of prompt payment discounts or is using shorter purchase terms as leverage in negotiating with suppliers for lower prices. An increase in the payment period may indicate that the business is having financial difficulties, requiring it to stretch out its payables; on the other hand, this situation could also indicate that the business is managing its payables well, taking greater advantage of interest-free financing by delaying payments to creditors.

Remember: Stretching payables may work in the short term, but will have long-term negative effects on credit reputation. If payments must be slowed, explain why to suppliers and try to make partial payments.

97 Current Liability Ratios

INTRODUCTION. Current liabilities are those due within 1 year, such as accounts payable, taxes payable, accrued expenses payable, and short-term notes payable.

Current liability ratios show the extent to which current debt payments will be required within the year. Understanding a business's liability position is critical, because if it is unable to pay current debt, it is illiquid.

HOW IS IT COMPUTED?

1. Current liabilities to noncurrent liabilities:

$$\frac{\text{Current liabilities}}{\text{Noncurrent liabilities}}$$

2. Current liabilities to total liabilities:

$$\frac{\text{Current liabilities}}{\text{Total liabilities}}$$

These ratios can be compared to industry averages.

Example   Assume the following financial data for a small business:

Current liabilities	$ 500,000
Noncurrent liabilities	600,000
Total liabilities	1,100,000

The relevant ratios are:

Current liabilities to noncurrent liabilities	83.3%
Current liabilities to total liabilities	45.5

These are compared to industry norms:

Current liabilities to noncurrent liabilities	45.0%
Current liabilities to total liabilities	24.0

The business's liquidity is unfavorable relative to the industry norm, as indicated by the business's high level of current debt.

HOW IS IT USED AND APPLIED?   A high ratio of current liabilities to total liabilities indicates low business liquidity, because the portion of current debt is greater. If the ratio is high, the owner should take steps to reduce the business's excessive short-term debt—steps such as financing on a long-term basis, or selling assets to obtain funds.

98 How Much Debt Do You Have, and Can You Pay It?

INTRODUCTION.   *Leverage ratios* indicate the degree of debt within a small business's capital structure and its ability to pay the debt. Financial leverage results from the owner's use of debt financing and leasing.

HOW IS IT COMPUTED?   Ten leverage ratios are used in analyzing a small business's financial position.

1. $\text{Debt/equity ratio} = \dfrac{\text{total liabilities}}{\text{total capital}}$

2. $\dfrac{\text{Long-term debt}}{\text{Total capital}}$

3. Debt ratio = $\dfrac{\text{total liabilities}}{\text{total assets}}$

4. Capital structure ratio =

$$\dfrac{\text{average long-term debt}}{\text{long-term debt plus owner's equity}}$$

5. $\dfrac{\text{Owner's equity}}{\text{Borrowed capital}}$

Owner's equity includes the owner's capital investment plus profit earned over the years less any withdrawals.

6. $\dfrac{\text{Interest}}{\text{Borrowed capital}}$

7. $\dfrac{\text{Average working capital}}{\text{Average funded debt}}$

8. $\dfrac{\text{Average current liabilities}}{\text{Owner's equity}}$

9. Financial leverage index = $\dfrac{\text{return on owner's equity}}{\text{return on total assets}}$

10. Financial leverage ratio = $\dfrac{\text{total assets}}{\text{owner's equity}}$

Note: Total capital and owner's equity are interchangeable terms.

Example Leverage ratio information is derived from a small business's balance sheet:

Long-term liabilities	$500,000
Total liabilities	700,000
Owner's equity	300,000
Cash flow provided from operations	100,000

The business's ratios are:

Long-term debt to owner's equity	1.67
Cash flow to long-term liabilities	0.2
Total liabilities to owner's equity	2.33

These are compared to average norms taken from competitors:

Long-term debt to owner's equity	0.8
Cash flow to long-term liabilities	0.3
Total liabilities to owner's equity	1.5

After comparing the business's ratios with the industry norms, it is clear that the owner's solvency is worse than that of competing small businesses. The business has significantly more total debt and long-term liabilities in its capital structure, and has lower cash flow to cover its debt.

HOW IS IT USED AND APPLIED? In evaluating a small business's performance, a high ratio of total liabilities to total owner's equity (financial leverage) indicates much risk because it may be a problem for the owner to pay interest and principal payments and also obtain reasonable future financing. A high debt/equity ratio is a particularly acute problem for small businesses with cash problems, especially during recessionary periods. Carrying excessive amounts of debt will result in less financial flexibility for the business, because it is more difficult to obtain money in a tight money market. Further, having to pay high fixed interest charges will result in negative effects on earnings.

A favorable leverage situation exists when the return on borrowed funds exceeds the interest charge, provided that the owner is not in debt over his or her head. A desirable debt/equity ratio depends on many factors, including the rates of other small businesses in the industry, access to further debt financing, and earnings stability.

A ratio greater than 1 for long-term debt to owner's equity indicates a higher long-term debt participation relative to equity capital.

The debt ratio (total liabilities to total assets) reveals the percentage of total funds obtained from creditors. The ratio indicates how much debt may be comfortably assumed, given the owner's financial status. Creditors would obviously rather see a low debt ratio.

Potential creditors are reluctant to provide financing to a business with a high debt posture; however, the size of debt taken on may be satisfactory, depending on the nature of the small business.

If analysis reveals that interest on borrowed funds has increased, it is essential to know why. Is it because lenders demand a higher interest rate because of increased risk? Is it because overall market interest rates have risen?

The ratio of current debt to owner's equity is used to measure if short-term creditors are providing excessive capital resources to support operations relative to materials, supplies, and services. The adequacy of the ratio depends on such variables as the turnover rate of inventory and receivables, liquidity status, and so on.

Where there is considerable debt, a sharp drop in sales or in receivables turnover may mean that the owner will be unable to pay debt obligations. Interest on borrowed funds may even be greater than earnings, resulting in a loss. Even though debt might be high, however, the business may still be able to meet its obligations—for example, there may be a quick turnover in current assets, allowing timely debt payments; some current liabilities may be stretched or due dates extended; long-term debt may be restructured for later payment; or a substantial boost in cash earnings may take place.

If borrowed capital exceeds invested capital, proprietary risk is shared with the creditors. In general, invested capital should exceed borrowed capital. Analyzing the trend in the ratio of owner's capital shows a business's financial policy and objectives. This provides insight into the owner's financing preferences, such as whether the owner is inclined toward taking excessive risk.

The impact of leverage on operating results is positive when the return on equity capital exceeds the return on total assets. Leverage is favorable when the return on assets is higher than the cost of debt.

The financial leverage ratio measures the relationship between total assets and the owner's equity capital that finances them. In a business that uses leverage profitably, a higher financial leverage ratio will enhance the return on equity; at the same time, the risk inherent in a change in profitability is also greater.

The ratio of working capital to funded debt is employed to determine whether a business could liquidate its long-term debt obligations from working capital. Even if a business shows adequate profitability, it may not have sufficient liquid funds to pay long-term debt obligations.

99 What Obligations Are Pressing?

INTRODUCTION. The ratio of "pressing" current to "patient" current liabilities describes the degree of flexibility of a small business with regard to paying debt. "Pressing" liabilities are those that must be paid without excuse, such as taxes and loans payable. "Patient" liabilities are those that provide flexibility when financial difficulties exist (e.g., accounts payable). For example, in troubled times, a supplier may postpone or even downwardly adjust the amount of the debt.

HOW IS IT COMPUTED?

$$\frac{\text{Pressing current liabilities}}{\text{Patient current liabilities}}$$

Example Assume that a small business's current liabilities consist of the following:

	19X1	19X2
Accounts payable (patient)	$400,000	$350,000
Taxes payable (pressing)	50,000	60,000
Bank loans payable (pressing)	250,000	280,000

The ratios of pressing debt to patient debt are:

	19X1	19X2
Pressing debt to patient debt	$\dfrac{\$300,000}{\$400,000} = 0.75$	$\dfrac{\$340,000}{\$350,000} = 0.97$

The higher ratio of pressing to patient short-term debt indicates that the business has greater liquidity risk in the second year than in the first.

HOW IS IT USED AND APPLIED? If more pressing current liabilities exist, a potential problem could occur during recessionary times, because short-term creditors would demand to be paid. Loan agreements, for example, may provide that the principal of the loan be paid even if an interest payment is not. On the other hand, having more patient current liabilities will work to the owner's advantage. It may also be easier to renegotiate payment terms with "patient" creditors.

100 Ratios of Off-Balance-Sheet Assets and Liabilities

INTRODUCTION. Unrecorded (off-balance-sheet) assets either represent resources of the small business or are anticipated to have future benefit but are not shown on the balance sheet. This makes the business more valuable. Off-balance-sheet assets include tax-loss carryforward benefits, expected rebates, and purchase commitments where the business has a contract to purchase an item at a price below the going rate. Unrecorded (off-balance-sheet) liabilities are those that are not reported on the balance sheet but may require future payments or services. These make the business less valuable. Examples are lawsuits and cosigned loans.

HOW IS IT COMPUTED?

$$1. \quad \frac{\text{Off-balance sheet assets}}{\text{Total assets}}$$

$$2. \quad \frac{\text{Off-balance sheet liabilities}}{\text{Total liabilities}}$$

Example A small business reports the following information:

	19X1	19X2
Off-balance-sheet liabilities	$ 20,000	$ 50,000
Total liabilities	100,000	130,000

The relevant ratios are:

	19X1	19X2
Off-balance-sheet liabilities to total liabilities	0.20	0.38

The increase in unrecorded liabilities may cause concern to the owner because of possible future payment. For example, there may be possible renegotiations of claims under city or county contracts.

HOW IS IT USED AND APPLIED? Off-balance-sheet assets are positive aspects of financial position even though they are not shown on the balance sheet. Obviously, a going concern is assumed, since unrecorded assets would typically not be realized in a distress situation. Off-balance-sheet liabilities are negative signs of financial position, because they may require the use of business resources.

101 Earnings Growth

INTRODUCTION. Earnings growth shows whether the business is able to generate increasing profit as sales grow. Deflated earnings growth is the growth in profitability after adjusting for inflation.

HOW IS IT COMPUTED?

Earnings growth

$$= \frac{\text{net income (current year)} - \text{net income (prior year)}}{\text{net income (prior year)}}$$

Deflated earnings growth

$$= \frac{(\text{net income} \times [\text{CPI (prior year)/CPI (current year)}]) - \text{net income (prior year)}}{\text{net income (prior year)}}$$

where CPI = Consumer Price Index.

Example A small business reported net income last year of $800,000 and this year it is $600,000. This is an unfavorable trend because there has been a percentage decline in profit of 25 percent, computed as follows:

$$\frac{\$600,000 - \$800,000}{\$800,000} = -\frac{\$200,000}{\$800,000} = -25\%$$

HOW IS IT USED AND APPLIED? There is a problem if sales rise but profits do not. If earnings are not consistent with revenue growth, possible reasons might be inadequate gross profit due to lower selling prices or increasing cost of goods sold, and/or the inability to keep expenses in check. Expenditures must positively benefit revenue to a greater extent.

Profit growth after adjusting for inflation is the key to assuring that the business is growing in real dollars.

A better measure is to compute average earnings growth over a 5-year period to show a reasonable trend.

102 Profit Margin

INTRODUCTION. The profit margin shows the earnings generated from sales. There are three ways of evaluating profitability, comprising net income, operating profit, and gross profit.

Gross profit must exist to cover operating expenses and earn a profit. It is easiest for the owner to improve gross profit because of the flexibility associated with buying and selling merchandise as well as cost containment.

HOW IS IT COMPUTED?

$$1.\ \text{Net profit margin} = \frac{\text{net income}}{\text{net sales}}$$

$$2.\ \text{Operating profit margin} = \frac{\text{income before taxes and interest}}{\text{net sales}}$$

$$3.\ \text{Gross profit margin} = \frac{\text{gross profit}}{\text{net sales}}$$

$$\text{Gross profit} = \text{sales} - \text{cost of sales}$$

Profit margin may vary widely within an industry, because it is subject to sales, pricing, and cost controls.

Example Analysis of a small business's profit margin is based on the following data:

	19X2	19X3
Gross profit	$15,000	$20,000
Net income	8,000	9,600
Sales	65,000	80,000

Relevant ratios are:

	19X2	19X3
Net profit margin	0.12	0.12
Gross profit margin	0.23	0.25

The net profit margin is constant, indicating that the earning power of the business has remained static. The improvement in gross profit is probably a result of increased sales and/or better control of cost of sales. A lack of control in operating expenses is most likely the reason that gross profit margin increased but net profit margin remained constant, even though sales have increased.

HOW IS IT USED AND APPLIED? Profit may be enhanced by obtaining additional revenue or by reducing costs. The profit of a business should be compared to that of competitors.

Profit margins vary among industries and among companies within the industry. Profit margin often depends on the type of product line; for example, profit margins are higher for fur coats but lower for groceries.

The profit margin shows the success of the owner in obtaining profit from operations. The higher the profit margin on each sales dollar generated, the better the business is doing financially. Profit may also be increased by controlling expenses. A high profit margin is advantageous because it indicates that the business is earning an attractive return on its cost of merchandise sold and operating expenses. A low profit margin may be due to a low gross profit arising from underpricing or lack of control over the cost of the merchandise. A low profit margin may also arise during expansion because adequate control may not be exercised over spending. High returns are prevalent in companies that have strong customer demand because of product quality or pricing and/or lack of competition.

By evaluating a business's profit margin relative to previous years and to industry norms, the owner can evaluate the business's operating efficiency and pricing strategy as well as its competitive position within the industry. The ratio of income to sales reveals the financial success of the business. The "bottom line" is what counts! Profit margin reveals the business's ability to generate earnings at a particular sales level.

A low gross profit margin may mean that the owner is overpaying for merchandise and/or that selling prices are too low. Another reason might be a change in sales mix from high-margin goods to low-margin ones. The gross profit margin may be maintained by the owner by pricing at a fixed multiple of cost of goods sold. For example, the markup might be consistently 2 times cost. Profit margins might be improved by charging the public at large on a direct order considerably more than that charged to the retailer. However, this approach works only if customers are loyal and competition is virtually nonexistent.

The gross profit margin is useful in comparing entities in different lines of business. However, one-time adjustments may distort the gross profit margin when comparisons are made.

103 Sales to Current Assets

INTRODUCTION. Current assets are assets that have a life of 1 year or less, such as cash, inventory, and accounts receivable. The ratio of sales to current assets examines the extent to which revenue is generated from current assets.

HOW IS IT COMPUTED?

$$\frac{\text{Sales}}{\text{Current assets}}$$

Example A small business reports the following information:

	19X1	19X2
Sales	$250,000	$400,000
Current assets	100,000	120,000

The relevant ratios are:

	19X1	19X2
Sales to current assets	2.5	3.33

A high ratio may mean that current assets are low, indicating deficient working capital. Perhaps current liabilities will become due before inventory and receivables turn to cash.

HOW IS IT USED AND APPLIED? The amount of sales relative to current assets indicates the adequacy of current assets. A low ratio implies excessive current assets or inadequate sales. Excessive current assets may mean a buildup in inventory that is tying up funds, or a buildup in customer balances. Ways to reduce the buildup are needed, such as offering cash discounts. If sales are insufficient, ways to boost sales should be devised, such as promotion plans.

104 Sales to Current Debt

INTRODUCTION. Current debt is debt due within 1 year, such as accounts payable, short-term notes payable, and accrued expenses payable.

The ratio of sales to current debt looks at the extent to which short-term liabilities finances sales growth.

HOW IS IT COMPUTED?

$$\frac{\text{Sales}}{\text{Short-term debt}}$$

Example A small business reports the following:

	19X1	19X2
Sales	$100,000	$130,000
Short-term debt	40,000	40,000

The results of the computation are:

	19X1	19X2
Sales to short-term debt	2.5	3.25

The analysis shows that in 19X2 the business is making better use of current debt in supporting its sales base.

HOW IS IT USED AND APPLIED? The amount of short-term credit a business is able to obtain from suppliers depends on its level of sales of goods or services. This ratio enables the owner to analyze the relationship between these factors. The advantage of a larger amount of short-term credit is that it is relatively low cost and, in turn, reduces the investment in working capital.

105 Analysis of Expenses

INTRODUCTION. Marketing involves getting, servicing, and keeping customers. Selling expenses are incurred to obtain sales (advertising, sales promotion, salesperson salaries and commissions) or to distribute merchandise (e.g., shipping).

Expenses are often related to sales to determine if proper cost controls exist and whether the expenditures are resulting in improved revenue and/or profitability.

Efficiency occurs when the business owner generates revenue (product and/or service) at the least practical expense.

If sales grow faster than total expenses, profit will increase. This is a positive indicator, particularly for a growing business.

HOW IS IT COMPUTED?

$$\text{Aggregate operating expense ratio} = \frac{\text{total operating expenses}}{\text{net sales}}$$

where operating expenses include general and administrative, and selling. Excluded are financial expenses (e.g., interest expense) and cost of goods sold.

For any specific expense that it is useful to compare to sales,

$$\text{Specific expense to net sales} = \frac{\text{specific expense}}{\text{net sales}}$$

$$\text{Selling expense ratio} = \frac{\text{selling expenses}}{\text{net sales}}$$

$$\text{Utilities ratio} = \frac{\text{utilities expense}}{\text{net sales}}$$

where utilities expense includes telephone, electricity, gas, and water provided by public utilities.

Percentage change in selling expenses

$$= \frac{\text{selling expenses (current year)} - \text{selling expenses (prior year)}}{\text{selling expenses (prior year)}}$$

Percentage change in total expenses

$$= \frac{\text{total expenses (current year)} - \text{total expenses (prior year)}}{\text{total expenses (prior year)}}$$

Percentage change in profit = percentage change in sales − percentage change in total expenses

Example 1 The following information is provided for a small business:

	19X8	19X9
Operating expenses	$ 500,000	$ 600,000
Utilities expense	30,000	40,000
Selling expense	200,000	250,000
Telephone expense	40,000	60,000
Sales	1,000,000	1,050,000

Relevant ratios are:

	19X8	19X9
Operating expenses to sales	50.0%	57.1%
Utilities expense to sales	3.0	3.8
Selling expense to sales	20.0	23.8
Telephone expense to sales	4.0	5.7

The trend in the expenses relative to sales is unfavorable. Each of the expense ratios has increased relative to sales, meaning that there will be less profitability. There is a need for a cost-reduction program.

HOW IS IT USED AND APPLIED? If actual sales are expected to be below budgeted sales, expenses must be trimmed to maintain profit margins. A lower total expense-to-sales ratio indicates that the owner is controlling business expenses.

If sales increase, expenses will probably do likewise. However, the latter should increase at a slower rate if earnings growth is to occur. However, a rapidly growing business may have expenses (primarily marketing and research) that increase at a faster rate than revenue because of the attempt to achieve higher sales levels in *future years*.

A specific expense-to-sales ratio can be analyzed to ascertain whether that expense item is being controlled. The item may be promotion and entertainment, fringe benefits, travel, training, supplies, automobiles, and so on.

The ratio of selling expenses to net sales shows the cost of making a sale of merchandise or rendering a service. A low ratio is favorable because it indicates the efficient use of selling efforts. A high ratio is unfavorable because it shows an inability to obtain sales efficiently. Further, a high ratio may mean that sales are increasing but earnings may not be because of high marketing costs. It should be noted that if sales decline significantly, the expense-to-sales ratios will increase but not due to cost excesses.

When marketing expenses increase more than sales on a percentage basis, it means an aggressive marketing strategy. The opposite is a contraction in marketing efforts. A multiyear period should be used in evaluating the success of marketing sales, because a marketing program may not "bear fruit" until a later year.

Utilities expenses are generally uncontrollable by the owner because rates are usually set by regulatory agencies. Further, a *minimum* use of utilities is necessary to keep plant facilities operational. However, telephone and energy bills are to some extent controllable by the owner and may be included in a cost-containment program.

106 Can You Cover Interest Payments?

INTRODUCTION. Interest coverage ratios show the number of times interest expense is covered by earnings or cash flow. The ratios show the degree of the decline in earnings that a small business can absorb and still be able to pay interest.

HOW IS IT COMPUTED? The two ways of figuring interest coverages are

$$\frac{\text{Income before taxes and interest}}{\text{Interest}}$$

and

$$\frac{\text{Cash flow from operations and interest}}{\text{Interest}}$$

Interest expense may also be compared to sales to determine if the business is relying too much on borrowed funds to finance sales growth and operating activities.

Example Interest coverage is evaluated for a business based on the following information from 2 years of operation:

	19X1	19X2
Income before taxes	$100,000	$105,000
Cash flow from operations	80,000	82,000
Interest expense	20,000	28,000

Relevant ratios are:

	19X1	19X2
Interest coverage based on earnings	6	4.8
Interest coverage based on cash flow from operations	5	3.9

The decline in interest coverage from 19X1 to 19X2 is a negative sign, since less earnings and cash flow from operations are available to pay interest charges. This decline in the ratio in the second year is a matter for concern.

In 19X2, there was $4.80 in income before taxes and interest for every $1.00 spent on interest. Further, $3.90 in cash earnings was the amount available to cover each $1.00 in interest expenses.

HOW IS IT USED AND APPLIED? A business that is unable to pay interest is in a dangerous financial position. The trend in the coverage ratios reveals how much interest-bearing debt burden the business can handle.

It is better to use cash flow from operations than income before taxes as a basis on which to compare interest expense, since cash flow indicates the amount of actual cash that can be used to pay interest.

An owner prefers high ratios for his or her business, because high ratios indicate that the business is able to meet its interest obligations with room to spare.

107 Operating Leverage

INTRODUCTION. *Operating leverage* refers to the existence of fixed costs in the cost structure of a small business, and represents operating risk. Fixed costs are expenses that remain constant regardless of changes in volume. Examples are rent, insurance, and property taxes.

HOW IS IT CALCULATED? The following ratios may be used to measure operating leverage:

1. $\dfrac{\text{Fixed cost}}{\text{Total cost}}$

2. $\dfrac{\text{Percentage change in operating income}}{\text{Percentage change in sales volume}}$

or

$\dfrac{\text{Change in profit/profit}}{\text{Change in quantity/quantity}}$

3. $\dfrac{\text{Net income}}{\text{Fixed charges}}$

An increase in ratios 1 and 2 or a decrease in ratio 3 indicates higher fixed charges for a small business. This situation indicates greater operating risk for the business, because it will have to meet its fixed cost commitments, which cannot be cut to meet declining sales volume in the short term.

Higher fixed charges also result in greater earnings instability, because high leverage magnifies changes in earnings that result from small changes in sales.

Example 1 Operating leverage is calculated based on data from the following comparative income statements for a small business:

	19X0	19X1
Net income	$100,000	$102,000
Fixed cost	40,000	55,000
Variable cost	25,000	27,000
Total cost	65,000	82,000

The small business's operating leverage in 19X1 relative to 19X0 was higher, as evidenced by the increase in the ratio of fixed costs to total cost and the decrease in the ratio of the net income to fixed costs.

	19X0	19X1
Fixed cost to total cost	61.5%	67.1%
Net income to fixed cost	2.5	1.85

Example 2 An owner wants to evaluate the operating leverage of his small business based on the following data:

Selling price per unit	$ 2.00
Fixed cost	50,000
Variable cost per unit	1.10

Profit is determined as follows:

Sales volume	Dollar sales	−	Fixed costs	−	Variable costs	=	Profit
100,000	$200,000	−	$50,000	−	$110,000	=	$40,000
130,000	260,000	−	50,000	−	143,000	=	67,000

The ratio of the percentage change in operating income to the percentage change in sales volume is:

$$\frac{(\$67,000 - \$40,000)/\$40,000}{(130,000 - 100,000)/100,000} = \frac{\$27,000/\$40,000}{30,000/100,000} = \frac{67.5\%}{30.0\%} = 2.25$$

HOW IS IT USED AND APPLIED? Owners are interested in knowing the degree of operating leverage of their small businesses. A high operating leverage means greater fixed cost commitments that have to be met even when sales volume declines. Owners must be aware that high degrees of operating leverage in combination with highly elastic product demand will result in high levels of variability in earnings, although such a condition may be inherent in the industry.

Small businesses should note that the effects of operating leverage diminish as revenue increases above the breakeven point (the point where sales equal total costs), since the bases to which increases in earnings are compared become progressively larger. Hence, owners should examine the relationship between sales and the breakeven point.

Owners should note that a small business with a high breakeven point is quite vulnerable to economic declines. A high ratio of variable cost to total cost indicates greater earnings stability, because variable cost can be adjusted more easily than fixed cost to meet a decline in product demand.

108 Fixed-Charge Coverage

INTRODUCTION. The fixed-charge coverage ratio indicates whether a small business is able to pay its fixed commitments (e.g., rent, interest) from profits and cash earnings.

HOW IS IT COMPUTED? Fixed-charge coverage involves two ratios:

$$1. \quad \frac{\text{Income before taxes and fixed charges}}{\text{Fixed charges}}$$

$$2. \quad \frac{\text{Cash flow provided from operations and fixed charges}}{\text{Fixed charges}}$$

Example The following information is given for a small business:

	19X1	19X2
Income before taxes	$360,000	$590,000
Cash flow provided from operations	300,000	500,000
Fixed charges	100,000	120,000

Relevant ratios are:

	19X1	19X2
Fixed-charge coverage based on income before tax	4.6	5.9
Fixed-charge coverage based on cash flow from operations	4.0	5.2

The analysis reveals that the business is better able to meet its fixed charges based on earnings and out of cash flow from operations in 19X2 than in 19X1. For example, in 19X2, for each $1 in fixed charges there was $5.90 of earnings and $5.20 in cash flow from operations.

HOW IS IT USED AND APPLIED? The fixed-charge coverage ratio is useful in gauging a business's ability to pay fixed costs. A low ratio indicates increased risk, because when business activity falls, the owner may be unable to meet fixed charges. In analyzing fixed charges, it is better for the owner to consider cash flow from operations than that from net income, since cash is used to meet fixed payments. A high fixed-charge ratio reflects favorably on the business's ability to refinance obligations as they mature.

In analyzing these ratios for a given business, it should be ascertained if the entity has stability in both operations and funds flow. Such stability provides more confidence in the business's ability to meet its fixed commitments.

The coverage ratios are influenced by the level of earnings and by the level of fixed charges, which depend significantly on the debt-to-equity relationship within the capital structure.

109 Is Your Funds Flow Adequate?

INTRODUCTION. The funds flow adequacy ratio shows the degree to which a small business can obtain adequate funds from operations to pay budgeted capital expenditures and increased inventories.

HOW IS IT COMPUTED?

$$\frac{\text{5-year sum of sources of funds from operations}}{\text{5-year sum of capital expenditures and inventory additions}}$$

A 5-year total is usually employed to eliminate cyclical and other distortions.

Example The following figures from a 5-year period are used to evaluate funds flow adequacy for a small business:

Capital expenditures	$ 800,000
Additions to inventory	500,000
Funds from operations	1,500,000

The funds flow adequacy ratio is:

$$\frac{\$1,500,000}{\$1,300,000} = 1.15$$

HOW IS IT USED AND APPLIED? The owner uses this ratio to determine whether internally generated funds are adequate to assure growth. A ratio of 1 means that the owner has covered his or her needs based on attained growth levels without resorting to external financing. A ratio below 1 indicates that there may be insufficient internally generated funds to maintain current growth.

110 Discretionary Cost Ratios

INTRODUCTION. *Discretionary cost ratios* are employed to evaluate costs that can easily be altered. Discretionary costs may be cut when the business is having problems and wants to stabilize its earnings. Discretionary costs include advertising, repairs and maintenance, and research and development.

HOW IS IT COMPUTED?

1. Discretionary costs/sales:

$$\frac{\text{Discretionary costs}}{\text{Sales}}$$

2. Discretionary costs/related asset:

$$\frac{\text{Discretionary costs}}{\text{Related assets}}$$

Example 1 A small business's discretionary costs for 2 years are:

	19X1	19X2
Repairs and maintenance	$ 10,000	$ 6,000
Sales	100,000	110,000
Fixed assets	200,000	230,000

The ratios are:

	19X1	19X2
Repairs and maintenance/sales	10%	5.5%
Repairs and maintenance/fixed assets	5%	2.6%

The declining trend in the ratio of repairs and maintenance to both sales and fixed assets indicates that there is insufficient maintenance of fixed assets, leading to possible future breakdowns. Although there are short-term profit benefits from cost reduction, the situation suggests that its continuance might have a detrimental impact in future years.

Example 2 The owner of a small business looked at the following relationship between advertising and sales:

	19X1	19X2	19X3
Sales	$120,000	$150,000	$100,000
Advertising	11,000	16,000	8,000

19X1 is the most typical year. Increasing competition is expected in 19X4.

Advertising to sales is 9.2 percent in 19X1, 10.7 percent in 19X2, and 8.0 percent in 19X3. In terms of base dollars, 19X1 is assigned 100. In 19X2, the index number is $16,000/$11,000 = 145.5; and in 19X3 it is $8,000/$11,000 = 72.7. These are negative indicators regarding 19X3. Advertising is at a lower level than in previous years. In fact, advertising should have risen due to the expected increased competition.

HOW IS IT USED AND APPLIED? The business owner should recognize that cost-reduction programs may sometimes eliminate costs that are necessary to compete and prosper effectively. However, a reduction in discretionary costs may be necessary when the prior business strategy was deficient or ill-conceived. Further, a reduction in discretionary costs (e.g., advertising) may be suitable when a major competitor has gone out of business.

The owner should determine if the current level of discretionary costs conforms with the business's prior trends and with present and future requirements. Index numbers may be used in comparing current discretionary expenditures with base-year expenditures. A substantial increase in discretionary costs may have a positive effect on the business's earning power and future growth.

111 "Z-Score" Model: Forecasting Business Failure

INTRODUCTION. The Z-score model is a quantitative model developed in an effort to predict bankruptcy (financial distress) of a business, using a blend of the traditional financial ratios and a statistical method known as multiple discriminant analysis (MDA).

The Z score is known to be about 90 percent accurate in forecasting business failure 1 year into the future and about 80 percent accurate in forecasting it 2 years into the future.

HOW IS IT COMPUTED?

$$Z = 1.2 \times X_1 + 1.4 \times X_2 + 3.3 \times X_3 + 0.6 \times X_4 + 0.999 \times X_5$$

where $X_1 = \dfrac{\text{working capital}}{\text{total assets}}$

$X_2 = \dfrac{\text{retained earnings}}{\text{total assets}}$

$X_3 = \dfrac{\text{earnings before interest and taxes (EBIT)}}{\text{total assets}}$

$X_4 = \dfrac{\text{market value of equity (or net worth for private firms}}{\text{book value of debt}}$

$X_5 = \dfrac{\text{sales}}{\text{total assets}}$

The following guidelines have been established for classifying firms:

Z score	Probability of failure
1.8 or less	Very high
1.81–2.99	Not sure
3.0 or higher	Unlikely

Example A manufacturer has the following financial data selected from its financial statements:

Total assets = $2000

EBIT = $266

Retained earnings = $750

Sales = $3000

Market value of common and preferred stock (net worth for private firms) = $1425

Book value of debt = $1100

The calculation of the company's Z score is shown below:

$$
\begin{aligned}
X_1 &= \$400/\$2000 \times 1.2 &&= 0.240 \\
X_2 &= \$750/\$2000 \times 1.4 &&= 0.525 \\
X_3 &= \$266/\$2000 \times 3.3 &&= 0.439 \\
X_4 &= \$1425/\$1100 \times 0.6 &&= 0.777 \\
X_5 &= \$3000/\$2000 \times 0.999 &&= \underline{1.499} \\
& && Z = 3.480
\end{aligned}
$$

Since the company's Z score of 3.480 is well into the "unlikely" zone, there is virtually no chance that it will go bankrupt within the next 2 years.

HOW IS IT USED AND APPLIED? The MDA may be used for a business or a group of businesses. The recent recessionary environment has witnessed an increasing trend in bankruptcies. Will your business go bankrupt? Is the business you are working for on the verge of bankruptcy? Who will go bankrupt? Your major customer? Your important supplier? Your borrower? If you can predict with reasonable accuracy that the business you are interested in is developing financial distress, you can better protect yourself and recommend means for corrective action. Some steps might be to curtail capital expansion, cut back on dividends, or engage in refinancing.

Measuring Business Performance

112 Choosing Profitability Goals

INTRODUCTION. Profit measures success. Making a profit is only the first step; making a profit large enough to survive and grow is the real challenge of a business. The ability to measure performance is essential in developing incentives and controlling operations toward the achievement of organizational goals.

HOW IS IT COMPUTED? Three widely used measures of success of a business are:

1. Earnings growth
2. Rate of return on investment (ROI)
3. Return on equity (ROE)

1. Earnings Growth. The earnings growth rate is used in many ways. One application is the growth rate in earnings or dividends (g) required for the *Gordon's dividend growth model*:

$$P_0 = \frac{D_1}{r - g}$$

where P_0 = current price of a security, D_1 = expected dividend at the end of the first year, and r = investor's required rate of return.

2. Return on Investment (ROI). ROI relates net income to invested capital (total assets). It provides a standard for evaluating how efficiently management employs the average dollar invested in a business's assets, and whether that dollar came from owners or creditors. Furthermore, a better ROI can also translate directly into a higher return on the owners' equity.

ROI is calculated as:

$$\text{ROI} = \frac{\text{net profit after taxes}}{\text{total assets}}$$

Example 1 Consider the following financial data:

Total assets	$100,000
Net profit after taxes	18,000

Then

$$\text{ROI} = \frac{\text{net profit after taxes}}{\text{total assets}} = \frac{\$18{,}000}{\$100{,}000} = 18\%$$

The problem with the ROI formula is that it tells you only how a business did and how well it fared within the industry. Other than that, it has very little value from the standpoint of profit planning.

3. Return on Equity (ROE).

Generally, a better management performance measure (i.e., a high or above-average ROI) produces a higher return to equity holders. However, even a poorly managed business that suffers from below-average performance can generate an above-average return on stockholders' equity, simply called the return on equity (ROE). This is because borrowed funds can magnify the returns a business's profits represent to stockholders.

The following formula ties together the ROI and the degree of financial leverage (use of borrowed funds). The financial leverage is measured by the equity multiplier, which is the ratio of a company's total asset base to its equity investment, or, stated another way, the ratio of how many dollars of assets held per dollar of stockholders' equity. It is calculated by dividing total assets by stockholders' equity. This measurement gives an indication of how much of a business's assets are financed by stockholders' equity and how much with borrowed funds.

The return on equity (ROE) is calculated as:

$$\text{ROE} = \frac{\text{net profit after taxes}}{\text{stockholders' equity}} = \frac{\text{net profit after taxes}}{\text{total assets}}$$

$$\times \frac{\text{total assets}}{\text{stockholders' equity}}$$

$$= \text{ROI} \quad \times \text{equity multiplier}$$

ROE measures the returns earned on the owners' (both preferred and common stockholders') investment. The use of the equity multiplier to convert ROI to ROE reflects the impact of leverage (use of debt) on stockholders' return.

The equity multiplier is

$$\frac{1}{\text{Stockholders' equity}} = \frac{1}{1 - \text{debt ratio}}$$

Example 2 For the company in Example 1, assume stockholders' equity of $45,000. Then

$$\text{Equity multiplier} = \frac{\text{total assets}}{\text{stockholders' equity}} = \frac{\$100,000}{\$45,000} = 2.22$$

$$= \frac{1}{1 - \text{debt ratio}} = \frac{1}{1 - 0.55} = \frac{1}{0.45} = 2.22$$

$$\text{ROE} = \frac{\text{net profit after taxes}}{\text{stockholders' equity}} = \frac{\$18,000}{\$45,000} = 40\%$$

$$\text{ROE} = \text{ROI} \times \text{equity multiplier} = 18\% \times 2.22 = 40\%$$

If the company used only equity, the 18 percent ROI would equal ROE. However, 55 percent of the firm's capital is supplied by creditors ($45,000/$100,000 = 45 percent is the equity-to-asset ratio; $55,000/$100,000 = 55 percent is the debt ratio). Since the 18 percent ROI all goes to stockholders, who put up only 45 percent of the capital, the ROE is higher than 18 percent. This example indicates that the company is using leverage (debt) favorably.

HOW IS IT USED AND APPLIED? Once you have calculated your ratios, compare them to your predetermined goals. Are your goals too high or too low? Have you compared your present profits (ratios and absolute amounts) for the last three years? Have you compared your profits to similar firms in your industry?

ROE provides an important view of the positive contribution that debt can make to a business, but within a certain limit. Too much debt can increase the firm's financial risk and thus the cost of financing.

If the assets in which the funds are invested are able to earn a return greater than the fixed rate of return required by the creditors, the leverage is positive and the common stockholders benefit. The advantage of this formula is that it enables the company to break its ROE into a profit margin portion (net profit margin), an efficiency-of-asset utilization portion (total asset turnover), and a use-of-leverage portion (equity multiplier). It shows that the company can raise shareholder return by employer leverage—taking on larger amounts of debt to help finance growth.

Since financial leverage affects net profit margin through the added interest costs, the manager must look at the various pieces of this ROE equation, within the context of the whole, to earn the highest return for stockholders. Financial managers have the task of determining just what combination of asset return and leverage will work best in the competitive environment. Most companies try to keep at least a level equal to what is considered "normal" within the industry.

113 Simple (Accounting) Rate of Return

INTRODUCTION. The *simple rate of return* relates the returns generated by a project, as measured by average accounting income after taxes, to the average dollar size of the investment.

HOW IS IT COMPUTED?

$$\text{Simple rate of return} = \frac{\text{expected future annual net income}}{\text{average investment}}$$

Example A proposal requires an initial investment of $6500, has an expected life of 20 years, and will generate expected annual net income of $675. The owner wants to calculate the simple rate of return.

$$\frac{\$675}{\$6500/2} = \frac{\$675}{\$3250} = 20.8\%$$

($6500 is divided by 2 to obtain an average.)

HOW IS IT USED AND APPLIED? The simple rate of return is one method used by the small business owner to compare the profitability among alternative investment opportunities and proposals; however, drawbacks of the method include its failure to (1) consider cash flows, (2) incorporate the time value of money, and (3) consider the payback period [see Sec. 59, How Many Years Does It Take to Get Your Money Back (Payback Period)?]

114 Return on Total Assets

INTRODUCTION. *Return on total assets* (ROA) equals net income after taxes divided by total tangible assets and measures the effectiveness of a small business's assets to create profits.

HOW IS IT COMPUTED?

$$ROA = \frac{\text{net income after taxes}}{\text{averaging total assets}}$$

where

Average total assets =
(beginning total assets + ending total assets)/2

Intangibles (e.g., goodwill) are usually not included in total assets because they are hard to measure and do not contribute to operating profits. However, an exception might be trademarks that do contribute profits.

Example The following data show a manufacturer's performance in two different years:

	19X4	19X5
Net income after taxes	$ 259,358	$ 384,346
Average total assets		
Beginning of year	1,548,234	1,575,982
End of year	1,575,982	1,614,932
Average	$1,562,108	$1,595,457
Return on total assets (ROA)	16.60%	24.09%

The analysis shows that there has been growth in the return on assets during the year, indicating greater productivity of assets in generating earnings.

HOW IS IT USED AND APPLIED? ROA is probably the single most widely used measure of an entity's success. It indicates the productive utilization of business resources. If ROA is acceptable to the owner or manager, the proper investment decision is to maintain and improve facilities. For managerial use, ROA should be viewed as the product of two factors, net profit margin and total asset turnover.

High-technology businesses with a proprietary product line (the company is the *only* provider of important and high-demand goods to consumers) have the potential to earn high return rates on assets.

115 Residual Income

INTRODUCTION. *Residual income* is the operating income that an investment center in a small business is able to earn above some minimum return on its assets.

HOW IS IT COMPUTED?

Residual income = net operating income

$\qquad$ − (minimum rate of return on investment

$\qquad\qquad$ × total operating assets)

The minimum rate of return is often based on the cost of financing to the small business.

Example Assume that a small business has operating assets of $100,000,000 and net operating income of $18,000,000. The minimum return on assets is 13 percent. Residual income is:

Net operating income	$18,000,000
Less: Minimum return × total operating assets	
(13% × $100,000,000)	13,000,000
Residual income	$ 5,000,000

HOW IS IT USED AND APPLIED? Residual income is an absolute amount of income rather than a rate of return, and it is used to evaluate departmental performance. An evaluation based on residual income encourages small business owners to accept investment opportunities that have rates of return greater than the charge for invested capital. A manager being evaluated using return on investment (ROI) may be reluctant to accept new investments that lower his or her current ROI, even though the investment would be desirable for the entire business.

The advantages of using residual income in evaluating performance include the following: (1) It is an economic income that takes into account the minimum return that must be earned on assets; (2) the minimum rate of return can vary depending on the riskiness of the division; (3) different assets can be required to earn different returns depending on their risk; (4) the same asset may be required to earn the same return regardless of the department it is in; and (5) the effect of maximizing dollars rather than a percentage leads to goal congruence.

A major disadvantage of residual income is that it cannot be used to compare departments of different sizes; residual income tends to favor larger departments due to the larger amount of dollars involved.

The small business owner should look favorably upon a higher residual income since it means that the business is not only earning a net income but it is also covering the opportunity cost of having assets tied up in the business.

The higher the ratio of residual income to net income, the better is the earnings quality. Residual income is viewed by many owners as a better measure of true earnings than net income.

116 Flexible-Budget Variance

INTRODUCTION. *A flexible budget* shows budgeted cost figures at various capacity levels (e.g., expected, optimistic, and pessimistic), and requires the separation of fixed and variable costs. A flexible budget enables the comparison of actual and budgeted results at virtually any level of activity, and is useful for evaluating the efficiency of both manufacturing and non-manufacturing activities.

HOW IS IT COMPUTED?

Flexible budget variance
         = budget versus actual at a particular capacity level

If idle capacity exists, total variable costs will increase with increased production but total fixed costs will remain the same.

Example The following shows how a small business would prepare a flexible budget to reflect a range of performance expectations.

	Pessimistic	Expected	Optimistic	Full capacity
Units	8,000	10,000	11,000	15,000
Capacity level relative to expected	80%	100%	110%	
Variable costs	$48,000	$60,000	$66,000	
Fixed costs	$90,000	$90,000	$90,000	

Assuming that 8000 units were actually produced, with actual costs of $50,000 in variable costs and $91,000 in fixed costs, the flexible budget variance would be:

	Actual	Flexible budget	Flexible budget variance	
Variable	$50,000	$48,000	$2,000	Unfavorable
Fixed	91,000	90,000	2,000	Unfavorable

HOW IS IT USED AND APPLIED? The flexible budget allows the owner to plan more effectively by assessing costs at different capacity levels. The owner can foresee which operating strategies may be most suitable and what costs may be expected.

117 Variance between Actual Sales and Budgeted Sales

INTRODUCTION. Sales variances analyze the deviation between expected and actual selling price and volume. Reasons for deviation are examined to improve the marketing of the small business's products and services.

If actual revenue is below expectations, this is a negative situation for the small business owner. Actual revenue may be less than budgeted revenue because of reduced selling price, decline in sales volume and market share, increase in sales returns because of poor quality, or advertising ineffectiveness.

HOW IS IT COMPUTED?

Total sales variance = expected sales revenue
$$- \text{ actual sales revenue}$$

The total sales variance should be separated into price and volume. Each should then be analyzed for the reasons behind the variance.

Sales price variance =
(actual selling price − budgeted selling price)
$$\times \text{ actual units sold}$$

Sales volume variance = (actual quantity − budgeted quantity)
$$\times \text{ budgeted selling price}$$

Example Marchler Retail's budgeted sales for 19X1 were:

Product A: 10,000 units at $6 per unit	$ 60,000
Product B: 30,000 units at $8 per unit	240,000
Expected sales revenue	$300,000

Actual sales for the year were:

Product A: 8,000 units at $6.20 per unit	$ 49,600
Product B: 33,000 units at $7.70 per unit	254,100
Actual sales revenue	$303,700

There is a favorable sales variance of $3700, consisting of the sales price variance and the sales volume variance.

The sales price variances are:

Product A: ($6.20 versus $6.00) × 8,000	$1,600	Favorable
Product B: ($7.70 versus $8.00) × 33,000	9,900	Unfavorable
Sales price variance	$8,300	Unfavorable

The sales volume variances are:

Product A: (8,000 versus 10,000) × $6.00	$12,000	Unfavorable
Product B: (33,000 versus 30,000) × $8.00	24,000	Favorable
Sales volume variance	$12,000	Favorable

HOW IS IT USED AND APPLIED? The sales variances (price and volume) are prepared for product sales reports to gauge the performance of the marketing function. The sales manager is responsible for sales variances and must explain deviations to the owner. The sales price variance indicates whether the product is being sold at a discount or a premium. Sales price variances may be due to uncontrollable market conditions or to owner decisions.

The analysis of sales volume includes consideration of budgets, sales plans, industry and competitive comparisons, and manufacturing costs. Note that high sales volume does not automatically mean high profits, since there may be high costs associated with the products.

An unfavorable sales volume variance may arise from poor marketing or price cuts by competitors. If the unfavorable volume variance is coupled with a favorable price variance, the business may have lost sales by raising its prices.

The sales volume variance reflects the effect on the total budgeted contribution margin that is caused by changes in the total number of units sold. The variance may be caused by unpredictable product demand, lack of product demand, or poor sales forecasting.

An unfavorable total sales variance may signal a problem with the sales manager, who controls sales, advertising, and often pricing. Another possible cause of an unfavorable sales variance may be a lack of quality control, substitution of poorer-quality components due to deficient purchasing, or deficient product design emanating from poor engineering.

A spreadsheet can be used to compute variances (refer to the July 1985 issue of LOTUS, pp. 46–48).

Corrective action is needed by the owner to improve lagging sales. Such action may take the following forms:

- Improve sales planning.

- Improve product quality, design, packaging, or sales mix.

- Dispose of outdated styles and slow-moving stock.

- To stimulate sales, offer better services, launch as many new products as possible, offer sales promotions, provide rebates, offer discounts, and give zero percent financing.

- Pay higher commission rates to salespeople to promote high-profit-margin items and slow-moving ones.

- Identify who is responsible for sales variances and take corrective action.

See Sec. 118, Variance between Actual Costs and Budgeted Costs.

118 Variance between Actual Costs and Budgeted Costs

INTRODUCTION. If actual costs significantly exceed budgeted costs in a small business, the owner should be alarmed as to the cause. While it may only be a tight budget estimate that the owner cannot realistically meet, it may be a serious problem indicating a lack of cost controls, misspending, and deficient planning. The business may be inefficient, requiring better cost management. Perhaps there is waste, and duplication of effort and facilities.

If only the budgetary process is at fault, budgets based on historical experience should incorporate the current operating environment. If a static (fixed) budget geared for only one level of activity is being used, a flexible (variable) budget should be implemented instead. In other words, if variances are due to poor estimation, improve the budgeting process.

HOW IS IT COMPUTED?

Variance = actual cost versus budgeted cost

If actual cost exceeds budgeted cost, the variance is unfavorable. It is favorable in the opposite case.

A variance should be computed for each major element within the small business, including costs by product, customer, territory, salesperson, and so on.

Flexible budgeting distinguishes between fixed and variable charges. It adjusts costs based on the actual volume achieved.

Price and quantity variances may be determined. The flexible budget compares actual costs for a specified output with budgeted costs for the same output level. Budgeted figures may easily be developed based on various activity levels. Flexible budgets aid in measuring performance.

Example 1 A small business owner compared her budgeted costs to the actual costs for the year as follows:

	Budget	Actual	Variance	Variance in percent†
Manufacturing costs	$150,000	$200,000	$50,000 U*	33.3
Selling expenses	30,000	42,000	12,000 U	40.0
General and administrative expenses	60,000	95,000	35,000 U	58.3
Total	$240,000	$337,000	$97,000 U	

*U = unfavorable variance.
†Variance in percent = variance amount/budgeted amount.

This small business is in trouble: Actual costs are excessive compared to expectations. The reasons for the significant variance must be found immediately and corrective action implemented. If this situation continues, the continued existence of the business may become questionable.

Example 2 To illustrate the difference between the static budget and the flexible budget, assume that a small business is budgeted to produce 6000 units during the year. The budget for direct labor and variable overhead costs is set as shown below:

Budgeted production	6,000 units	
Actual production	5,800 units	
Direct labor		$39,000
Variable overhead costs:		
Indirect labor		6,000
Supplies		900
Repairs		300
		$46,200

Note: Variable overhead costs are those that change with the volume of units produced.

Assume further that the business was able to produce only 5800 units. If a static budget approach is used, the performance report will appear as follows:

	Budget	Actual	Variance,* U or F†
Production in units	6,000	5,800	200 (U)
Direct labor	$39,000	$38,500	$500 (F)

	Budget	Actual	Variance,* U or F†
Variable overhead costs:			
Indirect labor	6,000	5,950	50 (F)
Supplies	900	870	30 (F)
Repairs	300	295	5 (F)
Total conversion costs	$46,200	$45,615	$585 (F)

*A variance represents the deviation of actual cost from the standard or budgeted cost.
†U = unfavorable variance; F = favorable variance.

Apparently, these cost variances are useless, since they have been derived by comparing the actual costs incurred at a 5800-unit level of activity to the budgeted costs at a different level of activity (6000 units). From a control standpoint, it makes no sense to compare costs at one activity level to costs at a different activity level. It is like comparing oranges to apples, instead of comparing oranges that grow in Florida to oranges that grow in California.

Redeveloping the budget based on the 5800 actual units of output gives the following performance report:

Budgeted production   6000 units
Actual production   5800 units

		Budget 5800 units	Actual 5800 units	Variance U or F
Direct labor	$6.50 per unit	$37,700	$38,500	$800 (U)
Variable overhead costs:				
Indirect labor	1.00	5,800	5,950	150 (U)
Supplies	0.15	870	870	0
Repairs	0.05	290	295	5 (U)
	$7.70	$44,660	$45,615	$955 (U)

Notice that all cost variances are unfavorable, as compared to the favorable cost variances on the performance report based on the static budget approach.

HOW IS IT USED AND APPLIED?   The reason and/or party responsible for the deviation between actual costs and budgeted costs should be determined, and corrective steps taken to correct unfavorable situations. However, a favorable variance (actual cost less than budgeted cost) should be learned from and taken advantage of.

When actual costs are out of line, the owner may consider doing the following:

- Implement a cost-reduction program to trim excessive expenditures. Use a flexible budget, which is extremely useful in cost control.

- Make volume purchases when discounts are attractive.

- Substitute cheaper materials.

- Restructure and reorganize to reduce "fat" in the business and make it leaner and more efficient.

- Eliminate duplicate activities and facilities.

- Merge operations to generate cost efficiencies.

- Combine facilities and equipment to achieve a more efficient productivity level and improve operations.

- Place "caps" on expense categories (such as travel and entertainment), requiring special permission to exceed maximum amounts.

- Change a production method or specification.

- Inspect at key points in the manufacturing cycle.

- Upgrade employee training.

- Improve supervision and scheduling.

- Computerize variance reporting for immediate feedback and analysis.

See Sec. 117, Variance between Actual Sales and Budgeted Sales.

119 Price Variance

INTRODUCTION. The *price variance* compares the difference between the standard price and actual price for materials issued to production, labor hours incurred, or overhead.

HOW IS IT COMPUTED?

Price variance = (actual price versus standard price)
$$\times \text{ actual quantity}$$

Note: Standard price means what the price *should* be.

Example Assume the following standards for a small business:

Direct materials: 5 pounds @ $4 per pound $20 per unit
Direct labor: 3 hours @ $12 per hour $36 per unit

Actual volumes and costs are:

Production   9,800 units
Purchases: 50,000 pounds @ $3 $150,000
Direct labor: 22,000 hours @ $10 $220,000

The materials price variance is:

$$(\$3 \text{ versus } \$4) \times 50,000 = \$50,000 \qquad \text{Favorable}$$

The labor price variance is:

$$(\$10 \text{ versus } \$12) \times 22,000 = \$44,000 \qquad \text{Favorable}$$

HOW IS IT USED AND APPLIED?   The owner uses the materials price variance to appraise purchasing efforts and to understand the impact of changes in raw material costs on profitability. To correct for an unfavorable materials price variance, the owner can raise selling price, substitute cheaper materials, modify a production process or specification, or undertake a cost-reduction program. The owner cannot control material price variances when higher prices are the result of inflation or market shortages.

Where salary rates are set by union contract, the labor price variance will typically be minimal, because the standard labor rate is based on the contracted hourly wage rate. Possible causes for a labor price variance are:

Reason	Party responsible
Use of overpaid or excessive number of workers	Production manager or union contract
Poor job descriptions	Personnel
Overtime	Production planning

If there is a shortage of skilled workers, it may be impossible to avoid an unfavorable labor price variance.

120 Quantity Variance

INTRODUCTION.   The *quantity variance* shows excess or deficit usage of materials or labor in production, and links this usage to cost consequences.

HOW IS IT COMPUTED?

Quantity variance = (actual quantity versus standard quantity)
$$\times \text{standard price}$$

The quantity variance is computed for both material and labor.

If the actual cost or quantity exceeds the standard cost or quantity, the variance is unfavorable.

Example Assume the following standards for a small business:

Direct materials: 5 pounds @ $4 per pound $20 per unit
Direct labor: 3 hours @ $12 per hour $36 per unit

Production volume: 9800 units
Direct materials used: 44,000 pounds
Direct labor: 22,000 hours @ $10 = $220,000

Then the materials quantity variance is:

(Actual quantity versus standard quantity) $\times$ standard price
$$= (44,000 \text{ versus } 49,000) \times \$4 = \$20,000$$

The labor quantity variance is:

(Actual quantity versus standard quantity) $\times$ standard price
$$= (22,000 \text{ versus } 29,400) \times \$12 = \$88,800$$

In both cases in this analysis, the quantity variances are favorable.

HOW IS IT USED AND APPLIED? Materials and labor quantity standards are usually estimated by an engineer based on an evaluation of the production process. The materials quantity variance is typically the responsibility of the production manager, while the purchasing manager is responsible for buying inferior goods to economize on cost.

The reasons and responsible people for unfavorable materials quantity variances are:

Reason	Party responsible
Improper specifications, insufficient quantities, failure to buy regularly	Purchasing
Poor mix of materials, poorly trained workers, improperly adjusted machines, poor production scheduling or design, lack of proper tools or machines, unexpected volume changes	Production manager
Failure to detect defective goods	Receiving
Inefficient labor, poor supervision, waste on the production line	Foreman

To control against an unfavorable labor efficiency variance due to inadequate materials or sales orders, a daily direct labor report should be prepared. The causes and responsible parties for unfavorable labor efficiency variances are:

Cause	Party responsible
Poor-quality workers, poor training	Personnel or training
Inefficient flow of materials, wrong mixture of labor for a given job, inferior tools, idle time from production delays	Foreman
Employee unrest	Personnel or foreman
Improper functioning of equipment	Maintenance
Insufficient material supply or poor quality	Purchasing

An unfavorable labor quantity variance may imply that better equipment is needed, plant layout needs to be modified, better operating methods are required, and/or better employee training and development are necessary.

121 Salesperson Variances

INTRODUCTION. *Salesperson variances* are used to determine the effectiveness of the sales force by looking at cost and time spent by these employees.

HOW IS IT COMPUTED? Several computations are utilized to gain insight into salesperson variances:

1. Total cost variance = actual cost versus standard cost

2. Variance in salesperson days = (actual days versus standard days) × standard rate per day

3. Variance is salesperson costs = (actual rate versus standard rate) × actual days

4. Total variance in calls = actual calls versus actual sales
   Total variance in calls = standard calls versus standard sales

5. Variance in calls = (actual calls versus standard calls) × standard sales

6. Variance in sales = (actual sales versus standard sales) × standard calls

7. Joint variance = (actual calls versus standard calls) × (actual sales versus standard sales)

Example 1 Assume the following sales data for a small business:

Standard cost	$240,000
Standard salesperson days	2,000
Standard rate per salesperson day	$120
Actual cost	$238,000
Actual salesperson days	1,700
Actual rate per salesperson day	$140

The total cost variance is:

Actual cost	$238,000	
Standard cost	240,000	
Variance	$ 2,000	Favorable

This analysis demonstrates a favorable variance.

The control variance is broken down into salesperson days and salesperson costs.

Variance in salesperson days = (actual days versus standard days)
$$\times \text{standard rate per day}$$

$$= (1{,}700 \text{ versus } 2{,}000) \times \$120$$

$$= \$36{,}000 \qquad \text{Favorable}$$

The variance is favorable because the territory was handled in fewer days than expected.

Variance in salesperson costs = (actual rate versus standard rate)
$$\times \text{actual days}$$

$$= (\$140 \text{ versus } \$120) \times 1{,}700$$

$$= \$34{,}000 \qquad \text{Unfavorable}$$

An unfavorable variance results because the actual rate per day is greater than the expected rate per day.

Example 2 Assume that a salesperson called on 55 customers and sold each an average of $2800 worth of merchandise. The standard number of calls is 50, and the standard sale is $2400. Variance analysis of calls and sales follows:

Total variance:		
Actual calls × actual sale: 55 × $2,800	$154,000	
Standard calls × standard sale: 50 × $2,400	120,000	
Variance	$ 34,000	
Variance in calls:		
(actual calls versus standard calls)		
× standard sale: (55 versus 50) × $2,400	$ 12,000	F

Variance in sales:
   (actual sale versus standard sale)
      × standard calls: ($2,800 versus $2,400) × 50 $ 20,000   F
Joint variance:
   (actual calls versus standard calls)
      × (actual sale versus standard sale):
         (55 versus 50) × ($2,800 versus $2,400) $ 2,000   F

HOW IS IT USED AND APPLIED?   Small business owners use salesperson variances to appraise the sales force within a territory, including time spent and expenses incurred. Owners can keep track of salesperson costs and compare them to budget figures to determine whether salespersons are using their time and calls effectively in generating profitable sales.

Cost variances for the selling function may be analyzed by geographic region, product, or type of personnel.

122 How Are Things at the Warehouse?

INTRODUCTION.   *Warehouse cost variances* compare actual costs and standard costs to reveal the efficiency with which warehousing is being performed.

HOW IS IT COMPUTED?   Variances in warehousing costs can be computed by examining the cost per unit to store the goods and the number of orders expected. Calculations include:

1. Total warehousing cost variance = total actual cost versus total standard cost

2. Variance in orders = (actual orders versus standard orders) × standard unit cost

3. Variance in cost = (actual cost per unit versus standard cost per unit) × actual orders

Example   Assume that a small business supplies the following data regarding a product and warehouse costs:

Standard cost	$12,100
Standard orders	5,500
Standard unit cost	$2.20
Actual cost	$14,030
Actual orders	6,100
Actual unit cost	$2.30

Total warehousing cost variance is:

Actual cost	$14,030
Standard cost	12,100
	$ 1,930 U

For the analysis, the total variance is segregated into the variance in orders and the variance in cost:

Variance in orders = (actual orders versus standard orders)× standard unit cost: (6100 versus 5500) × $2.20   **$1320**   U

Variance in cost = (actual cost per unit versus standard cost per unit) × actual orders: ($2.30 versus $2.20) × 6100   **$ 610**   U

HOW IS IT USED AND APPLIED? Variances in warehousing costs are used by the owner to determine whether the warehousing function is being conducted properly. Analyses of warehousing costs are made to identify possible problems requiring appropriate cost-saving measures.

123 Incremental Cost versus Incremental Revenue

INTRODUCTION. Extra (marginal) cost is the change in total cost associated with a unit change in quantity. Extra (marginal) revenue is the rate of change in total revenue with respect to quantity sold.

HOW IS IT COMPUTED? The calculation of *marginal revenue* (MR) indicates to a small business how total sales will change if there is a change in the quantity sold of a product. Marginal revenue must equal *marginal cost* (MC) in order for profit to be maximized, or MR = MC.

In a discrete range of activity—the activity in which small businesses operate in actual business—MR is the equivalent to *incremental* (or differential) *revenue* (IR). MC is also viewed as being equivalent to *incremental* (or differential) *cost* (IC), which is the increment in cost between the two alternatives or two volumes of output. Therefore, in reality, decisions affecting this type of activity should be made only when IR > IC.

The marginal cost of the five-hundredth unit of output can be calculated by finding the difference between total cost at 499 units of output and total cost at 500 units of output. Thus, MC is the additional cost of one more unit of output, calculated as:

$$MC = \frac{\text{change in total cost}}{\text{change in quantity}}$$

MC is also the change in total variable cost associated with a unit change in output, because total cost changes even though total fixed cost remains unchanged. MC may also be considered the rate of change in total cost as the quantity (Q) of output changes; it is simply the first derivative of the total cost (TC) function. Thus,

$$MC = \frac{d\text{TC}}{dQ}$$

Similarly, the marginal revenue of the five-hundredth unit of output can be calculated by finding the difference between total revenue at 499 units of output and total revenue at 500 units of output. MR is thus the additional revenue derived from one more unit of output. It is calculated as:

$$MR = \frac{\text{change in total revenue}}{\text{change in quantity}}$$

MR may also be thought of as the rate of change in total revenue as the quantity (Q) of output changes and is simply the first derivative of the total revenue (TR) function. Thus,

$$MR = \frac{d\text{TR}}{dQ}$$

For profit to be maximized, MR must equal MC.

Example

$$TR = \$1,000Q - \$5Q^2 \quad \text{and} \quad TC = \$20,000 + \$200Q$$

MR and MC are:

$$MR = \frac{d\text{TR}}{dQ} = \$1,000 - \$10Q \quad \text{and} \quad MC = \frac{d\text{TC}}{dQ} = \$200$$

At the profit-maximizing level, MR = MC; thus,

$$MR = \$1,000 - \$10Q = \$200 = MC$$

Solving for Q gives

$$Q = 980 \text{ units}$$

which is the profit-maximizing quantity of output.

HOW IS IT USED AND APPLIED? Marginal analysis utilizing the concepts of marginal revenue and marginal cost is a key principle in decision making that can be applied to financial and investment decisions. The analysis suggests that financial and investment decisions should be made and actions taken only when marginal revenues equal marginal costs. If this condition exists, a given decision should maximize the business's profits.

Owners making any type of decision—such as marketing, operational, production, purchasing, financing, investment, and personnel decisions—must always weigh the marginal cost to be incurred against the marginal revenue to be derived from that decision. In practice, since owners typically work with incremental data, they have to weigh the incremental (additional) cost associated with the decision against the incremental revenue to be gained.

Averages, Expectations, and Variability in Business Activities

124 Averages (Means): Simple and Weighted

INTRODUCTION. Averages are frequently used in business as a uniform method of stating values—for example, the average inventory, average cost, average income, average sales per salesperson, average units produced per worker, average sick days per employee, average overhead per department, etc. An average is more meaningful if it is compared to something else. An average should be compared over time. For example, the trend in the average revenue per salesperson will reveal the success of changes in sales policies such as pricing, advertising and promotion, and reassignment of territories.

HOW IS IT COMPUTED? A *simple average* (mean) is computed by adding all the numerical figures in a list and dividing by the number of figures in the list. The formula for a simple average is:

$$\text{Simple average} = \frac{S}{n}$$

where S = sum of the figures in the list and n = number of figures in the list. *Note:* Lotus 1-2-3 has a function key, @AVG(*list*), for the calculation of a simple average.

A *weighted average* (mean) is an average of observations having different degrees of importance or frequency. The formula for a weighted average is:

$$\text{Weighted average} = \Sigma wx$$

where x = the data values and w = relative weight assigned to each observation, expressed as a percentage or relative frequency.

Example 1 A monthly sales report shows the following:

Department A	$520,000
Department B	430,000
Department C	460,000
Department D	480,000

The simple average of sales is:

$$\frac{\$520,000 + \$430,000 + \$460,000 + \$480,000}{4} = \$472,500$$

Example 2 Total monthly sales are $1,200,000, and the number of salespeople is 20. The average salesperson generates sales of:

$$\frac{\$1,200,000}{20} = \$60,000$$

Example 3 A manufacturer uses three grades of labor to produce a finished product as follows:

Grade of labor	Labor hours per unit of labor	Hourly wages (x)
Skilled	6	$10.00
Semiskilled	3	8.00
Unskilled	1	6.00

The simple average (mean) labor cost per hour for this product can be computed as:

$$\text{Simple average} = \frac{\$10.00 + \$8.00 + \$6.00}{3} = \$8.00 \text{ per hour}$$

However, this implies that each grade of labor was used in equal amounts, and this is not the case. To calculate the average cost of labor per hour correctly, the weighted average should be computed as follows:

$$\text{Weighted average} = \$10.00\left(\frac{6}{10}\right) + \$8.00\left(\frac{3}{10}\right) + \$6.00\left(\frac{1}{10}\right)$$

$$= \$9.00 \text{ per hour}$$

where the weights used equal the proportion of the total labor required to manufacture the product.

Example 4 A prospective acquirer wants to determine the price to offer for a targeted business. It is decided that the business valuation should be based on 2 times the weighted-average earnings over the last 3 years. The most current year is always given the greatest weight.

Year	Net income	Weight	Weighted net income
19X1	$300,000	1	$ 300,000
19X2	260,000	2	520,000
19X3	350,000	3	1,050,000
		6	$1,870,000

$$\text{Weighted average earnings} = \frac{\$1,870,000}{6} = \$311,667$$

$$\text{Business valuation} = \$311,667 \times 2 = \$623,334$$

Example 5 Your small business has two loans outstanding. Loan 1 is for $300,000 with a 10 percent interest rate. Loan 2 is for $400,000 with an 8 percent interest rate. You want to determine the average interest rate.

A weighted-average interest rate is needed because the loans are for different amounts. The weighted-average interest rate equals 8.9 percent, computed as follows:

$$\left(\frac{\$300,000}{\$700,000 \times 10\%} \right) + \left(\frac{\$400,000}{\$700,000 \times 8\%} \right)$$

$$4.3\% \quad + \quad 4.6\% \quad = 8.9\%$$

Example 6 You invest in securities. The amount invested, the months held, and the profit earned are as follows:

Type	Investment	Months held	Profit
A	$ 80,000	6	$ 5,000
B	90,000	20	10,000
C	50,000	9	2,000
Total	$220,000		$17,000

You need to calculate a weighted-average rate of return because the amounts invested and the time period held vary with each investment.

Step 1. Compute the rate of return per investment.

$$\frac{\text{Profit}}{\text{Investment}}$$

$$\text{A:} \quad \frac{\$5,000}{\$80,000} = 6.25\%$$

$$\text{B:} \quad \frac{\$10,000}{\$90,000} = 11.11\%$$

$$\text{C:} \quad \frac{\$2,000}{\$50,000} = 4.00\%$$

Step 2. Annualize the rates of return so they are expressed on a common basis.

Annualized rate of return = (total return/number of months) × 12

A: $\left(\dfrac{6.25\%}{6}\right) \times 12 = 12.50\%$

B: $\left(\dfrac{11.11\%}{20}\right) \times 12 = 6.67\%$

C: $\left(\dfrac{4.0\%}{9}\right) \times 12 = 5.30\%$

Step 3. Determine the weighted-average rate of return.

Weighted-average rate of return

$= \dfrac{\text{amount invested in each security}}{\text{total amount invested}} \times \text{annualized rate of return}$

$= \left(\dfrac{\$80,000}{\$220,000} \times 12.50\%\right) + \left(\dfrac{\$90,000}{\$220,000} \times 6.67\%\right) + \left(\dfrac{\$50,000}{\$220,000} \times 5.3\%\right)$

$=\qquad 4.5\% \qquad + \qquad 2.7\% \qquad + \qquad 1.2\% \qquad = 8.4\%$

Note: To compute a return rate for less than 1 year, use:

Return rate (less than 1 year) $= \dfrac{\text{rate of return}}{12}$

$\times$ number of months held

Example 7 If the annual rate of return is 15 percent, the rate of return to be earned in 3 months is:

$$\dfrac{15\%}{12} \times 3 = 3.75\%$$

or

$$15\% \times \dfrac{3}{12} = 3.75\%$$

HOW IS IT USED AND APPLIED? Whenever each value has a different degree of importance or frequency, the weighted-average formula may be used. An arithmetic average is used only when the values are equally weighted. Expected value is basically a weighted average, the weights being the probabilities of occurrence.

Managers of all functional areas of business must have an understanding of the difference between the arithmetic mean and the weighted mean in order to calculate the correct average.

For multiproduct lines, it is necessary to predetermine the sales mix and then compute a weighted-average contribution margin (CM) in order to perform breakeven and cost-volume-profit (CVP) analysis. The weights used here are sales mix ratios. See Sec. 54, Cost-Volume-Profit Analysis.

Financial managers need to know the minimum rate of return, which is in effect the weighted average cost of capital, in order to decide whether or not to accept a project. See Sec. 8, Estimating the Cost of Debt and Equity Financing.

An average is more meaningful if it is compared over time or expressed relative to another average. Examples are reporting the change in average departmental sales per month, comparing the average sales figure to average marketing expenses needed to obtain that revenue, average telephone expense per person, and average orders processed per clerk. An average can identify abuses, such as when employees are using business facilities such as copiers for personal use.

An average may identify a problem in operations, such as when average sales increase but profits are declining, or when units produced are increasing but the number of defects are skyrocketing, causing the unit cost actually to increase.

125 Median and Mode

INTRODUCTION. The *median* is the middle value of a list of numbers, where the numbers in the data set are arranged by order of importance—that is, the midpoint in a range of values. The *mode* is the most commonly occurring value in a data set. It is a meaningful statistic only when a particular value clearly occurs more frequently than any of the others.

HOW IS IT COMPUTED?

Median. The formula for the position occupied by the median item is:

$$\frac{n + 1}{2}$$

where n is the number of items.

> **Example** An employer has nine employees, all of whom earn different hourly wages. The employer wants to determine the median wage of his employees, whose wages are listed below:

Unsorted Hourly Wages of Employees

Employee	Hourly wage rate
1	$3.75
2	5.25
3	4.25
4	6.25
5	6.50
6	4.00
7	4.50
8	5.75
9	8.00

The steps to calculate the median are as follows.

1. Sort the data by wage rate.

Sorted Hourly Wages of Employees

Employee	Hourly wage rate
1	$3.75
6	4.00
3	4.25
7	4.50
2	5.25
8	5.75
4	6.25
5	6.50
9	8.00

2. Locate the median item position:

$$\text{Median item position} = \frac{n+1}{2}$$

$$= \frac{9+1}{2} = \frac{10}{2} = \text{fifth position}$$

3. Ascertain the value of the component occupying the median position. By a simple process of observation, we determine that employee 2 is in the median position, receiving $5.25 per hour.

Mode. The mode is determined by observation, usually from a graph. On such a graph, the modal value is the value of the point of highest density of activity.

A simple mode is shown in Fig. 125.1.

Sometimes a distribution can be bimodal. For example, if a retailer wishes to find the modal values of the distribution of weekly sales volume, a graph may be drawn as shown in Fig. 125.2.

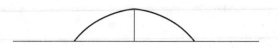

Figure 125.1 Simple mode.

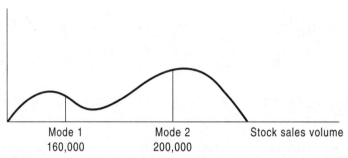

| Mode 1 | Mode 2 | Stock sales volume |
| 160,000 | 200,000 | |

Figure 125.2 Bimodal distribution.

HOW IS IT USED AND APPLIED? The median is an essential measure of central tendency, used in financial analysis when it is necessary to eliminate large deviations. For example, in a seasonal industry such as the manufacture and sale of snow skis, it may be essential to identify the midpoint sales month. Use of the median may be misrepresentative, however, if the values of the observed items do not cluster at the center of the data set. In this case, modal analysis may be more appropriate.

There are a wide variety of financial applications for modal analysis, including the evaluation of a product's selling periods when there are clear distinctions. Modal analysis is useful with any financial or other data graph to display the most commonly occurring value. Modal analysis can be applied to sales, income, utilization rates, population, and other data where there is a clearly recurring value. Use of a mode graph can be extremely effective in making business presentations.

126 Expected Value and Standard Deviation

INTRODUCTION. *Expected value* is a weighted average using probabilities as weights. For decisions involving uncertainty, the concept of expected value provides a rational means for selecting the best course of action.

Whenever we talk about expected value, one statistic that goes with it is standard deviation. *Standard deviation* is a statistic that measures the tendency of data to be spread out. It is intuitively a margin of error associated with a given expected value.

HOW IS IT COMPUTED?

Expected Value. The expected value $(\bar{r})$ is found by multiplying the probability of each outcome by its payoff:

$$\bar{r} = \Sigma r_i p_i$$

where r_i is the outcome for the ith possible event and p_i is the probability of occurrence of that outcome.

Example 1 Consider the possible rate of return, depending on the state of the economy—i.e., recession, normal, and prosperity—that a small business owner might earn next year on a $50,000 investment in proposal A or on a $50,000 investment in proposal B.

State of economy	Return (r_i)	Probability (p_i)
Proposal A		
Recession	− 5%	.2
Normal	20	.6
Prosperity	40	.2
Proposal B		
Recession	10%	.2
Normal	15	.6
Prosperity	20	.2

The expected rates of returns are:

Proposal A: $\bar{r} = (-5\%)(.2) + (20\%)(.6) + (40\%)(.2) = 19\%$

Proposal B: $\bar{r} = (10\%)(.2) + (15\%)(.6) + (20\%)(.2) = 15\%$

Standard Deviation. The standard deviation, denoted by σ (sigma), is defined as:

$$\sigma = \sqrt{\frac{\Sigma(r - \bar{r})^2}{n - 1}}$$

where $\bar{r}$ is the mean or expected value. In this case the r's are equally likely and therefore equally weighted. Note that for the sample data, we divide by $(n - 1)$. The standard deviation is used as a measure of risk.

Example 2 Quarterly returns for $1\frac{1}{2}$ years for Amko Motors are listed below.

Time period	r	$(r - \bar{r})$	$(r - \bar{r})^2$
1	10%	0	0
2	15	5	25
3	20	10	100
4	5	-5	25
5	-10	-20	400
6	20	10	100
	60		650

From the table,

$$\bar{r} = \frac{60}{6} = 10\%$$

$$\sigma = \sqrt{\frac{\Sigma(r - \bar{r})^2}{n - 1}} = \sqrt{\frac{650}{6 - 1}} = \sqrt{130} = 11.40\%$$

On average, Amko Motors stock has returned 10 percent over the last six quarters, and the variability about its average return was 11.40 percent. The high standard deviation (11.40 percent) relative to the average return of 10 percent indicates a risky situation.

Standard deviation is also a measure of the dispersion of a probability distribution. The smaller the deviation, the tighter is the distribution, and thus the lower is the riskiness of the investment. We use the square root of the mean of the squared deviations from the expected value $(\bar{r})$,

$$\sigma = (r - \bar{r})^2 p_i$$

where

$$\bar{r} = \Sigma r_i p_i$$

To calculate σ, we proceed as follows:

Step 1. Compute the expected rate of return (r).

Step 2. Subtract each possible return from r to obtain a set of deviations $(r - \bar{r})$.

Step 3. Square each deviation, multiply the squared deviation by the probability of occurrence for its return, and sum these products to obtain the variance (σ^2):

$$\sigma^2 = \Sigma(r - \bar{r})^2 p_i$$

Step 4. Finally, take the square root of the variance to obtain the standard deviation (σ).

Example 3 Using the same data as in Example 1, we will compute the standard deviations.
To work this step-by-step approach, it is convenient to set up a table, as follows:

Return (r)	Probability (p)	(Step 1) rp	(Step 2) $(r - \bar{r})$	$(r - \bar{r})^2$	(Step 3) $(r - \bar{r})^2 p$
		Proposal A			
-5%	.2	-1%	-24%	576	115.2
20	.6	12	1	1	.6
40	.2	8	21	441	88.2
		$\bar{r} = 19\%$			$\sigma^2 = 204$

$$\text{(Step 4) } \sigma = \sqrt{204}$$
$$\sigma = 14.28\%$$

Return (r)	Probability (p)	rp	$(r - \bar{r})$	$(r - \bar{r})^2$	$(r - \bar{r})^2 p$
		Proposal B			
10%	.2	2%	-5%	25	5
15	.6	9	0	0	0
20	.2	4	5	25	5
		$\bar{r} = 15\%$			$\sigma^2 = 10$

$$\text{(Step 4) } \sigma = \sqrt{10}$$
$$\sigma = 3.16\%$$

CAN A COMPUTER HELP? Spreadsheet programs and financial calculators often calculate standard deviation automatically. For example, Lotus 1-2-3 has a function called @STD(*list*) that performs the calculation.

HOW IS IT USED AND APPLIED? The standard deviation is used as an indicator of the risk involved in a project, since it measures the variability of returns around the expected return from an investment. Financial managers can also make important inferences from past data by using expected value and standard deviation. Other applications of standard deviation include determining the variability of sales and earnings. Unstable or erratic sales and earnings mean uncertainty, resulting in greater risk.

See Sec. 127, Coefficient of Variation.

127 Coefficient of Variation

INTRODUCTION. The *coefficient of variation* is a measure of relative dispersion, or relative risk. It represents the degree of risk per unit of return or profit.

HOW IS IT COMPUTED? The coefficient of variation is computed by dividing the standard deviation (σ) by the expected value $\Sigma(x)$, where

$$\Sigma(x) = \Sigma x_i p_i$$

where x_i is the outcome for the ith possible event and p_i is the probability of occurrence of that outcome; and

$$\sigma = \sqrt{\Sigma[x - \Sigma(x)]^2 p_i}$$

Example Consider two business proposals, A and B, with the following probability distributions of cash flows in each of the next 5 years:

	Cash inflows			
Probability	(.2)	(.3)	(.4)	(.1)
A	$ 50	$200	$300	$400
B	100	150	250	850

The expected value of the cash inflow for proposal A is:

$$\$50(.2) + 200(.3) + 300(.4) + 400(.1) = \$230$$

The expected value of the cash inflow for proposal B is:

$$\$100(.2) + 150(.3) + 250(.4) + 850(.1) = \$250$$

The standard deviations for proposals A and B are computed as follows:

Proposal A: $\sigma = \sqrt{(\$50 - 230)(.2) + (200 - 230)(.3) + (300 - 230)(.4) + (400 - 230)(.1)}$

$= \$107.70$

Proposal B: $\sigma = \sqrt{(\$100 - 250)(.2) + (150 - 250)(.3) + (250 - 250)(.4) + (850 - 250)(.1)}$

$= \$208.57$

Proposal B is more risky than proposal A, since its standard deviation is greater.
We note that:

Proposal	Expected value $[\Sigma(x)]$	Standard deviation (σ)
A	$230	$107.7
B	250	208.57

The coefficient of variation for each proposal is:

$$\text{Proposal A:} \quad \frac{\$107.70}{\$230} = 0.47$$

$$\text{Proposal B:} \quad \frac{\$208.57}{\$250} = 0.83$$

Therefore, because the coefficient is a relative measure of risk, proposal B is considered more risky than A.

HOW IS IT USED AND APPLIED? The standard deviation is an indicator of the risk involved in a proposal, since it measures the variability of returns around the expected return. Business managers can also make important inferences from past data using expected value and standard deviation. The problem with the standard deviation is that it is a measure of absolute risk. It can only be used to compare projects with the same expected returns. Therefore, businesspeople use the coefficient of variation to compare projects with *differing* expected returns.

128 Normal Distribution

INTRODUCTION. The *normal distribution* is a probability distribution that has the following important characteristics:

1. The curve has a single peak.
2. It is bell-shaped.
3. The mean (average) lies at the center of the distribution, and the distribution is symmetrical around the mean.
4. The two tails of the distribution extend indefinitely and never touch the horizontal axis.

5. The shape of the distribution is determined by its mean (μ) and its standard deviation (σ).

HOW IS IT COMPUTED?   As with any continuous probability function, the area under the curve must be equal to 1, and the area between two values of X (say, a and b) represents the probability that X lies between a and b, as illustrated in Fig. 128.1.

Further, since the normal distribution is symmetric, it has the nice property that a known percentage of all possible values of X lie within $\pm$ a certain number of standard deviations of the mean, as shown below:

Percent (%)	99.73%	99%	95.45%	95%	90%	68.27%
Number of $\pm\sigma$s:	3.00	2.58	2.00	1.96	1.645	1.00

That is, 68.27 percent of the values of any normally distributed variable lie within the interval (μ, σ). The probability of the normal distribution as given above is difficult to work with in determining areas under a curve, and each set of X values generates another curve (assuming that the means and standard deviations are different). To facilitate computations, every set of X values is translated to a new axis, a Z set, with the translation defined as

$$Z = \frac{x - \mu}{\sigma}$$

The resulting values, called Z values, are the values of a new variable called the *standard normal variate, Z*. The translation process is shown in Fig. 128.2.

The new variable Z is normally distributed with a mean of 0 and a standard deviation of 1. Tables of areas under this standard normal distribution have been compiled and widely published, so the area under any normal distribution can be found by translating the X values to Z values and then using the tables for the standardized normal.

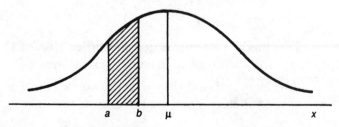

Figure 128.1 Normal distribution.

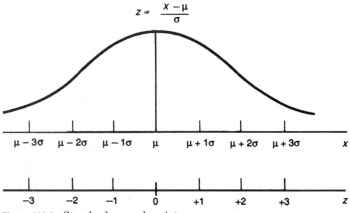

Figure 128.2 Standard normal variate.

Example Assume that the total book value of inventory is normally distributed with μ = $8000 and σ = $1000. What percent of the population lies between $6000 and $10,000?

To answer, we first translate the X values to Z values using the Z formula:

$$Z_1 = \frac{\$6,000 - \$8,000}{\$1,000} \qquad Z_2 = \frac{\$10,000 - \$8,000}{\$1,000}$$

$$= -2 \qquad\qquad\qquad = +2$$

Referring to the table of percentages, we see that 95.45 percent of the population lies between these two values. Interpreted as a probability, the statement can be made that total book value will lie between $6,000 and $10,000 with a probability of .9545.

HOW IS IT USED AND APPLIED? Normal distribution is perhaps the most widely assumed distribution in statistical applications to business. This widespread use is because a great many business data follow this familiar bell-shaped pattern. Applications are numerous, including:

1. Evaluating capital expenditure projects whose cash flows are uncertain

2. Determining the probability of meeting the delivery date for a project

3. Determining safety stock (see Sec. 43, Allowing for Safety Stock)

4. Finding the probability of a business not losing money (or at least breaking even)

Adequacy and Cost of Insurance Coverage

129 Determining How Much Insurance Is Needed

INTRODUCTION. *Commercial insurance* falls into two major classes—individual insurance and group insurance. Individual insurance differs from group insurance in that the contract covers a person or family as opposed to a group of persons. Each contract sold covers an individual or family and is sold separately.

Key-person insurance is insurance purchased by a business seeking to protect itself against financial losses caused by the death or disability of a key employee. This type of insurance seeks to protect a business from the death or disability of an individual possessing a high degree of skill and knowledge, which might lead to serious loss to the firm in terms of reduced sales, increased costs, or restricted credit.

Disability income contracts are designed primarily to provide income coverage during the period of disability, but may, in some cases, also provide medical insurance protection.

HOW IS IT COMPUTED? Ordinary insurance is generally sold in amounts of at least $1000. The premiums are calculated on an annual basis but may also be paid on a semiannual, quarterly, or monthly basis. The typical rule of thumb is that a worker with a spouse and two children should carry enough insurance to cover five times his or her annual income. Another year of income should be added for each additional dependent. Thus, the formula for determining life insurance coverage for a family of four is:

$$\text{Required life insurance protection} = \text{annual salary} \times 5$$

Key insurance coverage is based on the present value of lost revenue over a predetermined number of years.

For disability insurance, coverage must be at least 60 percent of salary, unless the small business owner has sufficient personal resources to cover disability income needs. Thus, the formula for disability coverage is:

$$\text{Salary} \times 60\% = \text{disability coverage}$$

Example 1 John Hamilton, a small business owner, is married with two children. His annual salary from his business is $60,000. His life insurance protection should be $300,000, calculated as follows:

$$\$60,000 \times 5 = \$300,000$$

Example 2 Marilyn Johnson, a small business owner, is married with three children. Her annual salary from her business is $75,000. Her life insurance protection should be $450,000, calculated as follows:

$$\$75,000 \times 5 = \$375,000 + \$75,000 = \$450,000$$

Example 3 It is estimated that the death of a key employee would reduce a firm's earnings by $50,000 annually for a period of at least 5 years. Key-person insurance for at least $210,600 should be purchased by the small business owner, assuming a 6 percent rate of interest, calculated as follows:

$50,000 × 4.212 (present value of 6% for 5 years; see Appendix Table 4)
$$= \$210,600$$

Example 4 Selena Combs, who earns a salary of $100,000 from a small business, seeks disability insurance. She should obtain coverage of $60,000, calculated as follows:

$$\$100,000 \times 60\% = \$60,000$$

HOW IS IT USED AND APPLIED? Life insurance should emphasize protection as opposed to investment. A contract with some investment element may also be proper if the business wants to meet protection and investment objectives with one contract. The small business owner may also want protection against a loss of profits due to the death of a key employee by obtaining a life insurance contract that contains an investment element. This technique would protect the business during the employee's period of employment, and also provide him or her with retirement income out of the investment value of the policy should the employee live and eventually retire.

130 Factoring in Coinsurance and Copayment

INTRODUCTION. The coinsurance principle has two basic purposes: (1) It prevents fire policyholders from underinsuring their property; and (2) it makes the insured bear a specified amount of the loss.

HOW IS IT COMPUTED? A coinsurance clause provides that if the small business owner will insure his property up to a given percentage of its value (usually 80 percent), the owner will be given the benefit of a lower premium. If the owner insures for less than a fixed percentage, he must bear a portion of the loss. The coinsurance formula is:

$$\frac{\text{Amount of insurance carried}}{\text{Amount of insurance required}} \times \text{loss} = \text{insurer's liability}$$

The coinsurance clause becomes inoperative if the loss is equal to or exceeds the stipulated percentage of value. Thus, assume that the insurance required (80 percent) is $80,000, the insurance obtained is $20,000, and the loss is $80,000. The insurance company will pay $20,000 or ($20,000/$80,000), the full value of the policy.

Insurance reimbursement is based on the lowest amount of either the face of the policy, the fair market value of the loss, or possible reimbursement.

Where property is insured with more than one company and the total concurrent insurance exceeds the actual loss, a standard pro rata clause applies; that is, the insured can collect from each company only its proportionate or pro rata share of the total amount of insurance.

Example 1 The Nevilo Company had inventory worth $10,000, on which the firm has a fire insurance policy of $6000 with an 80 percent coinsurance clause. Fire destroyed $4000 worth of inventory. The firm will recover $3000, calculated as follows:

$$\frac{\$6,000}{80\% \times \$10,000} \times \$4,000 = \$3,000$$

Example 2 Theo, Kramer, and Arlo are partners in a small business. The partnership obtained a $600,000 fire insurance policy on a building owned by the partnership. The policy contained an 80 percent coinsurance clause. Subsequently, the building was damaged by fire to the extent of $300,000. The building was worth $1,000,000 at the time the policy was issued and $800,000 at the time of the fire loss. The partnership will recover $281,250, calculated as follows:

$$\frac{\$600,000}{80\% \times \$800,000} \times \$300,000 = \$281,250$$

Because the partnership carried only $600,000 worth of insurance, it became a coinsurer with the insurance company for the difference of $40,000 ($640,000 − $600,000).

Example 3 The following demonstrates insurance recovery under three different calculations:

Case	Face of policy	Fair market value of property	Fair market value of loss
A	$ 4,000	$10,000	$ 6,000
B	6,000	10,000	10,000
C	10,000	10,000	4,000

Case A: $\dfrac{\$4,000}{80\% \times \$10,000} \times \$6,000 = \$3,000$ insurance reimbursement

Case B: $\dfrac{\$6,000}{80\% \times \$10,000} \times \$10,000 = \$7,500$ insurance reimbursement

Case C: $\dfrac{\$10,000}{80\% \times \$10,000} \times \$4,000 = \$5,000$ insurance reimbursement

Insurance reimbursement is based on the lowest of the face of the policy, the fair market value of the loss, or possible reimbursement. Therefore, in case B, the insured can recover only $6000, the amount of the policy. In case C, the insured can recover only $4000 (not $5000), the fair market value of the loss.

Example 4 A small business owner of a building worth $500,000, believing that her loss by fire will not exceed $200,000, obtains two standard fire policies with 80 percent coinsurance clauses, one from Company A for $120,000, and the other from Company B for $80,000. The firm subsequently sustains a fire loss of $200,000. Under the 80 percent coinsurance clause, the owner should have insured for 80 percent, or $400,000. She actually insured for $200,000, or half. She will therefore recover only half the loss, or $100,000. Under the pro rata clause, the recovery from each company will be as follows:

		Ratio	Loss	Amount recovered from each company
Company A	$120,000	12/20	× $100,000	$ 60,000
Company B	80,000	8/20	× 100,000	40,000
Total	$200,000			$100,000

HOW IS IT USED AND APPLIED?   The amount of insurance to be purchased is determined by the insured. In determining the proper amount, the small business owner must give careful consideration to the value of the property and to any changes in the value, so that the insurance coverage can be adjusted periodically if required. The coinsurance clause does not mean that the insurance company will pay only 80 percent of any loss, or that the insured is prohibited from obtaining any insurance beyond 80 percent of the value. The owner is free to insure the property to 100 percent of the value if he or she believes it necessary, so that any loss will be paid in full. However, if the insured is careful and obtains coverage amounting to 80 percent or more of the value of the property, any losses sustained will be covered in full, as if the policy contained no coinsurance clause. The owner of destroyed property can use the insurance reimbursement formula to compute the insurance proceeds due because of a casualty loss.

131 Evaluating Insurance Risk

INTRODUCTION. Every small business owner who is faced with the protection of a firm's assets must assess the various types of losses confronting his or her organization. The owner must then measure these potential losses with respect to such matters as their likelihood of occurrence and their effect on the profitability and operation of the firm.

HOW IS IT COMPUTED? To identify all potential losses, the small business owner must first prepare a checklist of all possible losses that could occur. The basic list should include (1) direct property exposures, and (2) liability losses. In measuring these losses, the two methods most commonly used to measure loss severity are the maximum possible loss to one unit per occurrence and the maximum probable loss for one unit per occurrence. The maximum possible loss is the worst loss that could possibly happen; the maximum probable loss is the worst loss that is likely to happen. The maximum probable loss is usually less than the maximum possible loss.

Example 1 Freeze Office Manufacturers owns a building with a fair market value of $400,000, excluding the land. The contents of the building, consisting of inventory, office equipment, and machinery, is worth $200,000. In case of complete destruction by fire or storm, the owner will lose $600,000, the maximum possible loss. However, assuming a maximum probable loss of less than $600,000 because the owner does not anticipate complete destruction of the premises, insurance coverage can be purchased for an amount less than $600,000.

Example 2 Fenwick Producers occupies a new warehouse and pays rent of $50,000 annually on a 5-year lease. The owner feels that if the building is destroyed by fire, similar property will cost $100,000 per year to rent. Thus, the proprietor wishes to purchase insurance to cover this possible contingency. She feels that there is an equal chance that the property could be destroyed during any one of the five years that the business occupies the warehouse. Therefore, the owner seeks to insure the *average cost* of the total increase in rental costs if the warehouse should burn down. Using the present value of a $1 at 8 percent, the present value of the rental cost for the 5-year period at $50,000, representing the increased annual rental cost, Fenwick should obtain a policy for approximately $100,000, computed as follows:

Year	Rental cost	Present value of $1 at 8%*	Amount
1	$50,000	0.926	$46,300
2	50,000	0.857	42,850
3	50,000	0.794	39,700
4	50,000	0.735	36,750
5	50,000	0.681	34,050
			$199,650/2 = $99,825

*See Appendix Table 3.

This amount would protect Fenwick against any increased costs due to a required move to more expensive quarters in case the property is destroyed by fire or some other catastrophe.

This policy would be in addition to any possible *business interruption insurance* that the owner might wish to obtain to insure against loss of profits during the period that the business cannot produce or sell goods due to destruction of the rented premises.

Example 3 Lux Realty rents a small building for 3 years, receiving $10,000 per year in rental income. If the building is destroyed by a fire, the rental income will be lost. Using the present value of $1 at 8 percent, the present value of income for the 3-year period is $25,770, computed as follows:

Year	Rental income	Present value of $1 at 8%*	Amount
1	$10,000	0.926	$ 9,260
2	10,000	0.857	8,570
3	10,000	0.794	7,940
			$25,770

*See Appendix Table 3.

Example 4 The Calx Company makes small personal computers. In the 10 years that the business has been assembling and selling computers, only one has caught fire. The fire caused extensive damage to the customer's office, so, in a gesture of goodwill, Calx paid for all fire damages and replaced the computer. The total cost to Calx was $50,000. Calx feels that, with improvements in computer technology, the probability of a computer fire is small and might occur only once a year and cause a maximum probable loss not exceeding $500,000.

Thus, Calx purchases a policy protecting against product liability with a limit of $500,000 per occurrence.

HOW IS IT USED AND APPLIED? The small business owner must first identify the continuous property and liability risk exposure of his or her business. The owner must also assess the frequency of product liability claims due to the "claims consciousness" of the public. Each potential loss must be assessed and evaluated in terms of current operating conditions and the prevailing economic environment. In determining the severity of a possible loss, the small business owner must include a broad spectrum of losses that might result from a given event as well as the ultimate impact upon the firm.

132 Estimating the Value of a Claim

INTRODUCTION. When the risk insured against causes a loss, it is essential for the small business owner to receive fair payment from the insurer. Settlement should be neither excessive nor inadequate. To obtain equitable compensation, the small business owner must have the ability to assess the actual loss sustained.

HOW IS IT COMPUTED? Determining the value of a claim can be a difficult task. The following procedures provide formulas for measuring the actual loss sustained.

To estimate a fire insurance loss, the insured should use one of two valuation bases: (1) replacement cost or (2) actual cash value (which is replacement cost less physical depreciation). The formula for replacement cost is:

Accumulated depreciation $\times$ 2 + original cost
$$= \text{estimated replacement cost}$$

(the factor 2 is used to reflect the effect of inflation on the original cost of the property).

To estimate the actual cash value, the following steps should be taken:

1. Determine the estimated replacement cost.
2. Estimate the physical, not tax, life of the property.
3. Deduct the estimated expended life of the property to arrive at the actual cash value.

To estimate the value of inventory lost through theft or fire, the *gross margin method* (gross margin/net sales revenue) should be used. The formula is:

Beginning inventory
+ Net purchases
= Cost of goods available for sale
− Cost of goods sold
= Ending inventory

Another method for estimating the value of lost inventory is the *retail inventory method*. The formula is:

$$\frac{\text{Cost}}{\text{Retail}} \times (\text{goods available for sale at retail}$$
$$- \text{ net sales revenue at retail})$$
$$= \text{ending inventory at cost}$$

Example 1 Pylar Lumber owned equipment with an original cost of $100,000 and accumulated depreciation of $40,000. The business suffered a fire and used the replacement cost method to estimate the insurance proceeds. The replacement cost was determined to be $180,000, calculated as follows:

Accumulated depreciation ($40,000 × 2)	$ 80,000
+ Original cost ($100,000)	100,000
= Estimated replacement cost	180,000

Example 2 The Green Pipe Company owned equipment with an original cost of $200,000 and accumulated depreciation of $60,000. The machinery had an estimated useful life of 10 years and had been in use for 4 years. The business suffered a fire and used the actual cash value method to estimate the expected insurance proceeds. The actual cash value of the loss was determined to be $192,000, calculated as follows:

Accumulated depreciation ($60,000 × 2)	$120,000
+ Original cost ($200,000)	200,000
= Estimated replacement cost	$320,000
− Depreciated life (4/10 years = 40% × $320,000)	128,000
= Actual cash value	$192,000

Example 3 Dupont Paint used the gross margin method to determine its fire loss. The firm's beginning inventory was $10,000, net purchases for the period were $70,000, net sales were $100,000, and the estimated gross margin was 40 percent. The estimated ending inventory lost was $20,000, calculated as follows:

Beginning inventory	$10,000
+ Net purchases	70,000
= Cost of goods available for sale	$80,000
− Cost of goods sold ($100,000 × 60%)*	60,000
= Ending inventory	$20,000

*(Retail 100% − gross margin 40%)

Example 4 Echo Parts used the retail sales method to determine its fire loss. The cost-to-retail ratio was 60 percent, and the goods available for sale at retail were $300,000. The net sales at retail for the period were $270,000. The ending inventory, at cost, lost in the fire was $18,000, calculated as follows:

$$60\% \times (\$300,000 - \$270,000) = \$18,000$$

HOW IS IT USED AND APPLIED? Property and liability insurance policies usually require that the insured give prompt notice of any loss to the insurance company. Within a stated period of time, usually 60 days, the insured must also provide a "proof of loss." The proof provides details of the theft or loss, detailed replacement or repair estimates, and a list of inventories lost or damaged. The insured is also expected to cooperate with the insurance company in processing the claim and supplying any receipts, accounting records, and legal documents requested.

Hiring and Compensating Employees

133 Permutations and Combinations

INTRODUCTION. *Permutations* enable business managers to determine the number of ways something can be arranged. *Combinations* determine the number of ways things can be combined when the arrangement or order is not important. Permutations and combinations can be used to assign personnel to jobs.

HOW IS IT COMPUTED? Permutations are computed by the following formula:

$$P = \frac{n!}{(n - r)!}$$

P means the number of ways to arrange n things taken r at a time. The "!" stands for *factorial,* and means that whatever the number is, multiply it times the series of whole numbers preceding it. Thus $5! = 5 \times 4 \times 3 \times 2 \times 1 = 120$. As a special case, $0! = 1$.

Example 1 Suppose that only three management internship positions are available for five qualified applicants. In how many different ways can three individuals from among the five be assigned to the three different management positions?

$$P = \frac{n!}{(n - r)!} = \frac{5!}{(5 - 3)!} = \frac{5 \times 4 \times 3 \times 2 \times 1}{2 \times 1} = 60$$

Combinations are computed by the following formula:

$$C = \frac{n!}{r!(n - r)!}$$

Note that only the "$r!$" was added in the denominator of the permutation formula. C is the number of combinations of n things taken r at a time.

Example 2 Referring to the situation described in Example 1, suppose that the three available positions can all be considered comparable, and not really different for practical purposes. In how many different ways can the three applicants be chosen from among the five qualified people to fill the three management positions?

$$C = \frac{n!}{r!(n - r)!} = \frac{5!}{3!(5 - 3)!} = \frac{5 \times 4 \times 3 \times 2 \times 1}{(3 \times 2 \times 1)(2 \times 1)}$$

$$= 10$$

HOW IS IT USED AND APPLIED? Permutations can be used to determine how many possible variations there are. For instance, a business owner may advertise two job openings, one for a copywriter and one for an artist. If 10 people who are qualified for either position apply, in how many ways can the openings be filled? Since the jobs are different, the order of selecting people matters: X as copywriter and Y as artist is different from Y as copywriter and X as artist. The solution is found by counting permutations:

$$P = \frac{10!}{(10 - 2)!} = \frac{10!}{8!} = 10 \times 9 = 90$$

Therefore there are 90 different ways to fill the openings.

Unlike permutations, where the order in which the objects are arranged is important, combinations are concerned with the number of possible different groupings of objects without regard to the order. For example, a business owner advertises two job openings for computer programmers, both with the same salary and job description. In how many ways can the openings be filled if 10 people apply? Since the two jobs are identical, the order of selecting the applicants is not important. Choosing X and Y for the positions is the same as choosing Y and X. Thus, the answer is a number of combinations that is half as large as the number of permutations in the previous example:

$$C = \frac{n!}{r!(n - r)!} = \frac{10!}{2!(10 - 2)!} = \frac{90}{2} = 45$$

There are many uses for combinations. Suppose that a business owner wants to analyze all possible failures of a system. There are a dozen different components of the system that can fail ($n = 12$), but the owner needs to evaluate only those cases where two fail at the same time ($r = 2$). At first glance the numbers may not look so bad, but

$$C = \frac{12!}{2!(12 - 2)!} = \frac{12 \times 11}{2} = \frac{132}{2} = 66 \text{ combinations}$$

Therefore, the owner may have to analyze all 66 situations.

134 Sizing up Human Resource Needs

INTRODUCTION. The determination of the human resources needs of a business must complement the operating structure of the organization. Human resource management requires a knowledge of the organization's needs and objectives. Part of this process is determination of the number of personnel with a specific expertise that must be provided if a business's sales and production goals are to be achieved.

HOW IS IT COMPUTED?   Time studies can be utilized to establish work standards. For example, if management sets a given number of units to be produced in a given period, and the number of employee hours necessary to produce the unit is determined, the total number of hours needed to produce the product is calculated and divided by the average number of hours in an employee's workweek. The result can be used to determine the number of employees needed to meet sales and production goals. This is shown mathematically as:

$$\frac{\text{Units to be produced} \times \text{number of employee hours necessary to produce unit}}{\text{Average number of hours in employee's workweek}}$$

$$= \text{number of employees needed to meet sales goals}$$

Absentee workers are workers who do not come to work. The most common measure for determining the number of employees that must be hired to compensate for absenteeism is to divide the number of employee days lost times 100 by the average number of employees times the number of workdays. This is shown mathematically as:

$$\frac{\text{Number of days lost} \times 100}{\text{Average number of employees}} \times \text{workdays}$$

$$= \text{required number of employees that must be hired to replace absentee workers}$$

Turnover may be due to retirement, death, resignation, or some other factor forcing separation from the business. Turnover statistics are calculated by taking the total number of people at the beginning and end of a period, averaging the numbers, and dividing the average into the total number of people who worked in the business for the period minus the average. The result multiplied by 100 is the *turnover rate*. This is shown mathematically as:

Turnover

$$= \frac{\text{total number of employees working for business for period}}{\text{total number of employees at beginning and end of period}/2}$$

$$- \text{ average number of employees} \times 100$$

Example 1 Pinetree Furniture Stores project that during the year it will produce 10,000 school desks for sale to schools. Prior experience indicates that each desk takes 20 hours to manufacture, and that all employees work 18,000 hours a year. Pinetree must employ 1000 persons, computed as follows:

$$10,000 \text{ desks} \times 20 \text{ hours} = \frac{200,000 \text{ hours}}{18,000 \text{ hours}}$$

$$= 11 \text{ employees (approximate)}$$

Example 2 Quality Appliances is concerned about the high rate of absenteeism in its workforce. The owner wishes to hire enough persons to meet production goals and to cover any "unauthorized vacations." Prior experience shows that 18 workdays are lost each month, that the average number of employees hired by the business over the last 6-month period was 783, and that there are an average of 23 workdays in a month. There are currently 1000 employees. Quality Appliances will have to hire an additional 100 persons for the month of July, computed as follows:

$$\frac{\text{Number of employee days lost} \times 100}{\text{Average number of employees} \times \text{number of workdays}}$$

$$= \frac{18 \text{ employees days lost} \times 100}{783 \text{ employees} \times 23 \text{ workdays}} \quad \frac{1,800}{18,009} = 10\%$$

$$10\% \times 1,000 \text{ employees} = 100 \text{ additional employees}$$

Example 3 The Shoe Box had 200 people employed at both the beginning and end of the year. It issued 300 W-2's, for people who were formerly employed during the year and for those still employed at year-end. The turnover ratio is 50 percent, calculated as follows:

$$\frac{200 + 200}{2} = 200$$

$$\frac{300 - 200}{200} = 0.50 \times 100 = 50$$

Thus, the manager must expect to hire 50 employees to compensate for employee turnover.

HOW IS IT USED AND APPLIED? When determining human resource needs, the inventory of current employees must be matched against the economic goals of the business. Although the business may have made long-range forecasts based on strategic business planning, more specific human resource planning must be made to meet immediate sales and production objectives. This strategy involves prediction of the number of sales units, or units to be produced, for the coming period, and translating this number into the number of persons necessary to meet these sales or production goals. Analysis of absenteeism and turnover rates must also be made to compensate for any shortfall in the work force. These procedures will provide the needed lead time necessary for effective recruitment.

135 Calculating the Cost of a Fringe Benefits Program

INTRODUCTION. Employee benefits are the current and deferred nonmonetary rewards that employees receive as a condition of their employment. The owner must define the firm's objectives, design a program to meet those objectives, implement the program, and administer it. Most employee benefits programs receive favorable tax treatment because they are a deductible expense, while the employer's cost is either nontaxable or deferred income to the employee. From a tax viewpoint, the benefits are particularly attractive because their nontaxability gives benefits a greater after-tax value as compared to a salary increase. "Cafeteria"-style fringe benefit programs have become extremely popular, because employees can periodically choose what particular benefits they desire within an overall cost limit.

HOW IS IT COMPUTED? The following fringe benefits are excludable from taxable income:

- No-additional-cost services such as free standby flights offered to airline employees.
- Qualified employee discounts if (1) they are available to employees on a nondiscriminatory basis, and (2) the discounts relate to qualified property or services offered for sale to customers in the same line of business in which the employee works.
- Working-condition fringe benefits such as the use of a company car for business purposes, bodyguard services, or on-the-job training.

- *De minimis* fringe benefits, such as the typing of personal letters by a secretary, the occasional personal use of a photocopying machine, and coffee and donuts furnished to employees.

- Employer-provided group term life insurance premiums paid by an employer for employee coverage up to $50,000 per person. If the employer-provided group term life insurance is for coverage in excess of $50,000, the cost of the excess coverage is taxable to the employee.

- Group accident and health insurance plan premiums paid by an employer on group accident and health insurance policies, as well as benefits collected.

- Certain dependent-care assistance plans, with a limit of $5000 on the tax exclusion.

- Employer-provided transportation between the employee's residence and place of work, provided that the van (1) has a seating capacity of eight adults plus a driver and (2) is used at least 80 percent of the time for transporting employees.

- Employer-provided meals and lodging furnished to the employee provided that (1) the meals have been furnished for the convenience of the employer and (2) the meals have been furnished on the employer's business premises.

- Incidental or indirect benefits provided by an employer, such as the payment of an employment agency fee by an employer for a new employee.

To qualify for tax-favored treatment, fringe benefits must be offered on a nondiscriminatory basis to essentially all employees.

Example 1 Barclay Equipment contemplates paying $2100 for group term life insurance and group health insurance in lieu of $2100 in additional salary.

Since the employer receives a $2100 tax deduction whether the expenditure is for salary or insurance, the employer is indifferent between the two alternatives. Assume that the employee is in a 30 percent tax bracket. While $2100 in salary gives rise to $1470 [$2100 × 70% (100% − 30%)] = cash after tax, the fringe benefits are nontaxable, so the employee keeps $2100 in benefits after tax. If, on the other hand, the employee were to purchase the fringe benefits directly and could not take a tax deduction for their cost, approximately $2100 of salary would be required to buy the same benefits, or $2100 (1 − 0.3) = $1470. The employees would most likely favor this arrangement, since they wind up with more on an after-tax basis. Happier employees will be more productive.

Example 2 Jane Raymond, an employee of Star Furniture, incurs expenses of $5000 for business meals and entertainment during the year. If Jane is reimbursed for these expenses, the reimbursement is nontaxable to her. If, on the other hand, Star Furniture provides a salary supplement, the payment is taxable but Jane can deduct 50 percent of the expenses under the Internal Revenue Code. If Star Furniture reimburses Jane, she reports no income or deductions, but Star can deduct only 50 percent of the $5000 reimbursement, or $2500. If Star is subject to a 25 percent corporate tax rate, then the reimbursement will cost the business $4375 in after-tax dollars, computed as follows:

Total reimbursement	$5000
Amount deductible (50%)	$2500
Corporate tax rate	25%
Tax benefit (deduction)	$625
Cost to Star Corporation in after-tax dollars ($5000 − $625)	$4375

HOW IS IT USED AND APPLIED? Unlike cash salary, fringe benefits such as life and health insurance plans or child-care assistance cannot be traded for other services. To some employees with no interest in life insurance, free group insurance, or child-care assistance, the benefits would be worthless. There are, however, other solutions. For such employees, a "cafeteria plan," wherein employees can pick and choose among several fringe benefits, may help mitigate this problem. Salary might also prove to be more satisfying compensation. Thus fringe benefits are really equivalent to the payment of ordinary cash compensation, producing a definite tax liability reduction based on the business's maximum tax rate.

There are also nontax factors that must be considered. These include the incentive effects as well as the administrative costs of reimbursement plans. Reimbursement plans may encourage overspending, although the absence of such benefits may lead to inefficiency in production, low employee morale, high employee turnover, and the inability of the small business owner to attract qualified personnel.

Although a large portion of employee benefits are not required by law, employers incur these costs because they accomplish organizational objectives.

136 Determining Profit-Sharing Bonus

INTRODUCTION. Studies have shown that employees can be motivated to be more productive by the use of individual incentive plans. A number of profit-sharing plans exist that are designed to effect large-group cooperation and promote efficiency and productivity while reducing waste. In essence, these plans constitute an attempt to share in productivity gains. They include the following: (1) the Scanlon plan, a bonus arrangement; (2) a percentage of profits after a target amount has been reached; (3) a fixed amount; (4) a formula that involves calculating the bonus both before and after deducting the bonus and/or income taxes; and (5) graduated or scaled amounts.

The Scanlon plan uses the compensation for normal labor cost per unit of product produced. If, through more cooperation and greater efficiency, labor costs are reduced, the entire amount saved (or some fraction) is distributed among the workers in the form of a bonus. For example, it is determined from past records that labor costs constitute 40 percent of sales. If, through cooperative efforts, these costs can be reduced to 35 percent, then 5 percent of sales is divided among employees on the basis of seniority and/or salary levels. The Scanlon plan, a group incentive plan, has become widely accepted in compensation circles for its motivational value and innovative usefulness within the business. The Scanlon plan employs both monetary compensation and a type of union–management relationship. The plan stresses labor–management cooperation and a system of processing suggestions. Under the Scanlon plan, production supervisors and union representatives meet to discuss individual suggestions and develop general production plans. Employees benefit through the production-savings bonus.

While an incentive bonus may be given to a key executive, the efforts of rank-and-file employees should also be recognized. A fixed bonus arrangement can be utilized for certain sales personnel having equal access to all the customers in a market. For example, paying a $1000 bonus to a car salesperson who sells the most cars in a 3-month period is fair and can be an effective reward for quality performance. This arrangement is equitable providing all employees are within the same salary range.

An employer can also use a graduated bonus percentage plan for a designated group of employees. The bonus can be a percentage of the employee's annual salary. The closer an employer gets to the company's operating sales objectives, the higher the bonus percentage is.

Profit-sharing plans are tax deductible. The Internal

Revenue Service requires that an approved plan (1) cover a majority of all employees, (2) stipulate a management commitment of periodic contributions to the fund based on profits (annual employer contributions are not required), (3) be communicated to all covered employees, and (4) specify a definite, predetermined formula for allocating employer contributions to individual employees and for establishing benefit payments.

Example 1   Corbin Textiles uses the Scanlon plan for employee motivational purposes. The ratio of 40 percent was established for the production year 19X3, computed as follows:

Average sales value of production for 19X3	$800,000
Average payroll costs for 19X3	320,000
Scanlon ratio ($320,000/$800,000)	40%
Bonus money for distribution in Jan. 19X4:	
Actual sales value of production	$800,000
Anticipated payroll costs for $800,000 in sales value	320,000
Actual payroll costs for $800,000 in sales value	240,000
Labor cost savings ($320,000 − $240,000)	80,000
Distribution of labor cost savings of $80,000:	
25% to company for production improvement	$ 20,000
75% to employees	60,000
20% × $60,000 to reserve account	12,000
80% × $60,000 for immediate distribution	48,000
Bonus to each employee (determined as a percentage of present pay):	
Bonus money available	$ 48,000
Actual payroll cost	240,000
Bonus to each employee	20%

Thus, an employee who earns $6000 in January 19X3 will receive a $1200 bonus ($6000 × 20%), making her total compensation for January 19X3 $7200 ($6000 + $1200).

Example 2   Fantasy Gifts agreed to give any sales personnel who had been with the business for at least one year 5 percent of any sales that exceed the targeted amount of $2,000,000 for 19X3. All employees earn approximately the same annual compensation. The 5 percent is to be shared equally. For 19X3, Fantasy had sales of $2,500,000. Ten salespersons had been with the company for the entire year. Each salesperson receives $2500 in January 19X3, calculated as follows:

Total 19X3 sales	$2,500,000
Targeted sales	2,000,000
Excess sales subject to 5% bonus	$ 500,000
× 5%	25,000
Bonus to each salesperson ($25,000/10)	$ 2,500

Example 3   The Danforth Corporation agreed to pay its chief executive a 10 percent bonus based on income before deducting the bonus and taxes. The executive earned $100,000 for 19X3, and corporate taxes for 19X3 were 30 percent. The bonus is:

$$\text{Bonus} = 0.10(\$100,000)$$
$$= \$10,000$$

Example 4 The Danforth Corporation agreed to pay its chief executive a 10 percent bonus based on income *after* deducting the bonus but *before* deducting taxes. The executive earned $100,000 for 19X3, and corporate taxes for 19X3 were 30 percent.

$$\text{Bonus} = 0.10(\$100,000 - \text{bonus})$$
$$= \$10,000 - 0.10(\text{bonus})$$
$$1.10(\text{bonus}) = \$10,000$$
$$\text{Bonus} = \$9,090.91$$

Example 5 The Danforth Corporation agreed to pay its chief executive a 10 percent bonus based on income *before* deducting the bonus but *after* deducting taxes. The executive earned $100,000 for 19X3, and corporate taxes for 19X3 were 30 percent.

$$\text{Bonus} = 0.10(\$100,000 - \text{taxes})$$
$$= 0.10(\$100,000 - \text{taxes})$$
$$\text{Taxes} = 0.30(\$100,000 - \text{bonus})$$

Substituting for taxes in the bonus equation and solving for the bonus:

$$\text{Bonus} = 0.10[\$100,000 - 0.30(\$100,000 - \text{bonus})]$$
$$= 0.10[\$100,000 - \$30,000 + 0.30(\text{bonus})]$$
$$= \$10,000 - \$3,000 + 0.03(\text{bonus})$$
$$0.97(\text{bonus}) = \$10,000$$
$$\text{Bonus} = \$10,309.28$$

Example 6 The Danforth Corporation agreed to pay its chief executive a 10 percent bonus based on income *after* deducting the bonus and taxes. The executive earned $100,000 for 19X3, and corporate taxes for 19X3 were 30 percent.

$$\text{Bonus} = 0.10(\$100,000 - \text{bonus} - \text{taxes})$$
$$\text{Taxes} = 0.30(\$100,000 - \text{bonus})$$

Substituting for taxes in the bonus equation and solving for the bonus:

$$\text{Bonus} = 0.10[\$100,000 - \text{bonus} - 0.30(\$100,000 - \text{bonus})]$$
$$= 0.10[\$100,000 - \text{bonus} - \$30,000 + 0.30(\text{bonus})]$$
$$= \$10,000 - 0.10(\text{bonus}) - \$3,000 + 0.03(\text{bonus})$$
$$1.07(\text{bonus}) = \$7,000$$
$$\text{Bonus} = \$6,542.06$$

Example 7 Silver Ridge Discounters agreed to pay its chief executive a graduated bonus percentage on her annual compensation. The plan scale is based on a percentage of the sales target for the business year. The scale is as follows:

Volume objective (% of sales)	Bonus (% of sales)
Below 90	0
90	1
91	2
92	3
93	4
94	5
95	6
96	8
97	9
98	10
99	15
100	20
Over 100	25

For the year 19X3, the business achieved 93 percent of its targeted sales goal. If the executive's annual compensation for 19X3 was $100,000, her bonus would be $4000 ($100,000 × 4%).

HOW IS IT USED AND APPLIED? Employee profit-sharing plans are useful compensation techniques that are adaptable to the financial goals of small businesses. Basically, a profit-sharing plan is an agreement by which the employees receive a share, fixed in advance, of the profits. Though the term "profit sharing" is not used precisely by many, a true plan generally involves a definite commitment on the part of the owner to pay, over and above a fair wage, extra compensation that bears a defined percentage relationship to profits.

Among the advantages claimed for profit sharing are that it (1) results in an increase in productive efficiency by reducing costs and increasing output; (2) improves employee morale; (3) provides for employee security in the event of death, retirement, or disability; (4) reduces turnover; and (5) improves public relations. A small business owner can also use profit sharing as a means of drawing labor and management closer together, thus inhibiting the development of a labor union. Other specific objectives can be incorporated through the mechanics of a plan. For example, one firm distributes profit shares solely on the basis of attendance, to reduce absenteeism. The administration of an employee profit-sharing plan is sometimes difficult to effect. Many small businesses go through the mechanics of computing and distributing profit shares, but receive little return. The employees must see a relationship between their efforts and the success of the enterprise. If high profits are paid to employees during profitable periods, it will generate a more favorable reaction on the part of employees during unprofitable periods. If a company is especially fearful of possible adverse effects during nonprofit periods, it should adopt a deferred-distribution type of plan.

137 Employee Efficiency

INTRODUCTION. Employee salaries, fringe benefits, and related costs (unemployment insurance, employment taxes) are for many businesses the most significant cost. It is important to control these expenditures in order to maintain profits.

A determination must be made as to whether employees are efficient in carrying out their duties. The revenue obtained should be sufficient considering the size of the force.

The personnel manager is interested in employee turnover because it may be a sign of worker discontent. Further, a significant amount of money and time is wasted in recruiting, training, and developing staff.

The average wage rate is taken into account in hiring decisions, bidding on jobs and contracts, and negotiating union agreements.

HOW IS IT COMPUTED?

Sales dollars to average number of employees (work force). The average number of employees should be expressed in terms of full-time equivalents when the staff includes part-time employees.

Sales volume to average number of employees.

Profit to average number of employees.

Sales to employee salaries. The value of employee fringe benefits may be added to salaries.

Profit to employee salaries.

Number of transactions to average number of employees.

Tangible assets to average number of employees. If assets have changed significantly during the year, average assets should be used.

Employee turnover: number of employees leaving/average number of employees. Employees leaving include those quitting, laid off, and fired.

Wage growth (adjusted for inflation):

(Average wages (current year)

× [CPI (prior year)/CPI (current year)]

    − average wages (prior year))/average wages (prior year)

where CPI is the Consumer Price Index.

Example 1 A small business experienced the following for the years 19X5 and 19X6:

	19X5	19X6
Net income	$60,000	$200,000
Number of employees	50	60

Worker efficiency has improved sharply, since profit generated per employee increased from $1200 per employee ($60,000/50) to $3333 per employee ($200,000/60). This is a very positive productivity trend.

Example 2 A small business's performance for year 1 is:

Unit sales	100,000
Dollar sales	$2,000,000
Number of employees	500
Salaries expense	$800,000

This year's ratios are:

$$\frac{\text{Sales}}{\text{Number of employees}} = \frac{\$2,000,000}{500} = \$4,000$$

$$\frac{\text{Sales volume}}{\text{Work force}} = \frac{\$100,000}{500} = 200$$

$$\frac{\text{Sales}}{\text{Salaries expense}} = \frac{\$2,000,000}{\$800,000} = \$1,600$$

Last year's figures were:

$$\frac{\text{Sales}}{\text{Number of employees}} = \$3600$$

$$\frac{\text{Sales volume}}{\text{Work force}} = 180$$

$$\frac{\text{Sales}}{\text{Salaries expense}} = \$1500$$

All the productivity ratios for employees have improved this year relative to last year—a favorable sign because greater revenue is being derived from employee efforts.

HOW IS IT USED AND APPLIED?   Efficiency measures can be used to see how productive the employees have been. The more revenue is generated per employee, the more profitable the business will be. High productivity ratios indicate good employee morale, training, and on-the-job performance. Are salary payments generating an acceptable level of sales and profits?

An increase in the ratio of sales to staff indicates better efficiency. The ratio may be improved through automation and other labor-saving devices. On the other hand, a decrease in the ratio may mean that there are too many employees relative to revenue, and that layoffs may be necessary. Sometimes this ratio is too low because union contracts prohibit the firing of workers, or contracts require too many workers per operation. If this is the case, renegotiate the union contract or, the next time the contract is up for renewal, insist that it be modified. In general, labor-intensive businesses have lower ratios than capital-intensive ones because the former emphasizes human resources rather than capital assets.

When the number of employees fluctuates significantly during the year, such as in the case of a cyclical or growth business, the *average* number of employees should be used in calculating the sales-to-number of employees ratio.

An increasing trend in profitability versus number of employees indicates greater productivity. In general, automated and high-technology businesses have higher ratios. Labor-intensive businesses typically have lower ratios.

Revenue and profit ratios versus the number of employees assist in computing profit sharing and bonuses, and wage rates in new contracts.

The number of transactions to the number of employees indicates the productivity of clerks in processing orders, delivery personnel in making shipments, and jobs completed by factory workers. This ratio can be used to test whether newly installed equipment, or modifications to work procedures and schedules, result in better employee efficiency.

It is a negative sign when the rate of growth in salaries exceeds the rate of growth in sales. Further, the ratio of profit to employees' salaries indicates whether the expenditure on human resources has been justified in the form of profitability. If labor costs are "eating into profits," there is a problem.

Tangible assets represent support to workers to improve efficiency. A higher ratio may mean greater productivity because additional resources such as labor-saving devices are being used. However, if these new assets do not generate greater earnings, the effort has not been worthwhile.

If high employee turnover is due to their quitting, the reasons should be found and corrective steps taken. Some possible reasons might be inadequate training, poor salaries and/or fringe benefits, unreasonable working hours, poor supervision and treatment, and a feeling that management does not care about them.

See Sec. 77, Efficiency Measurements.

Figuring Taxes

138 How to Compute Payroll and Payroll Taxes

INTRODUCTION. Employees are normally retained on a long-term basis. Employees include staff on straight salary, office workers who may or may not receive overtime, and unionized employees who are paid on an hourly basis plus overtime. Sales employees sometimes receive a commission, which is a percentage of the sales made by the employee.

HOW IS IT COMPUTED? The payroll can be in the form of a weekly salary, based on the number of pieces produced (called *piecework*), or based on the number of hours worked by an employee. Small businesses often pay workers based on the number of hours worked, with a higher rate of hourly pay for overtime. Overtime is generally considered to be over 40 hours a week. *Net pay* is gross pay less all employee deductions. This is the amount that an employee receives in cash, and is sometimes referred to as either *net take-home* pay or *after-tax dollars*.

If an individual is classified as an employee, a FICA (Federal Insurance Contribution Act) tax of 7.65 percent, composed of two separate rates (6.2 percent for retirement + 1.45 percent for Medicare), is imposed on the employee. The amount of salary subject to FICA taxes rises each year. For 1994, the FICA withholding rate of 6.2 percent ceased once the employee earned $60,600, with an equal amount imposed on the employer. For wages received after 1993, the 1.45 percent Medicare hospitalization portion of the FICA tax continued to apply to both the employer and the employee without limit. No withholdings of tax are required if an employer–employee relationship does not exist (e.g., if the individual performing the services is an independent contractor).

An employee is under the direct control of a supervisor or manager, and is also subject to federal, and sometimes state and local withholding and unemployment taxes. Optional deductions, such as contributions to an employee's savings plan and union dues, may also be withheld.

Example 1 Jane Harp earns $800 a week for a 40-hour workweek. Her employer pays her time-and-a-half for overtime and double time if she works on Saturday. During the week ended Saturday, May 14, she worked 40 regular hours, 3 hours overtime, and 5 hours on Saturday. Her total gross pay is $1090, calculated as follows:

Weekly salary (40 hours)	$ 800
Overtime: $800/40 hours = $20 per hour × 1.5 = $30 × 3 hours	90
Double time on Saturday: $20 per hour × 2 = $40 × 5 hours	200
	$1090

Example 2 Bill Bay works for Exeter Plumbing Parts. He is paid according to the number of pieces that he produces during the week. For the week ended June 28, Bay produced the following pieces:

	Number of items produced	Product produced	Payment per piece
Monday	100	Valve	$1.05
Tuesday	50	Tube	1.50
Wednesday	75	Nut	1.20
Thursday	60	Bolt	1.80
Friday	90	Joint	1.60

Bay's gross pay for the week is $522, calculated as follows:

	Number of items produced	Product produced	Payment per piece	Payment
Monday	100	Valve	$1.05	$105
Tuesday	50	Tube	1.50	75
Wednesday	75	Nut	1.20	90
Thursday	60	Bolt	1.80	108
Friday	90	Joint	1.60	144
Total				$522

Example 3 Raven Tools hired Jack Moore and Helen Hays for the year 1994. For the year 1994, their salaries were as follows:

Jack Moore	$ 40,000
Helen Hays	100,000

Assuming a flat FICA rate of 7.65 percent on salaries up to $60,600, how much in FICA taxes was withheld from each employee for the year?

	Salary	Maximum salary subject to FICA	FICA tax
Jack Moore	$ 40,000	$40,000 × 7.65%	$3,060.00
Helen Hays	100,000	60,600 × 7.65%	4,635.90*

*Also, an additional Medicare tax of $571.30 ($39,400 × 1.45%) is imposed on Hays, for a total FICA tax of $5207.20.

HOW IS IT USED AND APPLIED?   Accounting for payroll is important because payroll costs represent a major portion of the operating expenditures of most small businesses. A distinction must be made between an employee and an independent contractor. An employee is under the direct control of a supervisor or manager, and is subject to federal, state, and local withholding and unemployment taxes. An independent contractor, on the other hand, provides services for a fee and is not an employee. Thus, a small business is not liable for employee withholding and payroll taxes paid to an independent contractor. All businesses are required by law to keep detailed payroll records. These records are necessary in order to account for limitations on FICA taxes and to determine correct withholding and unemployment taxes. The information accumulated in the payroll records also serves as a basis for producing W-2 statements, which are used to report the annual earnings and withholdings of an employee to the Internal Revenue Service.

See Sec. 139, Determining Net Pay.

139 Determining Net Pay

INTRODUCTION.   The total earnings of an employee, before any deductions, is called *gross pay*. The periodic total wage or salary earned by an employee is not, however, the amount that the employee takes home. From the total or gross pay, a number of payroll deductions may be withheld for many purposes. The amount remaining after all deductions is *net pay*.

HOW IS IT COMPUTED?   The deductions from gross pay may be grouped into two broad classes:

1. Payroll taxes
    a. Federal Insurance Contributions Act or FICA (Social Security) taxes
    b. Federal income tax withholding
    c. State and local income tax withholdings
2. Voluntary deductions
    a. Pension and retirement plans
    b. Group health insurance
    c. Group life insurance
    d. State disability
    e. Union dues
    f. Payroll savings plans (e.g., U.S. Savings Bonds)

g. Charitable contributions

h. Repayment of all or part of a loan made by the employer

The amount that an employer must withhold depends on the amount of earnings, the number of personal exemptions claimed, and the frequency of the payroll period. Upon employment, each new employee must furnish an Employee's Withholding Allowance Certificate, Form W-4, showing his or her taxpayer identification number (TIN) and indicating the number of allowances to be claimed at the start of his or her employment. An amended withholding certificate may be required or permitted due to certain changes in the employee's circumstances.

The FICA tax is levied in equal amounts on both employees and employers. Thus, the employer must pay a matching sum for all FICA deductions from employee pay. The FICA tax is imposed on employees at a 7.65 percent rate (for 1994) on wages up to $60,600. An equal amount is imposed on the employer. For wages received after 1993, the hospitalization portion is not subject to a ceiling amount.

The Federal Unemployment Tax Act (FUTA) establishes a program whereby employers are required to pay federal and state unemployment taxes to fund the payment of unemployment benefits to former employees who become unemployed. There is no withholding from the employee's gross pay for this purpose, and the entire cost is paid by the employer. The FUTA rate is 6.2 percent on the first $7000 of wages. Eligible employers may take a credit against federal tax of up to 5.4 percent of their FUTA-taxable payrolls for unemployment taxes paid to the state, making their net federal tax 0.8 percent (6.2% − 5.4%). The amount of unemployment tax paid to the state is usually based on the amount and frequency of prior unemployment claims charged to the employer.

Employers must deposit the tax for each of the first three quarters by the last day of the calendar month following the end of each quarter (i.e., April 30, July 31, October 31). Larger amounts of withholding require earlier deposits. Form 941 is used to remit withholding taxes and FICA deductions to the Internal Revenue Service. For the last calendar quarter, the employer must compute the balance of tax due for the entire year and make any required payment.

Example 1 A small business paid the following salaries to their employees for 1994:

John Manley	$ 10,000
Barbara Owen	40,000
Norman Vincent	60,000
Raymond Connelly	100,000

The Social Security expense and additional Medicare portion imposed on the employer is $13,622.20, calculated as follows:

	Salary	Maximum salary subject to Social Security tax	Tax
John Manley	$ 10,000	$10,000 × 7.65%	$ 765.00
Barbara Owen	40,000	40,000 × 7.65%	3,060.00
Norman Vincent	60,000	60,000 × 7.65%	4,590.00
Raymond Connelly	100,000	60,600 × 7.65%	4,635.90
			$13,050.90

Add: Medicare portion
Raymond Connelly ($100,000 − $60,600 = $39,400 × 1.45%) 571.30
Total Social Security and Medicare tax portion imposed on the employer $13,622.20

Example 2 On January 1, 1994, the Rex Manufacturing Corporation hires three executives to head its manufacturing branches at the following salaries:

Ronnie Boyle	$160,000
Larry Cork	200,000
Tina Lambert	240,000

The total amount of taxes paid (including employer and employee shares) to the Social Security Administration for each applicable quarter is $22,950.00, $8,293.20, $4,350.00, and $4,350.00, calculated as follows:

	Annual salary	1st quarter	2d quarter	3d quarter	4th quarter
Ronnie Boyle	$160,000	$ 40,000	$ 40,000	$ 40,000	$ 40,000
Larry Cork	200,000	50,000	50,000	50,000	50,000
Tina Lambert	240,000	60,000	60,000	60,000	60,000
	$600,000	$150,000	$150,000	$150,000	$150,000

Amounts subject to Social Security taxes at 6.2 percent:

	Annual salary	1st quarter	2d quarter	3d quarter	4th quarter
Ronnie Boyle	$160,000	$ 40,000	$20,600	$-0-	$-0-
Larry Cork	200,000	50,000	10,600	-0-	-0-
Tina Lambert	240,000	60,000	600	-0-	-0-
	$600,000	$150,000	$31,800	$-0-	$-0-

Amounts subject to Medicare tax at 1.45 percent:

	Annual salary	1st quarter	2d quarter	3d quarter	4th quarter
Ronnie Boyle	$160,000	$ 40,000	$ 40,000	$ 40,000	$ 40,000
Larry Cork	200,000	50,000	50,000	50,000	50,000
Tina Lambert	240,000	60,000	60,000	60,000	60,000
	$600,000	$150,000	$150,000	$150,000	$150,000

The employer's tax payments are calculated as follows:

	1st quarter	2d quarter	3d quarter	4th quarter
Withheld from employee:				
Social Security @ 6.2%	$ 9,300.00	$1,971.60	-0-	-0-
Medicare @ 1.45%	2,175.00	2,175.00	$2,175.00	$2,175.00
Total	$11,475.00	$4,146.60	$2,175.00	$2,175.00
Equal cost paid by employer	11,475.00	4,146.60	2,175.00	2,175.00
Total payments per quarter	$22,950.00	$8,293.20	$4,350.00	$4,350.00

Example 3 Walter Sheldon, a commission salesperson employed by Ace Corporation, generated sales of $700,000 in January 1994. Sheldon works for a 10 percent commission on all sales and is paid at the end of every month. In addition to FICA taxes withheld, he had the following monthly deductions: federal withholding taxes of $10,500, state withholding taxes of $5,000, and city withholding taxes of $1,000. His medical insurance premiums were $250 for the pay period. He also purchases a U.S. Savings Bond every pay period. Sheldon's net take-home pay for January is $48,563.80, calculated as follows:

(1)		(2)	(3) = (1 × 2)	(4) Amount subject to Social Security and Medicare Tax
Month	Sales	Commission rate	Commissions	
Jan.	$700,000	10%	$70,000	$70,000
	Social Security	$60,600 × 7.65% =	$4,635.90	
	Medicare	9,400 × 1.45% =	136.30	
		$70,000	$4,772.20	

Gross earnings in Jan.		$70,000.00
Deductions:		
FICA	$ 4,772.20	
Federal withholding taxes	10,500.00	
State withholding taxes	5,000.00	
City withholding taxes	1,000.00	
Medical insurance premiums	250.00	
U.S. Savings Bond	100.00	
Total deductions		21,622.20
Net (take-home) pay		$48,377.80

Example 4 Marvin Goodson, a commission salesperson employed by the Norman Computer Equipment Corporation, generated sales of $400,000 in January 1994 and $300,000 in February. Goodson works for a 10 percent commission on all sales and is paid once at the end of every month. In addition to FICA taxes withheld, he had the following monthly deductions: federal withholding taxes of $5500, state withholding taxes of $1500, and city withholding taxes of $500. His medical insurance premiums were $200 for the pay period. He also gives $100 every pay period to the Red Cross. His net take home pay for February 1994 is $20,487.80, calculated as follows:

Social Security calculation:

Month	(1) Sales	(2) Commission rate	(3) = (1 × 2) Commissions	(4) Amount subject to Social Security tax
Jan.	$400,000	10%	$40,000	$40,000
Feb.	$300,000	10%	30,000	20,600
			$70,000	$60,600

Amount subject to Social Security—Feb. $20,600
                                        × 7.65%
                                        $1,575.90

Medicare calculation:

Month	(1) Sales	(2) Commission rate	(3) = (1 × 2) Commissions	(4) Amount subject to Medicare tax
Jan.	$400,000	10%	$40,000	$40,000
Feb.	$300,000	10%	30,000	30,000
			$70,000	$70,000

Less: Amount taxed at 7.65%   60,600

Amount subject to Medicare tax—February $9,400
                                              × 1.45%
                                              $136.30

Social Security $1,575.90
Medicare   136.30
Total FICA taxes withheld $1,712.20

Gross earnings in February		$30,000.00
Deductions:		
FICA	$1,712.20	
Federal withholding taxes	5,500.00	
State withholding taxes	1,500.00	
City withholding taxes	500.00	
Medical insurance premiums	200.00	
Charitable contribution (Red Cross)	100.00	
Total deductions		9,512.20
Net (take-home) pay		$20,487.80

Example 5 For the week ending January 7, 1994, Deluxe Manufacturing, a small business, paid $5000 in wages to its five employees. Assume that each employee earned $1000 for the week. The following amounts are paid by the employer for the Social Security and federal and state payroll tax expense for the week:

$$\text{Employer's FICA expense:} \quad \$5000 \times 7.65\% = \$382.50$$

$$\text{Federal unemployment tax:} \quad \$1000 \times 5 \text{ employees} = \$5000 \times 0.008$$
$$= \$40$$

$$\text{State unemployment tax:} \quad \$1000 \times 5 \text{ employees} = \$5000 \times 0.054$$
$$= \$270$$

The total payroll tax expense for the period is $692.50, calculated as follows:

FICA tax payable	$382.50
Federal unemployment tax payable	40.00
State unemployment tax payable	270.00
Total payroll tax expense	$692.50

HOW IS IT USED AND APPLIED? Virtually all businesses utilize the following payroll procedures:

1. The employee is hired by the personnel department. This department maintains records such as the date the employee was hired, his or her rate of pay, authorized deductions, and date of termination of employment.

2. The employee fills out a federal withholding form W-4, authorizing payroll deductions.

3. A form authorizing the employee's rate of pay, including overtime, is completed.

4. If the employee is a factory worker, the individual fills out a daily time card indicating when the employee started and stopped work and what job he or she worked on.

5. A check is prepared at the end of the payroll period indicating gross pay, withholdings, and net pay and is entered into the business's books and records.

6. At the end of the year, the employee is issued a W-2 form (Annual Wage and Tax Statement), which shows the employee's annual salary and payroll withholdings. The employee uses this statement to complete his or her tax return.

7. The employer submits periodic and annual wage and tax reports to the proper federal, state, and city tax collection agencies.

In summary, the typical payroll function begins with the filling out of payroll records in the personnel department upon employment, followed by periodic timekeeping and payroll preparation, payment to employees and the preparation of payroll tax records, and subsequent payment of taxes.

140 Income Taxes and Different Forms of Business

INTRODUCTION. In order to make sound financial and investment decisions regarding an operating entity, an investor or lender must have a full understanding of the tax impact on a financial transaction. While identical profit-directed operations projects may generate the same before-tax cash flows, the form of the organization can result in distinctly different after-tax cash consequences. Sole proprietorships, partnerships, and corporations are the usual organizational forms in which business activities are undertaken.

HOW IS IT COMPUTED? To illustrate the characteristics of these tax differentials, the tax rules affecting partnerships and corporations must be considered. A *partnership* is a legal organization that, like a *sole proprietorship,* serves as a tax conduit between the business and its owners or partners. The partnership files its own tax return (Form 1065). Each partner receives his or her allocable share of the partnership's ordinary income for the year, and any other specially treated items. As a result, the partnership itself pays no federal income tax on its own income, but the partner's own individual tax liabilities are affected by the activities of the entity. For example, if the partnership has a profitable year and generates a profit of $200,000, a 50 percent partner has income of $100,000 for the year, regardless of whether the partnership made an actual distribution of the profits.

While the sole proprietorship and general partnership are subject to single taxation, the *corporate form* of doing business is subject to double taxation. This tax burden is frequently cited as the major disadvantage of doing business in the corporate form. Corporations are required to pay an entity-level tax on their taxable income. They file tax returns (Form 1120) and pay tax on corporate taxable income in ways very similar to individuals. Shareholders pay additional tax (at their own individual rates) on dividends that are paid from the corporation's earnings and profits. This means that corporate stockholders are effectively taxed twice on income, one at the corporate level and again when profits are distributed by way of a dividend. Current corporate tax rates are as follows:

Taxable income	Tax
First $50,000	15% of taxable income
Over $50,000, but not over $75,000	$7,500 + 25% of taxable income over $50,000
Over $75,000, but not over $100,000	$13,750 + 34% of taxable income over $75,000
Over $100,000, but not over $335,000	$22,250 + 39% of taxable income over $100,000
Over $335,000, but not over $10,000,000	$113,900 + 34% of taxable income over $335,000
Over $10,000,000, but not over $15,000,000	$3,400,000 + 35% of taxable income over $10,000,000
Over $15,000,000, but not over $18,333,333	$5,150,000 + 38% of taxable income over $15,000,000
Over $18,333,333	$6,416,667 + 35% of taxable income over $18,333,333

A corporation can, under certain circumstances, attempt to avoid double taxation and subject its earnings to a lower marginal rate (at the individual level) by electing *S corporation* status and filing Form 1120S. A small business corporation, to elect S corporation status, must possess the following characteristics:

- Be a domestic corporation (one incorporated or organized in the United States)

- Have no more than 35 shareholders (husband and wife are generally considered to be one shareholder for purposes of the 35-shareholder limitation)

- Have as its shareholders only individuals, estates, and certain trusts

- Have no nonresident aliens as shareholders

- Issue only one class of stock (authorized and unissued stock or treasury stock of another class does not disqualify the corporation)

Example 1 B is a 50 percent partner in the BC Partnership. In 1994, the partnership generated $200,000 in ordinary net income. Because the partnership was expanding, the partners decided not to make any cash withdrawals for the year. B is taxed on her $100,000 ($200,000 × 50%)

share even if no cash distribution is paid to her in 1994. If B's marginal tax rate is 31 percent, the profit produces a tax liability of $31,000 ($100,000 × 31%).

Example 2 G Corporation has taxable income of $80,000 for 1994. Its tax liability is $15,450, determined as follows:

Taxable income	Tax rate	Tax
First $50,000	15%	$ 7,500
Next 25,000	25%	6,250
Next 5,000	34%	1,700
$80,000		
	Total tax	$15,450

Example 3 Exeter Extrusion Corporation has a $100,000 operating profit for 1994. It did not elect S corporation status, and it paid all after-tax profits to its shareholders. The shareholders, all of whom are subject to a 31 percent marginal tax rate, enjoy cash flow of $53,647, determined as follows:

Taxable income	Tax rate	Tax
First $ 50,000	15%	$ 7,500
Next 25,000	25%	6,250
Next 25,000	34%	8,500
$100,000		
	Total tax	$22,250

Taxable income	$100,000
Less: Corporate tax liability	22,250
Balance available for the payment of dividends	$ 77,750
Tax paid by shareholders on dividend distributions ($77,750 × 31%)	24,103
Cash flow enjoyed by shareholders	$ 53,647

Example 4 Beacon Parts Corporation has a $100,000 operating profit for 1994. The company has elected S corporation status. The shareholders, all of whom are subject to a 31 percent marginal tax rate, enjoy cash flow of $69,000, determined as follows:

Distribution to shareholders	$100,000
Tax paid by shareholders on corporate distributions ($100,000 × 31%)	31,000
Cash flow enjoyed by shareholders	$ 69,000

HOW IS IT USED AND APPLIED? The sole proprietorship is a "natural" form of doing business whereby the owner may operate without the formalities associated with other types of organizational forms. In addition, the sole proprietorship is not subject to the "double tax" applicable to corporate earnings. The partnership operates under the "conduit principle," meaning that the partnership pays no federal income tax. Instead, the profits and losses of each individual partner are taxed only at the individual level. A corporation has permanence. Unlike a partnership, where the death of a partner dissolves the partnership, a shareholder's death has no effect on the continuity of the corporation. Business ventures that might otherwise be financially risky to wealthy individuals can be initiated through the use of a corporation. Furthermore, by meeting certain statutory requirements and electing S corporation status, the shareholders eliminate the tax on the ordinary income of the shareholders and instead are taxed only at the shareholder level.

In addition, changes in tax rates across several accounting periods might affect an investor's preference for selecting the corporation over the partnership as an operating vehicle. To maximize after-tax returns, small business owners must account for both tax and nontax factors.

141 What Is the Real Tax Rate?

INTRODUCTION. The small business owner often makes business decisions using the effective or average rate of tax. Although corporate marginal tax rates extend between 15 and 39 percent, the true effective tax rate is somewhere between these rates.

HOW IS IT COMPUTED? In making financial decisions, it is frequently important to distinguish between average and marginal tax rates. The effective tax rate is the tax liability divided by taxable income. The marginal tax rate is the extra dollar that an enterprise must pay if the company earned one more dollar.

Current corporate tax rates are as follows:

Taxable income	Tax
First $50,000	15% of taxable income
Over $50,000, but not over $75,000	$7,500 + 25% of taxable income over $50,000
Over $75,000, but not over $100,000	$13,750 + 34% of taxable income over $75,000
Over $100,000, but not over $335,000	$22,250 + 39% of taxable income over $100,000
Over $335,000, but not over $10,000,000	$113,900 + 34% of taxable income over $335,000
Over $10,000,000, but not over $15,000,000	$3,400,000 + 35% of taxable income over $10,000,000
Over $15,000,000, but not over $18,333,333	$5,150,000 + 38% of taxable income over $15,000,000
Over $18,333,333	$6,416,667 + 35% of taxable income over $18,333,333

Example 1 Green Corporation has taxable income of $80,000 for 1994. Its tax liability is $15,450, determined as follows:

Taxable income	Tax rate	Tax
First $50,000	15%	$ 7,500
Next 25,000	25%	6,250
Next 5,000	34%	1,700
$80,000		
	Total tax	$15,450

The average effective tax rate is 19.31 percent, calculated as follows:

$$\frac{\text{Total taxes}}{\text{Total taxable income}} = \frac{\$15,450}{\$80,000} = 19.31\%$$

Example 2 Tree Corporation has taxable income of $400,000 for 1994. Its tax liability is $136,000, determined as follows:

Taxable income	Tax rate	Tax
First $ 50,000	15%	$ 7,500
Next 25,000	25%	6,250
Next 25,000	34%	8,500
Next 235,000	39%	91,650
Next 65,000	34%	$ 22,100
$400,000		
	Total tax	$136,000

At income levels of $335,000 or over, the marginal tax rate and average tax rate are always the same, 34 percent, calculated as follows:

$$\frac{\text{Total taxes}}{\text{Total taxable income}} = \frac{\$136,000}{\$400,000} = 34\%$$

HOW IS IT USED AND APPLIED? The effective tax rate is used to determine the impact of tax on the business's taxable income. While the average tax rate may be used to gauge the extent to which a small business is paying its fair share of taxes, it is not very useful for tax-planning purposes. In making such economic choices as investment or financing decisions, it is the marginal rate that is important, since any new cash flows and profits are taxed at the marginal rate.

Buying or Selling a Small Business

142 Determining How Much Your Small Business Is Worth*

INTRODUCTION. In determining the value of your small business, consider the nature of the business and its principal activities, the age of the firm, industry conditions, the economic environment, competition, marketing status, customer base, risk, past and potential profitability, growth rate, cash flow, and overall financial position.

HOW IS IT COMPUTED? The business valuation methods to be covered include gross revenue multiplier, simple earnings, weighted-average earnings, capitalization of excess earnings, capitalization of cash flow, present value of future cash flows, book value of net assets, fair market value of net assets, and integration of methods.

Values of comparable businesses in the industry may provide useful norms. A source of comparative industry information for small businesses is *Financial Studies of the Small Business* (Washington, D.C.: Financial Research Associates, 1984).

Valuation Based on Profitability. A major emphasis should be placed on profit in valuing a small business. An evaluation of past earnings is typically a good start. Historical earnings are a barometer of future profitability.

The value of the small business may be determined by multiplying net income by a multiplier indicating what the owner could sell the business for.

Net income should be adjusted for unusual income statement items. For example, personal expenses which are not business-related, such as personal auto, travel, entertainment, and *fringe* benefits (e.g., health plan, pension, life insurance). Further, excessive salary equal to the difference between the owner's salary and a reasonable salary, should be added back. The entire compensation package should be taken into account, including "perks." For example, if the owner's salary is $250,000 and an equivalent qualified worker would receive $200,000, then $50,000 should be added back to profit. Interest expense should also be added back to net income because it is a financial rather than an operating expense.

---

*This section was coauthored by Abraham J. Simon, Ph.D., CPA, Professor of Accounting at Queens College, and a financial consultant to business.

If rental payments arise from a low-cost lease, net income should be adjusted to arrive at a fair rental charge. Extraordinary items (e.g., a gain on the sale of property) should be removed from profit to derive typical earnings.

If business assets are being depreciated at an accelerated pace, profit should be adjusted upward by an amount equal to the difference between the straight-line method and the accelerated depreciation method being used.

Net income should be reduced for investment income so as to obtain income from operations.

Adjust net income for business valuation purposes as follows:

Net income
Adjustments:
  Add
  Subtract
Restated net income

An illustration of the adjustment of historical net income follows:

Reported net income	$325,000
Adjustments:	
Personal expenses	50,000
Owner's fringe benefits	10,000
Excessive owner's salary relative to a reasonable salary	20,000
Interest expense	5,000
Restated net income	$410,000

The adjusted net income should be multiplied by a multiplier to estimate the business's value. The multiplier should be higher for a low-risk business and lower for a high-risk one. For example, the multiplier for a high-risk business might be 2, while that for a low-risk business might be 4. A 5-year average restated historical earnings figure is representative of earning power. The computation is:

Average adjusted earnings (5 years) × multiplier = valuation

Simple average earnings is the total earnings for each of the years divided by the number of years. An illustration is:

19X1	$ 80,000
19X2	60,000
19X3	100,000
19X4	125,000
19X5	115,000
Total	$480,000

$$\text{Average earnings (5 years)} = \frac{\$480,000}{5} = \$96,000$$

The multiplier depends on many variables, including stability, risk, growth rate, earning potential, financial health, industry conditions, and economic environment.

Weighted-average adjusted historical earnings gives greater weight to the most recent years, and is more representative than a simple average. Current earnings take into account current prices and recent business activity. For a 5-year weighted average, the current year is given a weight of 5 while the initial year is assigned a weight of 1. The multiplier is then applied to the weighted-average 5-year restated historical earnings to come up with the valuation. An example follows.

Year	Net income	× Weight	=	Total
19X9	$100,000	5		$ 500,000
19X8	90,000	4		360,000
19X7	80,000	3		240,000
19X6	110,000	2		220,000
19X5	70,000	1		70,000
		15		$1,390,000

Weighted-average 5-year earnings ($1,390,000/15)	$92,667
× multiplier	× 4
Capitalization-of-earnings valuation	$ 370,668

Another approach is the capitalization of excess earnings, computed as follows:

Weighted-average restated profit (5 years)
Less: Normal return rate of weighted-average tangible net assets
Excess earnings
× multiplier
Goodwill
Add: Fair market value of net tangible assets
Business valuation

Capitalization of cash flow involves multiplying adjusted cash earnings by an appropriate factor and then subtracting liabilities as follows:

Restated cash earnings
× multiplier
Capitalization of cash flow
Less: Liabilities
Business valuation

Valuation Based on Present Value of Future Cash Flows. A business may be valued at the present value of future cash earnings and the present value of the expected selling price. The growth rate in cash earnings may be based on prior growth and future expectations. The discount rate should be the return rate earned by the business. Refer to the present-value tables in the Appendix.

The format is:

Present value (discounted) of future cash earnings
Add: Present value of expected selling price
Value of business

Step 1: Present value of cash earnings. Once the future earnings are determined, they should be discounted. Future earnings may be based on prior years' earnings and the current profit margin applied to sales.

Step 2: Present value of sales price. The present value of the expected selling price of the business at the date of sale should be determined.

Valuation Based on Book Value (Net Worth). The business may be valued at the book value of the net assets at the most *current* balance sheet date. Net assets equals total assets less total liabilities. However, this method is unrealistic because it does not take into account current values. It may be appropriate only when it is impossible to determine the fair value of net assets and/or goodwill.

Valuation Based on Fair Market Value of Net Assets. The fair market value of the net tangible assets of a small business may be determined through independent appraisal. Expert appraisers for different types of tangible assets may be used, such as specialized appraisers for real estate, equipment, and trucks. Further, reference may be made to published values for particular assets, such as the "blue book" for business automobiles. Typically, the fair value of the net tangible assets (assets less liabilities) is higher than book value. To this, add the value of the goodwill (if any). Note that goodwill applies to such aspects as reputation of the business, customer base, and quality of merchandise or services.

A business broker, who facilitates the sale of small businesses, may be retained to perform an appraisal of property, plant, and equipment. According to Equitable Business Brokers, about 25 percent of businesses that change hands are sold through business brokers.

The general practice is to value inventory at a maximum value of cost.

Unrecognized and unrecorded liabilities should be considered when determining the fair market value of net assets, since such off-balance-sheet liabilities represent future commitments and contingencies. An example is an unrecorded lawsuit.

Off-balance-sheet assets, such as tax loss carryforward benefits, represent unrecorded assets that will increase the value of the business.

Gross Revenue Multiplier. A business value may be computed by multiplying sales by a revenue multiplier typical in the line of business. For example, if revenue is $3 million and the multiplier is 0.2, the valuation is $3,000,000 \times 0.2 = $600,000.

Values of Similar Businesses. Recent sales prices of similar businesses may be used. While a perfect match will usually not exist, the businesses should be reasonably similar (e.g., size, product line, location). Sources of industry data include Dun & Bradstreet, trade association reports, and on-line databases. For example, assume that a competing business was sold 6 months ago for $3,000,000. If you believe that your business is worth 80 percent of the competing business, the valuation is $2,400,000.

Integration of Methods. The value of the small business may be estimated by determining the average value by two or more methods. For example, assume that the fair market value of net assets method provides a value of $3,000,000 and the capitalization of excess earnings method provides a value of $2,750,000. The value of the business is the simple average of these two methods, or $2,875,000 [($3,000,000 + $2,750,000)/2].

It is even better to value the small business using a weighted-average value of several approaches. The most weight should be placed on the earnings methods and the least weight on the asset approaches.

Example 1 Assume that the fair market value using the net assets method provides a value of $3 million and the earnings method gives a value of $2.4 million. If the earnings method is assigned a weight of 2 and the fair market value of net assets method is assigned a weight of 1, the business valuation is computed as follows:

Method	Amount	× Weight	=	Total
Fair market value of net assets	$3,000,000	1		$3,000,000
Capitalization of excess earnings	2,400,000	2		4,800,000
		3		$7,800,000
Valuation ($7,800,000/3)				$2,600,000

Example 2 This example is based on the capitalization-of-earnings valuation.

Year	Net income	×	Weight	=	Total
19X9	$120,000		5		$ 600,000
19X8	100,000		4		400,000
19X7	110,000		3		330,000
19X6	90,000		2		180,000
19X5	115,000		1		115,000
			15		$1,625,000

Weighted-average 5-year earnings ($1,625,000/15)	$108,333
× capitalization factor	× 5
Capitalization-of-earnings valuation	$541,665

Example 3 In this example, valuation using weighted-average net tangible assets is computed.

Year	Amount	×	Weight	=	Total
19X1	$ 950,000		1		$ 950,000
19X2	1,000,000		2		2,000,000
19X3	1,200,000		3		3,600,000
19X4	1,400,000		4		5,600,000
19X5	1,500,000		5		7,500,000
			15		$19,650,000

Weighted-average net tangible assets ($19,650,000/15)	$1,310,000
Weighted-average adjusted net income (5 years) —assumed	$ 200,000
Reasonable rate of return on weighted-average tangible net assets ($1,310,000 × 10%)	131,000
Excess earnings	$ 69,000
Capitalization rate (20%)	× 5
Value of intangibles	$ 345,000
Fair market value of net tangible assets	3,000,000
Capitalization-of-excess-earnings valuation	$3,345,000

Example 4 In 19X1, net income is $200,000. Earnings are expected to grow at 8 percent per year. The discount rate is 10 percent. You estimate that the business is worth the discounted value of future earnings. The valuation is computed as follows:

Year	Net income	$\times$	Present-value factor	$=$	Present value
19X1	$200,000		0.909		$181,800
19X2	216,000		0.826		178,416
19X3	233,280		0.751		175,193
19X4	251,942		0.683		172,076
19X5	272,098		0.621		168,973
Present value of future earnings					$876,458

If the expected selling price at the end of year 19X5 is $600,000, the valuation of the business is found as:

Present value of earnings	$ 876,458
Present value of selling price ($600,000 $\times$ 0.621)	372,600
Valuation	$1,249,058

HOW IS IT USED AND APPLIED?   The owner may want to value his or her business to determine a potential selling price. The owner may also want to value a targeted small business to determine an offering price for the acquisition. In a lawsuit between parties, a business valuation may be required as a basis on which to settle the claim. If a business wants to expand its credit line, the bank will likely require a business valuation. Valuations are required in some tax situations, such as to determine the tax liability associated with a business liquidation.

A business may also be valued in a divorce action for equitable distribution between spouses.

Partners may want to value a partnership if there is an admission or withdrawal of a partner, a dispute between the parties requiring a settlement, or to establish a selling price.

143 Valuing a Franchise

INTRODUCTION.   If you are thinking of buying a franchise (e.g., Baskin and Robbins), you will want to determine how much it is worth to you. Can you earn enough money from the franchise to justify its initial and recurring franchise fees?

In valuing a franchise, consideration has to be given to the franchise tax. Many states have such a tax, which may be based on the net worth of the franchise. A franchise in a state imposing a high tax should be assigned a lower value by the franchisee.

HOW IS IT COMPUTED?   To determine whether to buy a franchise, perform the following computation:

Add: Present value of future cash earnings to be derived from the franchise (excluding franchise fees)
Less: Initial franchise fee
Less: Present value of future franchise fees and franchise taxes
Advantage or disadvantage of the franchise

A franchise with a long track record and reputation will have a higher value than an emerging or problem franchise. The franchise value depends on many factors, including territorial rights, length of agreement, exclusiveness, restrictions, and what must be supplied by the franchisor. A long-term agreement is worth more in the case of a lucrative franchise.

Example   You are considering buying a Burger King franchise. The initial fee for the right to open up the store is $300,000. You plan to operate the store for 10 years. The annual year-end franchise fee is $100,000, payable to Burger King. You estimate the following stream of cash earnings (cash revenue less cash expenses) for the next 10 years:

Year	Net cash earnings
1	$ 90,000
2	125,000
3	140,000
4	150,000
5	165,000
6	170,000
7	180,000
8	200,000
9	210,000
10	225,000
Total	$1,655,000

Your desired rate of return is 6 percent.
    The franchise should be bought because it results in a net positive present value of $136,900 as computed below:

Year	Amount	×	Present value factor (at 6%)	=	Present value
0	$ − 300,000		1.00		$ − 300,000
1–10	− 100,000		7.36*		− 736,000
1	+ 90,000		0.94†		+ 84,600
2	+ 125,000		0.89		+ 111,250
3	+ 140,000		0.84		+ 117,600
4	+ 150,000		0.79		+ 118,500
5	+ 165,000		0.75		+ 123,750
6	+ 170,000		0.71		+ 120,700
7	+ 180,000		0.67		+ 120,600
8	+ 200,000		0.63		+ 126,000
9	+ 210,000		0.59		+ 123,900
10	+ 225,000		0.56		+ 126,000
Net present value					$ + 136,900

*Using the present value of ordinary annuity table for $n = 10$, $i = 6\%$. See Appendix Table 4.

†Using the present value of $1 table. See Appendix Table 3.

HOW IS IT USED AND APPLIED? By calculating the value of a franchise, the potential franchisee can determine whether it is worth the price he or she will have to pay the franchisor for the franchise. Further, an existing franchisee may need to determine what the franchise may be worth if he or she now wants to sell it to another individual, assuming the franchise contract so permits.

Appendix

TABLE 1 The Future Value of $1.00

(Compounded Amount of $1.00)

$T_1(i,n)$

Periods	4%	6%	8%	10%	12%	14%	20%
1	1.040	1.060	1.080	1.100	1.120	1.140	1.200
2	1.082	1.124	1.166	1.210	1.254	1.300	1.440
3	1.125	1.191	1.260	1.331	1.405	1.482	1.728
4	1.170	1.263	1.361	1.464	1.574	1.689	2.074
5	1.217	1.338	1.469	1.611	1.762	1.925	2.488
6	1.265	1.419	1.587	1.772	1.974	2.195	2.986
7	1.316	1.504	1.714	1.949	2.211	2.502	3.583
8	1.369	1.594	1.851	2.144	2.476	2.853	4.300
9	1.423	1.690	1.999	2.359	2.773	3.252	5.160
10	1.480	1.791	2.159	2.594	3.106	3.707	6.192
11	1.540	1.898	2.332	2.853	3.479	4.226	7.430
12	1.601	2.012	2.518	3.139	3.896	4.818	8.916
13	1.665	2.133	2.720	3.452	4.364	5.492	10.699
14	1.732	2.261	2.937	3.798	4.887	6.261	12.839
15	1.801	2.397	3.172	4.177	5.474	7.138	15.407
16	1.873	2.540	3.426	4.595	6.130	8.137	18.488
17	1.948	2.693	3.700	5.055	6.866	9.277	22.186
18	2.026	2.854	3.996	5.560	7.690	10.575	26.623
19	2.107	3.026	4.316	6.116	8.613	12.056	31.948
20	2.191	3.207	4.661	6.728	9.646	13.743	38.338
30	3.243	5.744	10.063	17.450	29.960	50.950	237.380
40	4.801	10.286	21.725	45.260	93.051	188.880	1469.800

TABLE 2 The Future Value of an Annuity of $1.00*

(Compounded Amount of an Annuity of $1.00)

$T_2(i,n)$

Periods	4%	6%	8%	10%	12%	14%	20%
1	1.000	1.000	1.000	1.000	1.000	1.000	1.000
2	2.040	2.060	2.080	2.100	2.120	2.140	2.200
3	3.122	3.184	3.246	3.310	3.374	3.440	3.640
4	4.247	4.375	4.506	4.641	4.779	4.921	5.368
5	5.416	5.637	5.867	6.105	6.353	6.610	7.442
6	6.633	6.975	7.336	7.716	8.115	8.536	9.930
7	7.898	8.394	8.923	9.487	10.089	10.730	12.916
8	9.214	9.898	10.637	11.436	12.300	13.233	16.499
9	10.583	11.491	12.488	13.580	14.776	16.085	20.799
10	12.006	13.181	14.487	15.938	17.549	19.337	25.959
11	13.486	14.972	16.646	18.531	20.655	23.045	32.150
12	15.026	16.870	18.977	21.385	24.133	27.271	39.580
13	16.627	18.882	21.495	24.523	28.029	32.089	48.497
14	18.292	21.015	24.215	27.976	32.393	37.581	59.196
15	20.024	23.276	27.152	31.773	37.280	43.842	72.035
16	21.825	25.673	30.324	35.950	42.753	50.980	87.442
17	23.698	28.213	33.750	40.546	48.884	59.118	105.930
18	25.645	30.906	37.450	45.600	55.750	68.394	128.120
19	27.671	33.760	41.446	51.160	63.440	78.969	154.740
20	29.778	36.778	45.762	57.276	75.052	91.025	186.690
30	56.085	79.058	113.283	164.496	241.330	356.790	1181.900
40	95.026	154.762	259.057	442.597	767.090	1342.000	7343.900

*Payments (or receipts) at the *end* of each period.

TABLE 3 Present Value of $1

$T_3 (i,n)$

Periods	4%	5%	6%	8%	10%	12%	14%	16%	18%	20%	22%	24%	26%	28%	30%	40%
1	0.962	0.952	0.943	0.926	0.909	0.893	0.877	0.862	0.847	0.833	0.820	0.806	0.794	0.781	0.769	0.714
2	0.925	0.907	0.890	0.857	0.826	0.797	0.769	0.743	0.718	0.694	0.672	0.650	0.630	0.610	0.592	0.510
3	0.889	0.864	0.840	0.794	0.751	0.712	0.675	0.641	0.609	0.579	0.551	0.524	0.500	0.477	0.455	0.364
4	0.855	0.823	0.792	0.735	0.683	0.636	0.592	0.552	0.516	0.482	0.451	0.423	0.397	0.373	0.350	0.260
5	0.822	0.784	0.747	0.681	0.621	0.567	0.519	0.476	0.437	0.402	0.370	0.341	0.315	0.291	0.269	0.186
6	0.790	0.746	0.705	0.630	0.564	0.507	0.456	0.410	0.370	0.335	0.303	0.275	0.250	0.227	0.207	0.133
7	0.760	0.711	0.665	0.583	0.513	0.452	0.400	0.354	0.314	0.279	0.249	0.222	0.198	0.178	0.159	0.095
8	0.731	0.677	0.627	0.540	0.467	0.404	0.351	0.305	0.266	0.233	0.204	0.179	0.157	0.139	0.123	0.068
9	0.703	0.645	0.592	0.500	0.424	0.361	0.308	0.263	0.225	0.194	0.167	0.144	0.125	0.108	0.094	0.048
10	0.676	0.614	0.558	0.463	0.386	0.322	0.270	0.227	0.191	0.162	0.137	0.116	0.099	0.085	0.073	0.035
11	0.650	0.585	0.527	0.429	0.350	0.287	0.237	0.195	0.162	0.135	0.112	0.094	0.079	0.066	0.056	0.025
12	0.625	0.557	0.497	0.397	0.319	0.257	0.208	0.168	0.137	0.112	0.092	0.076	0.062	0.052	0.043	0.018
13	0.601	0.530	0.469	0.368	0.290	0.229	0.182	0.145	0.116	0.093	0.075	0.061	0.050	0.040	0.033	0.013
14	0.577	0.505	0.442	0.340	0.263	0.205	0.160	0.125	0.099	0.078	0.062	0.049	0.039	0.032	0.025	0.009
15	0.555	0.481	0.417	0.315	0.239	0.183	0.140	0.108	0.084	0.065	0.051	0.040	0.031	0.025	0.020	0.006
16	0.534	0.458	0.394	0.292	0.218	0.163	0.123	0.093	0.071	0.054	0.042	0.032	0.025	0.019	0.015	0.005
17	0.513	0.436	0.371	0.270	0.198	0.146	0.108	0.080	0.060	0.045	0.034	0.026	0.020	0.015	0.012	0.003
18	0.494	0.416	0.350	0.250	0.180	0.130	0.095	0.069	0.051	0.038	0.028	0.021	0.016	0.012	0.009	0.002
19	0.475	0.396	0.331	0.232	0.164	0.116	0.083	0.060	0.043	0.031	0.023	0.017	0.012	0.009	0.007	0.002
20	0.456	0.377	0.312	0.215	0.149	0.104	0.073	0.051	0.037	0.026	0.019	0.014	0.010	0.007	0.005	0.001
21	0.439	0.359	0.294	0.199	0.135	0.093	0.064	0.044	0.031	0.022	0.015	0.011	0.008	0.006	0.004	0.001
22	0.422	0.342	0.278	0.184	0.123	0.083	0.056	0.038	0.026	0.018	0.013	0.009	0.006	0.004	0.003	0.001
23	0.406	0.326	0.262	0.170	0.112	0.074	0.049	0.033	0.022	0.015	0.010	0.007	0.005	0.003	0.002	
24	0.390	0.310	0.247	0.158	0.102	0.066	0.043	0.028	0.019	0.013	0.008	0.006	0.004	0.003	0.002	
25	0.375	0.295	0.233	0.146	0.092	0.059	0.038	0.024	0.016	0.010	0.007	0.005	0.003	0.002	0.001	
26	0.361	0.281	0.220	0.135	0.084	0.053	0.033	0.021	0.014	0.009	0.006	0.004	0.002	0.002	0.001	
27	0.347	0.268	0.207	0.125	0.076	0.047	0.029	0.018	0.011	0.007	0.005	0.003	0.002	0.001	0.001	
28	0.333	0.255	0.196	0.116	0.069	0.042	0.026	0.016	0.010	0.006	0.004	0.002	0.002	0.001	0.001	
29	0.321	0.243	0.185	0.107	0.063	0.037	0.022	0.014	0.008	0.005	0.003	0.002	0.001	0.001	0.001	
30	0.308	0.231	0.174	0.099	0.057	0.033	0.020	0.012	0.007	0.004	0.003	0.002	0.001	0.001	0.001	
40	0.208	0.142	0.097	0.046	0.022	0.011	0.005	0.003	0.001	0.001						

TABLE 4 Present Value of Annuity of $1

$T_4(i,n)$

Periods	4%	5%	6%	8%	10%	12%	14%	16%	18%	20%	22%	24%	26%	28%	30%	40%
1	0.962	0.952	0.943	0.926	0.909	0.893	0.877	0.862	0.847	0.833	0.820	0.806	0.794	0.781	0.769	0.714
2	1.886	1.859	1.833	1.783	1.736	1.690	1.647	1.605	1.566	1.528	1.492	1.457	1.424	1.392	1.361	1.224
3	2.775	2.723	2.673	2.577	2.487	2.402	2.322	2.246	2.174	2.106	2.042	1.981	1.868	1.816	1.816	1.589
4	3.630	3.546	3.465	3.312	3.170	3.037	2.914	2.798	2.690	2.589	2.494	2.404	2.320	2.241	2.166	1.879
5	4.452	4.330	4.212	3.993	3.791	3.605	3.433	3.274	3.127	2.991	2.864	2.745	2.635	2.532	2.436	2.035
6	5.242	5.076	4.917	4.623	4.355	4.111	3.889	3.685	3.498	3.326	3.167	3.020	2.885	2.759	2.643	2.168
7	6.002	5.786	5.582	5.026	4.868	4.564	4.288	4.039	3.812	3.605	3.416	3.242	3.083	2.937	2.802	2.263
8	6.733	6.463	6.210	5.747	5.335	4.968	4.639	4.344	4.078	3.837	3.619	3.421	3.241	3.076	2.925	2.331
9	7.435	7.108	6.802	6.247	5.759	5.328	4.946	4.607	4.303	4.031	3.786	3.566	3.366	3.184	3.019	2.379
10	8.111	7.722	7.360	6.710	6.145	5.650	5.216	4.833	4.494	4.192	3.923	3.682	3.465	3.269	3.092	2.414
11	8.760	8.306	7.887	7.139	6.495	5.988	5.453	5.029	4.656	4.327	4.035	3.776	3.544	3.335	3.147	2.438
12	9.385	8.863	8.384	7.536	6.814	6.194	5.660	5.197	4.793	4.439	4.127	3.851	3.606	3.387	3.190	2.456
13	9.986	9.394	8.853	7.904	7.103	6.424	5.842	5.342	4.910	4.533	4.203	3.912	3.656	3.427	3.223	2.468
14	10.563	9.899	9.295	8.244	7.367	6.628	6.002	5.468	5.008	4.611	4.265	3.962	3.695	3.459	3.249	2.477
15	11.118	10.380	9.712	8.559	7.606	6.811	6.142	5.575	5.092	4.675	4.315	4.001	3.726	3.483	3.268	2.484
16	11.652	10.838	10.106	8.851	7.824	6.974	6.265	5.669	5.162	4.730	4.357	4.033	3.751	3.503	3.283	2.489
17	12.166	11.274	10.477	9.122	8.022	7.120	6.373	5.749	5.222	4.775	4.391	4.059	3.771	3.518	3.295	2.492
18	12.659	11.690	10.828	9.372	8.201	7.250	6.467	5.818	5.273	4.812	4.419	4.080	3.786	3.529	3.304	2.494
19	13.134	12.085	11.158	9.604	8.365	7.366	6.550	5.877	5.316	4.844	4.442	4.097	3.799	3.539	3.311	2.496
20	13.590	12.462	11.470	9.818	8.514	7.469	6.623	5.929	5.353	4.870	4.460	4.110	3.808	3.546	3.316	2.497
21	14.029	12.821	11.764	10.017	8.649	7.562	6.687	5.973	5.384	4.891	4.476	4.121	3.816	3.551	3.320	2.498
22	14.451	13.163	12.042	10.201	8.772	7.645	6.743	6.011	5.410	4.909	4.488	4.130	3.822	3.556	3.323	2.498
23	14.857	13.489	12.303	10.371	8.883	7.718	6.792	6.044	5.432	4.925	4.499	4.137	3.827	3.559	3.325	2.499
24	15.247	13.799	12.550	10.529	8.985	7.784	6.835	6.073	5.451	4.937	4.507	4.143	3.831	3.562	3.327	2.499
25	15.622	14.094	12.783	10.675	9.077	7.843	6.873	6.097	5.467	4.948	4.514	4.147	3.834	3.564	3.329	2.499
26	15.983	14.375	13.003	10.810	9.161	7.896	6.906	6.118	5.480	4.956	4.520	4.151	3.837	3.566	3.330	2.500
27	16.330	14.643	13.211	10.935	9.237	7.943	6.935	6.136	5.492	4.964	4.525	4.154	3.839	3.567	3.331	2.500
28	16.663	14.898	13.406	11.051	9.307	7.984	6.961	6.152	5.502	4.970	4.528	4.157	3.840	3.568	3.331	2.500
29	16.984	15.141	13.591	11.158	9.370	8.022	6.983	6.166	5.510	4.975	4.531	4.159	3.841	3.569	3.332	2.500
30	17.292	15.373	13.765	11.258	9.427	8.055	7.003	6.177	5.517	4.979	4.534	4.160	3.842	3.569	3.332	2.500
40	19.793	17.159	15.046	11.925	9.779	8.244	7.105	6.234	5.548	4.997	4.544	4.166	3.846	3.571	3.333	2.500

TABLE 5 Monthly Installment Loan Payments (to Repay a $1000, Simple-interest Loan)

Rate of interest	Loan term						
	6 months	12 months	18 months	24 months	36 months	48 months	60 months
$7\frac{1}{2}\%$	$170.33	$86.76	$58.92	$45.00	$31.11	$24.18	$20.05
8	170.58	86.99	59.15	45.23	31.34	24.42	20.28
$8\frac{1}{2}$	170.82	87.22	59.37	45.46	31.57	24.65	20.52
9	171.07	87.46	59.60	45.69	31.80	24.89	20.76
$9\frac{1}{2}$	171.32	87.69	59.83	45.92	32.04	25.13	21.01
10	171.56	87.92	60.06	46.15	32.27	25.37	21.25
$10\frac{1}{2}$	171.81	88.15	60.29	46.38	32.51	25.61	21.50
11	172.05	88.50	60.64	46.73	32.86	25.97	21.87
$11\frac{1}{2}$	172.30	88.62	60.76	46.85	32.98	26.09	22.00
12	172.55	88.85	60.99	47.08	33.22	26.34	22.25
$12\frac{1}{2}$	172.80	89.09	61.22	47.31	33.46	26.58	22.50
13	173.04	89.32	61.45	47.55	33.70	26.83	22.76
14	173.54	89.79	61.92	48.02	34.18	27.33	23.27
15	174.03	90.26	62.39	48.49	34.67	27.84	23.79
16	174.53	90.74	62.86	48.97	35.16	28.35	24.32
17	175.03	91.21	63.34	49.45	35.66	28.86	24.86
18	175.53	91.68	63.81	49.93	36.16	29.38	25.40

TABLE 6 Area in the Right Tail of a Chi-Square (χ^2) Distribution

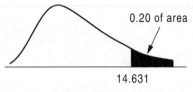

0.20 of area

14.631

Value of χ^2

Example: In a chi-square distribution with 11 degrees of freedom, find the appropriate chi-square value for 0.20 of the area under the curve (the shaded area in the right tail), look under the 0.20 column in the table, and proceed down to the 11 degrees of freedom row; the appropriate chi-square value there is 14.631.

	Area in right tail				
Degrees of freedom	0.99	0.975	0.95	0.90	0.800
1	0.00016	0.00098	0.00398	0.0158	0.0642
2	0.0201	0.0506	0.103	0.211	0.446
3	0.115	0.216	0.352	0.584	1.005
4	0.297	0.484	0.711	1.064	1.649
5	0.554	0.831	1.145	1.610	2.343
6	0.872	1.237	1.635	2.204	3.070
7	1.239	1.690	2.167	2.833	3.822
8	1.646	2.180	2.733	3.490	4.594
9	2.088	2.700	3.325	4.168	5.380
10	2.558	3.247	3.940	4.865	6.179
11	3.053	3.816	4.575	5.578	6.989
12	3.571	4.404	5.226	6.304	7.807
13	4.107	5.009	5.892	7.042	8.634
14	4.660	5.629	6.571	7.790	9.467
15	5.229	6.262	7.261	8.547	10.307
16	5.812	6.908	7.962	9.312	11.152
17	6.408	7.564	8.672	10.085	12.002
18	7.015	8.231	9.390	10.865	12.857
19	7.633	8.907	10.117	11.651	13.716
20	8.260	9.591	10.851	12.443	14.578
21	8.897	10.283	11.591	13.240	15.445
22	9.542	10.982	12.338	14.041	16.314
23	10.196	11.689	13.091	14.848	17.187
24	10.856	12.401	13.848	15.658	18.062
25	11.524	13.120	14.611	16.473	18.940
26	12.198	13.844	15.379	17.292	19.820
27	12.879	14.753	16.151	18.114	20.703
28	13.565	15.308	16.928	18.939	21.588
29	14.256	16.047	17.708	19.768	22.475
30	14.953	16.791	18.493	20.599	23.364

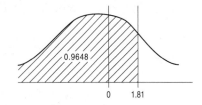

0.9648

0   1.81

TABLE 7   Normal Distribution Table

Areas under the normal curve

Z	0	1	2	3	4	5	6	7	8	9
0.0	0.5000	0.5040	0.5080	0.5120	0.5160	0.5199	0.5239	0.5279	0.5319	0.5359
0.1	0.5398	0.5438	0.5478	0.5517	0.5557	0.5596	0.5636	0.5675	0.5714	0.5753
0.2	0.5793	0.5832	0.5871	0.5910	0.5948	0.5987	0.6026	0.6064	0.6103	0.6141
0.3	0.6179	0.6217	0.6255	0.6293	0.6331	0.6368	0.6406	0.6443	0.6480	0.6517
0.4	0.6554	0.6591	0.6628	0.6664	0.6700	0.6736	0.6772	0.6808	0.6844	0.6879
0.5	0.6915	0.6950	0.6985	0.7019	0.7054	0.7088	0.7123	0.7157	0.7190	0.7224
0.6	0.7257	0.7291	0.7324	0.7357	0.7389	0.7422	0.7454	0.7486	0.7517	0.7549
0.7	0.7580	0.7611	0.7642	0.7673	0.7703	0.7734	0.7764	0.7794	0.7823	0.7852
0.8	0.7881	0.7910	0.7939	0.7967	0.7995	0.8023	0.8051	0.8078	0.8106	0.8133
0.9	0.8159	0.8186	0.8212	0.8238	0.8264	0.8289	0.8315	0.8340	0.8365	0.8389
1.0	0.8413	0.8438	0.8461	0.8485	0.8508	0.8531	0.8554	0.8577	0.8599	0.8621
1.1	0.8643	0.8665	0.8686	0.8708	0.8729	0.8749	0.8770	0.8790	0.8810	0.8830
1.2	0.8849	0.8869	0.8888	0.8907	0.8925	0.8944	0.8962	0.8980	0.8997	0.9015
1.3	0.9032	0.9049	0.9066	0.9082	0.9099	0.9115	0.9131	0.9147	0.9162	0.9177
1.4	0.9192	0.9207	0.9222	0.9236	0.9251	0.9265	0.9278	0.9292	0.9306	0.9319
1.5	0.9332	0.9345	0.9357	0.9370	0.9382	0.9394	0.9406	0.9418	0.9430	0.9441
1.6	0.9452	0.9463	0.9474	0.9484	0.9495	0.9505	0.9515	0.9525	0.9535	0.9545
1.7	0.9554	0.9564	0.9573	0.9582	0.9591	0.9599	0.9608	0.9616	0.9625	0.9633
1.8	0.9641	0.9648	0.9656	0.9664	0.9671	0.9678	0.9686	0.9693	0.9700	0.9706
1.9	0.9713	0.9719	0.9726	0.9732	0.9738	0.9744	0.9750	0.9756	0.9762	0.9767
2.0	0.9772	0.9778	0.9783	0.9788	0.9793	0.9798	0.9803	0.9808	0.9812	0.9817
2.1	0.9821	0.9826	0.9830	0.9834	0.9838	0.9842	0.9846	0.9850	0.9854	0.9857
2.2	0.9861	0.9864	0.9868	0.9871	0.9874	0.9878	0.9881	0.9884	0.9887	0.9890
2.3	0.9893	0.9896	0.9898	0.9901	0.9904	0.9906	0.9909	0.9911	0.9913	0.9916
2.4	0.9918	0.9920	0.9922	0.9925	0.9927	0.9929	0.9931	0.9932	0.9934	0.9936
2.5	0.9938	0.9940	0.9941	0.9943	0.9945	0.9946	0.9948	0.9949	0.9951	0.9952
2.6	0.9953	0.9955	0.9956	0.9957	0.9959	0.9960	0.9961	0.9962	0.9963	0.9964
2.7	0.9965	0.9966	0.9967	0.9968	0.9969	0.9970	0.9971	0.9972	0.9973	0.9974
2.8	0.9974	0.9975	0.9976	0.9977	0.9977	0.9978	0.9979	0.9979	0.9980	0.9981
2.9	0.9981	0.9982	0.9982	0.9983	0.9984	0.9984	0.9985	0.9985	0.9986	0.9986
3.0	0.9987	0.9990	0.9993	0.9995	0.9997	0.9998	0.9998	0.9999	0.9999	1.0000

TABLE 8 *t*-Distribution Table

Values of t

d.f.	$t0.100$	$t0.050$	$t0.025$	$t0.010$	$t0.005$	d.f.
1	3.078	6.314	12.706	31.821	63.657	1
2	1.886	2.920	4.303	6.965	9.925	2
3	1.638	2.353	3.182	4.541	5.841	3
4	1.533	2.132	2.776	3.747	4.604	4
5	1.476	2.015	2.571	3.365	4.032	5
6	1.440	1.943	2.447	3.143	3.707	6
7	1.415	1.895	2.365	2.998	3.499	7
8	1.397	1.860	2.306	2.896	3.355	8
9	1.383	1.833	2.262	2.821	3.250	9
10	1.372	1.812	2.228	2.764	3.169	10
11	1.363	1.796	2.201	2.718	3.106	11
12	1.356	1.782	2.179	2.681	3.055	12
13	1.350	1.771	2.160	2.650	3.012	13
14	1.345	1.761	2.145	2.624	2.977	14
15	1.341	1.753	2.131	2.602	2.947	15
16	1.337	1.746	2.120	2.583	2.921	16
17	1.333	1.740	2.110	2.567	2.898	17
18	1.330	1.734	2.101	2.552	2.878	18
19	1.328	1.729	2.093	2.539	2.861	19
20	1.325	1.725	2.086	2.528	2.845	20
21	1.323	1.721	2.080	2.518	2.831	21
22	1.321	1.717	2.074	2.508	2.819	22
23	1.319	1.714	2.069	2.500	2.807	23
24	1.318	1.711	2.064	2.492	2.797	24
25	1.316	1.708	2.060	2.485	2.787	25
26	1.315	1.706	2.056	2.479	2.779	26
27	1.314	1.703	2.052	2.473	2.771	27
28	1.313	1.701	2.048	2.467	2.763	28
29	1.311	1.699	2.045	2.462	2.756	29
Inf.	1.282	1.645	1.960	2.326	2.576	Inf.

The t-value describes the sampling distribution of a deviation from a population value divided by the standard error.

Degrees of freedom (d.f.) are in the first column. The probabilities indicated as subvalues of t in the heading refer to the sum of a one-tailed area under the curve that lies outside the point t.

For example, in the distribution of the means of samples of size $n = 10$, d.f. $= n - 2 = 8$; then 0.025 of the area under the curve falls in one tail outside the interval $t \pm 2.306$.

Glossary

ABC analysis A selective classification and analysis of inventory SKUs (stockkeeping units) according to annual dollar importance.

Absolute value The value of a number without considering its sign. For example, the absolute value of -2.18 is 2.18.

Accounts receivable turnover Annual credit sales divided by average accounts receivable.

Accuracy The degree to which a measurement is correct.

Acid test ratio The most liquid current assets (cash, marketable securities, accounts receivable) divided by current liabilities.

Activity-based costing (ABC) A costing system which first traces costs to activities and then to products. It separates overhead costs into overhead cost pools, where each cost pool is associated with a different cost driver. Then a predetermined overhead rate is computed for each cost pool and each cost driver. In consequence, this method has enhanced product costing accuracy.

After-tax cash flow The net cash flow (cash revenue less cash expenses) after taxes have been subtracted. It is the cash flow generated from operations.

Algorithm A computer program instructing that some mathematical computation be performed.

Alpha (α) A multiplier used in averaging amounts assigned to data in a time series so that the importance of older values is lessened.

Amortized loan A loan that is paid off in periodic equal installments and includes varying portions of principal and interest during its term.

Analysis of variance (variance analysis) An analysis and investigation of causes for variances between standard costs and actual costs. A variance is considered favorable if actual costs are less than standard costs; it is unfavorable if actual costs exceed standard costs. Unfavorable variances need further investigation for their causes, so corrective action may be taken.

Annuity A series of equal periodic payments or receipts.

Asset turnover Sales divided by average total assets, which reveals the efficiency of assets in generating revenue.

Average A measure of central tendency summarizing a collection of values.

Average inventory The average balance of inventory on hand; in the case of constant demand, average inventory is about half of maximum inventory.

Backorder An order which is yet to be filled.

Beta (β) The variability in the price of a stock relative to the variability in a stock market index (e.g., Standard & Poor's 500). If the company's stock price fluctuates more than the stock market index, it is a risky security.

Billing cycle The time period between periodic billings for merchandise or services rendered, typically 1 month. It could also be the periodic mailing of statements within a month to distribute the work load efficiently.

Blanket rate The same rate paid for transportation charges for delivery of merchandise to buyers within a given geographic area.

Bond A written promise by a company to pay the face amount of a debt instrument at the maturity date.

Book value per share The worth of each share of stock per the books, based on historical cost.

Breakeven analysis A branch of cost-volume-profit (CVP) analysis that determines the breakeven sales, which is the level of sales where total costs equal total revenue. At the breakeven point, there is no profit or loss.

Breakeven point The level of sales at which total costs equal total revenue.

Budget A quantitative plan of activities and programs expressed in terms of assets, liabilities, revenues, and expenses.

Business risk The uncertainties surrounding the operating and/or financial activities of a business which may result in problems and lower profitability.

Capital asset pricing model (CAPM) The theory of asset pricing used to analyze the relationship between risk and rates of return in securities.

Capital budget   A budget or plan of proposed acquisitions and replacements of long-term assets and their financing. A capital budget is developed using a variety of capital budgeting techniques, such as the discount cash flow method.

Capital budgeting   The process of making long-term planning decisions for capital investments.

Capital rationing   The selection of the mix of acceptable projects that provides the highest overall net present value of future cash flows when a company has a limit on the budget for capital spending.

Capital structure   The composition of common stock, preferred stock, retained earnings, and long-term debt maintained by the business entity in financing its assets.

Carrying costs   The costs incurred in maintaining inventory, including storage and handling costs.

Cash budget   A budget for cash planning and control that presents anticipated cash inflow and cash outflow for a specified time period. The cash budget helps the owner keep cash balances in reasonable relationship to needs. It assists in avoiding idle cash and possible cash shortages. The cash budget shows beginning cash, cash receipts, cash payments, and ending cash.

Cash flow   (1) Cash receipts minus cash disbursements from a given operation or asset for a given period. Cash flow and cash inflow are often used interchangeably. (2) The monetary value of the expected benefits and costs of a project. It may be in the form of cash savings in operating costs or the difference between additional dollars received and additional dollars paid out for a given period.

Cash flow statement   A statement showing from what sources cash has come into the business and on what the cash has been spent. Cash flow is broken down into operating, investing, and financing activities.

Coefficient of determination   A statistical measure of how good the estimated regression equation is. It is a measure of "goodness of fit" in the regression.

Collection period   The number of days it takes to collect accounts receivable. The collection period equals 365 days divided by the accounts receivable turnover. The collection period should be compared to the terms of sale.

Combination   An arrangement of a set of objects in which the order is not important.

Common costs   Costs shared by different departments, products, jobs; also called joint costs or indirect costs.

Compensating balance   The balance a borrower must maintain on deposit in a bank, representing a given percentage of a loan. No interest is earned on this balance, which increases the effective interest rate on the loan.

Consumer Price Index (CPI)　A measure of the change in consumer prices.

Contribution　Price per unit less variable cost per unit.

Contribution margin (CM)　The difference between sales and the variable costs of the product or service, also called marginal income. It is the amount of money available to cover fixed costs and generate profits.

Conversion costs　The sum of the costs of direct labor and factory overhead.

Correlation coefficient　A number between -1 and $+1$ that measures how closely two variables are related to each other.

Cost behavior analysis　An analysis of mixed costs. Mixed costs must be separated into variable and fixed elements in order to be included in a variety of business planning analyses such as cost-volume-profit (CVP) analysis.

Cost center　A unit within the organization in which the manager is responsible only for costs. A cost center has no control over sales or over the generating of revenue. An example is the production department of a manufacturing company. The performance of the cost center is evaluated by comparing actual costs to budgeted costs.

Cost driver　A factor that causes a cost item to be incurred (e.g., direct labor hours, number of setups, or number of inspections).

Cost management　A system that measures the cost of significant activities, recognizes non-value-added costs, and identifies activities that will improve overall performance.

Cost of accumulation　The collection of costs in an organized fashion by means of a cost accounting system. There are two primary approaches to cost accumulation: a job-order system and a process cost system.

Cost of capital　The weighted average of the costs of debt and equity funds.

Cost pool　A group of related costs that are assigned together to a set of cost objectives (such as jobs, products, or activities).

Cost-volume formula　A cost function in the form of $y = a + bx$. For example, the cost-volume formula for factory overhead is $y = \$200 + \$10x$, where y = estimated factory overhead and x = direct labor hours, which means that the factory overhead is estimated to be $200 fixed, plus $10 per hour of direct labor. Cost analysts use the formula for cost prediction and flexible budgeting purposes.

Cost-volume-profit (CVP) analysis　An analysis that deals with how profits and costs change with a change in volume. It looks at the effects on profits of changes in such factors as variables costs, fixed costs, selling prices, volume, and mix of products sold.

Coupon rate   The interest rate on the face amount of a debt security.

Credit limit   A specified amount beyond which a credit customer may not buy on credit.

Credit line   A specified amount of money available to a borrower from a bank, usually for 1 year. A credit line is a moral, not a contractual, commitment, and no commitment fee is charged.

Credit rating   A rating to help the business determine if a credit applicant should be granted credit. It is based on factors such as the applicant's job history, income, assets owned, and credit history.

Current ratio   Current assets divided by current liabilities.

Customer acquisition   A marketing technique designed to obtain a greater customer base.

Debt-equity ratio   Total liabilities divided by total stockholders' equity.

Decision tree   A pictorial representation of sequential decisions, states of nature, probabilities attached to the state of nature, and conditional benefits and losses.

Decomposition   A procedure to identify the component factors (such as trend, seasonality, and cycle) that influence each of the periodic values in a time series.

Deflation   A decline in price levels.

Departmental rate   A predetermined factory overhead rate for each production department.

Discount loan   A loan in which the whole interest charge is deducted in advance from the face value of a loan reducing the proceeds received. This increases the effective interest cost of the loan.

Discretionary (fixed) costs   The fixed costs that change because of managerial decisions, also called management (fixed) costs or programmed (fixed) costs. Examples of this type of fixed costs are advertising, training, and research and development.

Du Pont formula   The breakdown of return on investment (ROI) into profit margin and asset turnover.

Economic order quantity (EOQ)   The order size that should be ordered at one time to minimize the sum of carrying and ordering costs. At the EOQ amount, total ordering cost equals total carrying cost.

Effective interest rate   The real rate of interest on a loan, equal to the nominal interest divided by the proceeds of the loan.

EOQ   Economic order quantity.

Expected value   A weighted average of the outcomes of an item, transaction, or experiment.

Exponential smoothing A forecasting method of continually revising a forecast in the light of more recent experience.

External standard A norm obtained from outside the business. An example is the industry average for the current ratio.

Face value The nominal amount of a debt obligation or equity security as stated in the instrument.

Financial leverage A portion of a firm's assets financed with debt rather than equity.

Fixed cost A cost that remains the same each period in the short run, regardless of activity. Examples are rent, insurance, and property taxes.

Flexible budget A budget based on cost-volume relationships and developed for the actual level of activity. It is an extremely useful tool for comparing the actual cost incurred to the cost allowable for the activity level achieved.

Float (1) The amount of funds represented by checks that have been issued but not yet collected. (2) The time between the deposit of checks in a bank and payment. Due to the time difference, many firms are able to "play the float," that is, to write checks against money that is not presently in the firm's bank account.

Floor space The square footage of plant and office space used by a business.

Frequency distribution A table in which possible values for a variable are grouped into classes, and the number of observed values which fall into each class is recorded.

Gross profit margin The ratio of gross profit to net sales. A high gross profit margin is a positive sign, since it shows that the business is earning an attractive return over the cost of its merchandise sold.

Illiquid (1) Lacking enough liquid assets, such as cash and marketable securities, to cover short-term obligations. (2) Current liabilities exceed current assets.

Index numbers The percentages that show changes over time relative to a base year. The base year selected should be that one which is typical of operations.

Indicator A measurement or inference of something. For example, poor accounts receivable is indicated by increased customer uncollectibility due to a recession.

Industry norm A typical ratio for the industry, based on averaging companies' values.

Insolvency The failure of a company to meet its obligations as they become due. An analysis of insolvency concentrates on the operating and capital structure of the business. The proportion of long-term debt in the capital structure must also be considered.

Integer   A whole number, such as 105.

Internal rate of return (IRR)   The rate of return on a proposal that equates the initial investment with the present value of future cash inflows.

Internal standard   A standard derived within the business, such as a limit on promotion and entertainment expenses.

Inventory turnover   The number of times inventory is sold during the year. It equals cost of goods sold divided by the average dollar balance. Average inventory equals the beginning and ending balances divided by 2.

Investment center   A responsibility center within an organization that has control over revenue, cost, and investment funds. It is a profit center whose performance is evaluated on the basis of the return earned on invested capital.

Job-order costing   The accumulation of costs by specific jobs, contracts, or orders. This costing method is appropriate when direct costs can be identified with specific units of production. Job-order costing is widely used by custom manufacturers such as printing, aircraft, construction, auto repair, and professional services.

Judgmental forecast   A forecasting method that brings together in an organized way personal judgments about the process being analyzed.

Just-in-time (JIT)   A demand-pull system under which demand for customer output (not plans for using input resources) triggers production. Production activities are "pulled," not "pushed," into action. JIT, in its purest sense, is buying and producing in very small quantities, just in time for use.

Labor efficiency variance   The difference between the amount of labor time that should have been used and the labor that was actually used, multiplied by the standard rate.

Labor rate variance   A deviation from standard in the average hourly rate paid to workers, multiplied by the actual hours worked.

Lead time   The time (usually measured in days) required for inventory to arrive after an order is placed.

Learning curve   A curve that represents the efficiencies gained from experience. It is based on the statistical findings that as the cumulative output doubles, the cumulative average labor input time required per unit will be reduced by some constant percentage, ranging between 10 and 40 percent.

Least-squares method   A method of fitting a trend line which minimizes the sum of the squares of the errors between the estimated points on the trend line and the actual observed points that were used to fit the line.

Leverage The use of borrowed money to magnify potential returns from the business. It is hoped that investment through leverage will earn a rate of return greater than the after-tax costs of borrowing.

Like-kind numbers The numbers in the ratio can be logically related.

Linear programming (LP) A technique used to find an optimal solution to the resource allocation problem under constrained conditions.

Liquidity The ability of current assets to meet current liabilities when due.

Markdown A reduction in the original retail selling price.

Market risk The uncertainty that prices or services will decline.

Markup (1) An increase in the original selling price. (2) The adding of a profit to cost to determine a selling price.

Master (comprehensive) budget A plan of activities expressed in monetary terms of the assets, liabilities, equities, revenues, and costs which will be involved in carrying out the plans. It is a set of projected or planned financial statements.

Material requirements planning (MRP) A system which recognizes the dependent nature of individual components in an inventory system and calculates quantities and schedule times accordingly.

Materials price variance The difference between what is paid for a given quantity of materials and what should have been paid, multiplied by the actual quantity of materials used.

Materials quantity (usage) variance The difference between the actual quantity of materials used in production and the standard quantity of materials allowed for actual production, multiplied by the standard price per unit.

Maturity value The amount to be paid at the maturity date of a financial instrument.

Mean A statistical average found by dividing the sum of a set of observations by the number of observations.

Median A statistical average found by arranging the data in increasing or decreasing order. It will be either the middle number or the mean of the two middle ones.

Mixed costs The costs that vary with changes in volume but, unlike variable costs, do not vary in direct proportion; also called semivariable costs.

Mode A statistical average that is the observation occurring most often.

Model A mathematical abstract of a real-life system.

Moving average An average that is updated as new information becomes available.

Multiple regression analysis A statistical procedure that attempts to assess the relationship between the dependent variable and two or more independent variables. For example, the demand for a particular product or service is related to both price and advertising.

Naive models A group of forecasting techniques that assume that recent periods are the best predictors of the future.

Negative cash flow A situation in which cash inflows are less than cash outflows. This is an unfavorable situation because it may result in liquidity problems.

Net present value (NPV) The difference between the present value of cash inflows generated by a project and the amount of the initial investment.

Nominal interest rate The stated interest rate on the face of a debt security or loan.

Noninteger numbers A number that is not included among the whole numbers used for counting. For example, 2.5, or 40 percent (0.40).

Operating cycle The average time period between buying inventory and receiving cash proceeds from its eventual sale. It is determined by adding the number of days inventory is held and the collection period for accounts receivable.

Opportunity cost The revenue forfeited by rejecting an alternative use of time or facilities.

Optimum production lot size The particular quantity which, if produced in one production run, will minimize the total annual cost of setting up and carrying finished goods inventory.

Ordering costs The costs of getting an item into inventory; these costs are incurred each time an order is placed. An example is the cost of processing an order.

Out-of-pocket costs The actual cash outlays made during the period for payroll, advertising, and other operating expenses. Depreciation is not an out-of-pocket cost, since it involves no current cash expenditure.

Payback period The number of years it takes to recover an initial investment. The payback period equals the initial investment divided by the annual cash inflow.

Permutation An arrangement of a set of objects in which order is important.

Predetermined overhead rate An overhead rate, based on budgeted factory overhead cost and budgeted activity, that is established before a period begins.

Present value The current worth of a future sum of money.

Primary data sources The sources of all original data.

Probability The chance that something will happen.

Profit margin The ratio of net income to net sales. It reveals the entity's ability to generate profit at a given sales level. The ratio gives the owner an indicator of the operating efficiency and pricing strategy of the business.

Profitability index The ratio of the total present value of future cash inflows to the initial investment.

Profit-volume chart A chart that indicates how profits vary with changes in volume.

Program evaluation and review technique (PERT) A useful management tool for planning, coordinating, and controlling large, complex projects such as formulation of a master budget, construction of a building, installation of computers, and scheduling the closing of books.

Proprietary product A good available from one company that is highly desirable.

Reciprocal The number 1 divided by another number. For example, 0.02 is the reciprocal of 50.

Regression analysis A statistical procedure for estimating mathematically the average relationship between the dependent variable (sales, for example) and one or more independent variables (price and advertising, for example).

Regression model A forecasting model which relates the dependent variable (sales, for example) to one or more independent variables (Gross National Product and Index of Economic Activity, for example).

Relevant cost The expected future cost that will differ among the alternatives being considered.

Reorder point The inventory level at which it is appropriate to replenish stock.

Residual The difference between an actual value and its forecast value, also called an error or a deviation.

Residual income (RI) The operating income which an investment center is able to earn above some minimum return on its assets. It equals operating income less the minimum rate of return times total assets.

Responsibility accounting The collection, summarization, and reporting of financial information about various decision centers (responsibility centers) throughout an organization; also called activity accounting or profitability accounting.

Responsibility center A unit in the organization which has control over costs, revenues, or investment funds. For accounting purposes, responsibility centers are classified as cost centers, revenue centers, profit centers, and investment centers, depending on what each center is responsible for.

Return The reward for making an investment in the form of earnings and appreciation in value.

Return on investment (ROI) (1) For the company as a whole, net income after taxes divided by invested capital. (2) For a segment of an organization, net operating income divided by operating assets. (3) For capital budgeting purposes, also called simple, accounting, or unadjusted rate of return, expected future net income divided by initial (or average) investment.

Risk (1) Variability about income, returns, or other financial variable. (2) The possibility of losing value.

Risk averse Opposed to risk. It is a subjective attitude against risk taking.

Risk management The analysis of and planning for potential risks and subsequent losses. The objective of risk management is to try to minimize the financial consequence of random losses.

Risk reduction An attempt by a business owner to minimize risk by taking some action, such as diversifying or obtaining insurance coverage.

Risk-return trade-off A comparison of the expected return from an investment with the risk associated with it. The higher the risk undertaken, the more ample should be the return. Conversely, the lower the risk, the more modest should be the return.

Safety stock Extra units of inventory carried as protection against possible stock-outs.

Sample In statistics, a subset of the population.

Scatter diagram A plot of data points on an *X-Y* graph.

Seasonality A fluctuation in business conditions that occurs on a regular basis. It may be caused by such factors as weather and vacations. An example is the toy industry, which has its largest sales in November and December.

Secondary data sources Already-published data originally collected for purposes other than the particular research or forecasting need at hand.

Segmented reporting The process of reporting activities of various segments of an organization, such as divisions, departments, product lines, services, sales territories, or customers.

Set A collection of similar numbers.

Simple interest The interest charge computed on the original principal.

Simple regression   A regression analysis which involves one independent variable. For example, total factory overhead is related to one activity variable (either direct labor hours or machine hours).

SKU   Stockkeeping unit; a specific different item in an inventory.

Spreadsheet   A working paper having numbers in rows and columns.

Standard deviation   A measure of the spread of the data around the mean.

Step method   The allocation of service department costs to other service departments as well as production departments in a sequential manner.

Time series   A chronologically arranged sequence of data on a specific variable.

Time value of money   The value of money at different time periods. As a result, $1 today is worth more than $1 tomorrow. The time value of money is a critical consideration in financial decisions.

Total quality control (TQC)   A quality program in which the goal is complete elimination of product defects.

Total return   The return received over a specified time period from periodic income and capital gain on sale.

Trend   The movement and direction of an item over time.

Trend line   A line fitted to sets of data points which describes the relationship between time and the dependent variable.

Turnover   The number of times an asset, such as inventory, turns over during an accounting period.

Variance   (1) In statistics, the square of the standard deviation. (2) In cost analysis, the deviation between the actual cost and the standard cost.

Volume-based cost driver   A cost driver that is based on production volume, such as machine hours or direct labor hours.

Zero-based budgeting   A method of budgeting in which cost and benefit estimates are built up from scratch, from the zero level, and must be justified.

Index

ABOUT THE AUTHORS

JOEL G. SIEGEL is a certified public accountant and small business consultant who has authored 45 other books, including the best-selling *The Vest Pocket MBA*. He is currently professor of accounting and finance at Queens College, City University of New York. Dr. Siegel is the chairperson of the National Oversight Board. He is listed in *Who's Who in the World*.

JAE K. SHIM is president of the National Business Review Foundation, a financial consultant to small business, and professor of accounting and finance at California State University, Long Beach. His 38 previous books include *The McGraw-Hill Pocket Guide to Finance* (with Joel Siegel).

DAVID MINARS is professor of accounting, tax, and law at Brooklyn College, City University of New York. A small business consultant, he is the author of 12 other books, including *Shepard's/McGraw-Hill Tax Dictionary for Business* and (with Joel Siegel and Jae Shim) *The Financial Troubleshooter*.